YEMEN

HEART
BREAK
& HOPE

PETER CROOKS

Yemen, Heartbreak and Hope. Written by Peter Crooks

First Edition 2013.
© Peter Crooks. All rights reserved

ISBN: 978-1-291-30531-9

Also written by Peter Crooks – 'Lebanon: the pain and the glory'

ABOUT THE AUTHOR

Peter and Nancy Crooks met in Aqaba in Jordan in 1973. They were married three years later in Durham. Peter served in turn on the staff of two London churches – Holy Trinity, Brompton and St John's, Wembley – before they returned, with their son Timothy, to the Middle East.

The next ten years took them to posts in Beirut, Damascus and latterly Jerusalem, where Peter was Dean of St George's Anglican Cathedral. There followed nine years of rural ministry in Warwickshire, England.

More recently they have worked in Aden, Yemen, sharing responsibility for running two busy clinics and the care of the little international congregation of Christ Church. It is a post they describe as the 'happiest and most rewarding' of their lives. In 2009 Peter was awarded an MBE for work with seafarers and the community in Yemen.

They currently live in Dolgellau in north Wales, have a Rottweiler Labrador cross called Lottie, are enthusiastic grandparents to Jessica, and are involved with several church congregations in Snowdonia. They continue to visit the Middle East and Yemen in particular.

With special gratitude to Linda, who not only tidied the text but has encouraged us wherever we have been.

CONTENTS

FORWARD

Peter Crooks writes out of wide and deep experience in the Middle East and years spent serving and relishing its people. Always in partnership with his wife Nancy, he has given immeasurably, even as he has immeasurably received. Peter's courteous gentleness, his persistence in seeing justice done and truth told, and the combination of a clear mind and an unaffected delight in those around him, make him a true ambassador for Christ: God indeed makes his gentle and persistent appeal through him. These reflections and tales from several largely poor and troubled countries stand as testimony to authentic Christian mission: God's outpouring of his loving self through Christ who suffered, and died, and lives eternally.

Michael Lewis
Bishop of the Anglican Diocese of Cyprus and the Gulf
Province of Jerusalem and the Middle East

THE COMING

And God held in his hand
A small globe. Look, he said.
The son looked. Far off
As through water, he saw
A scorched land of fierce
Colour. A light burned
There, crested buildings
Cast their shadows: a bright
Serpent, a river
Uncoiled itself, radiant
With silver.

On a bare
Hill a bare tree saddened
The sky. Many people
Held out their thin arms
To it, as though waiting
For a vanished April
To return to its crossed
Boughs. The son watched
Them. Let me go there, he said.

R.S. Thomas

R.S.Thomas Collected Poems, 1945-1990, p. 234. Printed by permission of The Orion Publishing Group, London Copyright ©1993 R.S. Thomas

THE SECOND COLLECT, FOR PEACE

O God, who art the author of peace and lover of concord, in knowledge of whom standeth our eternal life, whose service is perfect freedom: Defend us thy humble servants in all assaults of our enemies; that we, surely trusting in thy defence, may not fear the power of any adversaries; through the might of Jesus Christ our Lord. Amen.

The Book of Common Prayer

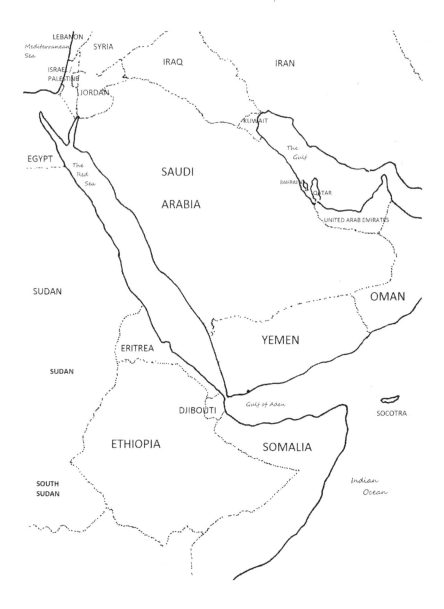

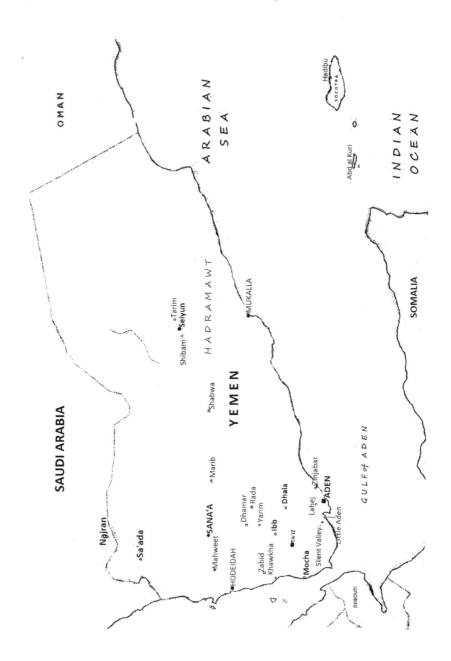

ADEN

N

To Sheikh Othman & Little Aden
◆ Airport

To Abayan,
Zinjabar &
Mukalla

Khormaksar

Port

Steamer Point

Ma'alla
• Cemetery

Tawahi
◆ Christ Church & clinics

Elephant Bay

Gold Mohur

Lighthouse

△
Jebel
△ Shamsan

△

Crater

◆ Cemetery

⊢————————⊣ 2 miles

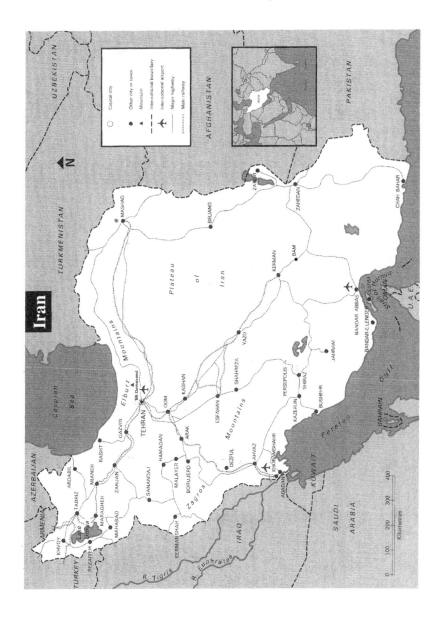

(CHAPTER ONE)
BY ROAD TO MOCHA

She looked like a lady accustomed to command and when I saw her she was commanding. She spoke into a diminutive dark-coloured phone in clipped, authoritative tones. I could not make out the words. She was facing my way but looking through me and beyond me with a fixed, resolute gaze. Perhaps she was giving instructions to a junior colleague in the City, or to the nanny in Kew, but to those standing behind in the queue waiting to be served at Prêt à Manger, neither the content of the phone conversation nor the identity or location of the person being called mattered. They had made their selection from the menu – chosen their coffee option and just wished that the lady in the smart suit, with the phone and elegant leather shoulder bag would make hers.

The tall young woman behind the counter with blond hair and company apron smiled conspiratorially at her waiting customers, ventured an audible cough and enquired of the black back with the phone what she would like. She knew just what she wanted and, with hardly a turn of the head, gave the order. The order was put together speedily and efficiently – with a smile. Then, without even a gesture of thanks, the order, which I noticed included a limp croissant, was borne purposefully by the lady in black to a window settee.

My brother, seated opposite me in a very large leather armchair, looked up from his laptop – quizzically and slightly disapproving of my interest in the lady in black. I turned to my enormous cup of mocha coffee and raised it to my lips in anticipation.

I was in every sense a very long way from the ruined, windswept, and now forgotten Red Sea port of Mocha from which, several centuries ago, coffee had been shipped in great quantities to the ports of Europe for the coffee shops of London, Vienna, and Amsterdam and whose name had passed to the brew which I held. Later, wily Dutch and British merchants had smuggled the plant out to their respective East Indian and East African colonies, leading to the sad and rapid demise of Mocha's fortunes.

I licked with appreciation the sweet coffee froth from my lips and momentarily marvelled at the way in which 'Mocha - by - the - Sea' as we came affectionately to call the dusty town, had worked its way into our lives, a little like a stray dog one has succumbed to adopting. It had come about incidentally with a cautionary phone call one evening from the British Ambassador, Mike Gifford – in Yemen's capital city Sanaa – some seven hours' drive north of Aden, where we were then living.

"We have," he said simply, "notice of specific threats against British interests in Yemen and I'm afraid that on this occasion, that means you and me." I thanked him for the information and asked if he had any specific advice for us, in the light of it. "Vary your routine, get away if you can, and keep your heads down." I thought of past advice offered us by other British Embassy personnel at other times of uncertainty in our different Middle East assignments. Most memorable and laconic was that made by a senior diplomat in the British Embassy in Beirut after it had been relocated to the east side of the city during the later years of Lebanon's terrible civil war. We were still living as a family in West Beirut. I asked how things were on his side. He replied, "Standards are falling dreadfully." It was true.

I told Nancy, my wife, what the ambassador had said and without a great deal of discussion we resolved to visit Mocha the next day – thereby breaking routine and getting away – albeit briefly, as directed.

We had not long been in Yemen – and had never visited Mocha. It sounded exotic and the locally produced guidebook also made it sound promising. It described palm-lined boulevards, extensive sandy beaches and delicious fish. We phoned Mansour, the clinic's long-standing administrator – resourceful, devout, enormously conscientious and unfailingly kind – to ask him to prepare a sheaf of identical letters with our address, personal details and particulars in Arabic on the clinic's official letter-heading to hand over to the many military checkpoints we knew we would encounter on the road to Mocha. We did not tell him the reason for our unexpected request and he did not ask to know. Already he was growing used to the unexpected and occasionally unorthodox behaviour and requests of the new director and priest. We had not been long in post when he swivelled round in his chair in the office we all shared to announce with a chuckle, "The staff have problem with you." He paused for effect and continued, "You tell them strongly not to be late and at the same time you smile at them; they are confused." Later on in our time I asked Mansour if he could possibly procure a donkey for a procession through the garden beside the church for the approaching Palm Sunday celebrations. He was confident that he could, but explained apologetically, though understandably, that he could not actually be present himself to supervise as he would at the time in question be attending Friday prayers in his mosque. True to his word, the donkey and its young barefooted handler arrived in good time. He bore 'Jesus' – a Sudanese refugee – without demur, and was untroubled by the palm branches waved enthusiastically above him or laid by others in his path. It was a moving and memorable service. The next day Mansour asked Nancy how it had all gone. He was delighted to hear. He then commented dryly, "If Mr Peter wants a lion one day, we can do it."

On the morning after the ambassador's warning we left early, before the clinics opened, a large brown envelope of travel passes on the back seat, lots of water and a tank of petrol.

A Victorian traveller visiting Aden wrote in his diary, 'What a sense of desolation and dreariness Aden presents to the newcomer. And how soon he gets to like the place in spite of it all.' One hundred years later we found ourselves feeling exactly the same way about the city. And, as we turned out of the clinic compound into the moving traffic and waved to the duty guard on the gate, hoped our stay in the city would not be cut short.

Christ Church and the clinics that nestle around it are in a district called Tawahi at the farthest eastern tip of Aden's huge horseshoe-shaped natural harbour. Opposite our gate was a government-run boatyard with several slipways, where in a noisy and leisurely fashion, small boats, pilot cutters, the odd tugs and occasional landing craft had their bottoms scraped or their engines overhauled. Sometimes we met intrepid and unfortunate foreign yachtsmen who had entrusted their vessels with mechanical problems, whether gearbox or steering, pumps or generators, to the yard. The problems were always sorted out but the process was often protracted and expensive. Sometimes employees came across to the clinic for minor ailments or eye tests, while their wives would bring their children for vaccinations or any other medical needs.

Occasionally I visited the yard. I went once in search of some chain which we needed as a prop in a Christmas performance of Dickens', 'A Christmas Carol'. It was to be dragged and clanked by Marley's ghost. The foreman was amused and helpful; there were heaps of rusty chain. Eventually, we found some whose links were thinner than a man's wrist – and they rattled and clanked most effectively. I was also offered a redundant rubber-tyred Cole's crane and an old road roller made by a now long extinct British company. I assured my kind friend that the chain was all I needed.

My first visit to the yard was a sad one. It was on the very day when I began work as Director of the Ras Morbat Clinics, and Chaplain of Christ Church.

Nancy and I were in the office when Dr Shadda, one of two sisters on the staff who were both doctors, rushed in in great agitation asking if either of us spoke French as she had a very sick Frenchman from a boat in the consulting room. We got up immediately and followed her across the courtyard. A very pale, slim man lay on her couch. His wife explained that they were staying on their boat in the yard opposite while it was being repaired. The husband had been complaining of feeling sick for several days but tragically she had not known where to turn. Her hasty explanation completed, her husband gasped loudly and died. All attempts to revive him proved futile. We were completely stunned.

It was decided that it would be best to take her husband's body to the nearby military hospital on the hill behind us to obtain a death certificate and store his body. The honorary French consul was contacted and proved conscientious and very kind. We later learned that the couple, both in their early 50s, had bought their yacht in Marseilles and had been en route to the island of Réunion in the Indian Ocean when it had developed engine problems and was diverted to the yard. The voyage was to have been the realisation of a dream of a lifetime. With the help of colleagues we put the body on a stretcher, laid it across the seats of the staff minibus and headed gently out of the gates up the hill to the hospital. Sahil, our senior Group 4 guard - tall, able, handsome and of Somali Yemeni background - drove the bus. I sat beside him. The winding road up to the hospital was horribly pot-holed. We passed a group of cheerful goats pillaging an overflowing orange garbage trolley, and a little later an old British era cinema, divided - we learned later - with curtains and hardboard into accommodation, of a sort, for over twenty families, some of whom were among the clinics' regular patients.

The hospital, constructed in the heyday of Britain's long tenure of Aden, was dramatically situated with spectacular views across the sea - and at that time known as the RAF Hospital. Built before the days of air conditioning, it was positioned to enjoy the steady on-shore breezes, and with wide, shaded verandas remained cool even in Aden's hottest and most oppressive months. It remains in its present shabby decline still a beautiful and striking building.

On arrival, we explained our business to a military guard and went in search of a doctor. We entered a ward off the main entrance. It was a sorry sight. There were two sleeping patients, several beds that were clearly broken and discarded bandages lying on the floor. In the centre of the ward stood an abandoned, rusty metal stand from which there hung an empty saline drip. We did find a doctor. He was asleep, his head resting on his arms on an old, glass topped, grey metal desk. We woke him up. He helped us. Later we carried the unfortunate Frenchman in to the mortuary before a rapidly growing crowd of curious onlookers. There were cats in the mortuary.

We returned to the clinics in subdued and reflective mood. I expressed my wish to the young doctors on our return that should I expire unexpectedly I would prefer not to be taken to the nearby military hospital.

On the morning of that first journey to Mocha, we turned out of the clinics and drove through our immediate area of Tawahi. It had once been a thriving, bustling, commercial district, living well off the sale of transistor radios and fashionable Rolex watches to numerous British servicemen and their dependents stationed in Aden, and to the passengers of cruise liners docked in the port to refuel. Many would have passed through customs on arrival at Steamer Point, where there stands a fine, single storey stone building - something between an English rural railway station and an elegant pavilion. Heavily embossed copper signs are still there on the walls indicating where passengers should line up for embarkation or demarcation. The building was constructed in 1919.

Over the years, tens of thousands of British military and administrative personnel and their families must have passed through the building. Aden was, for well over a hundred years, a key bunkering or refuelling port. A Scottish visitor to the port in the early 1850s wrote of the sight of coal being handled in Aden's sweltering heat by, 'armies of Herculean Africans shovelling immense heaps of coal for the steamships' of the British Empire. It was also visited, as elderly Adenis will tell you with relish, by famous passenger liners. The faded letters 'P & O' can still be seen hanging a little precariously from the side of a nearby building. Opposite is Victoria Park, recently imaginatively restored and tidied up under the solemn eyes of the Queen herself - cast in bronze and seated on a high plinth in the garden. She has reigned over the park now for many years but has from time to time been removed for safekeeping by her admirers, when anti-British sentiment has run high in the city.

The peace of the park and that of the neighbourhood was suddenly, rudely shattered by a loud explosion late on a hot September afternoon in 2011, when a young man blew himself up at the Police checkpoint nearby. We heard the explosion very clearly from the apartment at Christ Church where we were staying on a brief return visit to the city. It was one of several similar attacks launched against military and Police installations in Aden at the time and popularly attributed to young men recruited from the thousands of people displaced by fighting in the province of Abayan. The Tawahi bomber's head was later found in the park. Some of the staff at the clinic thought the young man was only sixteen years old.

Aden, unlike most big Middle Eastern cities, knows almost nothing of traffic congestion except during the Eid times when northerners from Sanaa and Yemenis returning from Saudi Arabia clog its main beachfront roads with huge, shiny, family-filled Toyota Land Cruisers. Half an hour's drive from home found us passing the British Petroleum refinery on the far end of Aden's great harbour. It still functions. Then we turned right and headed west to follow Yemen's southern shore, towards Bab al Mandab, 'the Gate of Tears', where Yemen's coastline edges out towards Djibouti and Africa - a bare twenty five miles away.

A few minutes' drive on from the oil refinery and just short of the first of the many military checkpoints we were to encounter on the road to Mocha, we stopped to look across Silent Valley, the hauntingly lonely resting place of some 120 British - military and civilian personnel - killed in the troubled years immediately preceding Britain's hasty, untidy, and bloody departure from Aden in November 1967. It is a dramatic setting. High, pointed, pock-marked hills rise suddenly up behind the distant low stone wall of the cemetery. The area defined by the wall, which runs all around the cemetery, is big. Those who laid it out anticipated a greater occupancy. The wind whistles continuously through it, and nesting birds in the hills behind add their own raucous cries.

On the 40th anniversary of the departure of the British from Aden I wrote to someone in England who had grown up as a teenager in Aden, and whose mother had died in a terrorist attack in the city at the time. I asked if she could write something of her memories from that time that we could read at the forthcoming Remembrance Day Service in Silent Valley. She kindly agreed and wrote back with her own moving memory of her mother's death and the funeral service in Silent Valley, overseen by many armed and vigilant British soldiers. It was a generous letter without a trace of bitterness. Our service fell on the 40th anniversary of the day that her mother died.

During our time in Aden we often received letters and e-mails from men who had done their National Service there, wanting to know whether a particular building they recalled was still standing, or if shark nets still hung in Elephant Bay or, and most often, asking us to trace, and if possible photograph, the grave of a friend they had served with, who had been killed and buried in Aden. In this context we got to know the cemeteries of Maalla and Silent Valley well and were nearly always able to trace and photograph the requested grave. The notes of thanks we received for these little errands were often effusive in their gratitude. Aden was a tough place to serve in their time and yet still evokes affection amongst many sent there. And the Aden Veterans Association, made up of those who served there in the military, is active and strong and has proved a thoughtful and generous supporter of the clinics at Christ Church.

We are still haunted by an e-mail received from New Zealand sent by a man who did his National Service in Aden in the grim months immediately preceding the departure of the British. In it he recalled his nineteenth birthday when he cradled in his arms the head of his best mate who had just been shot dead by a sniper. He went on to recount too, the death of a Somali girl of whom he had been fond, who was murdered as a suspected collaborator. The e-mail was heartrending and poignant, but ended abruptly; 'For all that I liked the place and the people. So glad you're there. Best of luck.' Nancy was always diligent in looking after these unexpected friends and the enquiries of past servicemen or their families.

We drove on and handed the first of our travel papers to the soldier at the nearby checkpoint. He had been watching us. He looked at it in a desultory way, and with a half-hearted wave, indicated we could go on.

The road from there was wide, smooth and new and the traffic, light. It grew even less after we had passed the Kharaz refugee camp - reluctant home to some 10,000 Somali refugees. Many more opt to live in a sprawling shanty town called Basateen, just off the main road, north of Aden. And every day, except in the stormiest of weather, dozens of other Somalis and smaller numbers of Ethiopians take passage for Yemen in small open boats, desperate to flee famine and war at home.

A significant number never make it. Boats overturn. And often the thugs who handle the boats don't actually make landfall but force their numb and exhausted passengers overboard to swim for shore. In our congregation at Christ Church there was a lovely vibrant Kenyan, Irene, who worked for the UNHCR. For a while she was posted to a reception centre for newly arrived refugees on the far east coast of Yemen. Interviewed in a church service about the work, she asked us one day to pray for Moses – a Somali child born on arrival on the beach in Yemen. His mother had died there after giving birth to him. It was some weeks before Irene was free again to worship with us. When she was we asked about Moses. Irene laughed an enormous laugh and explained, "I didn't check properly – he's a girl and doing well! Please pray now for Miriam."

We drove on. The little traffic we met was heading in the opposite direction to us and consisted mostly of small trucks with insulated fibreglass bodies carrying fish. A lone camel carrying bundles of brushwood appeared seemingly from nowhere, ridden by a small figure swathed in white and headed on towards an empty horizon. Sometimes where the road hugged the shoreline we passed through remote fishing hamlets, the homes made from driftwood off the beach. A few larger villages boasted a cinder block school and almost all a simple mosque – made of the same material – flat roofed and painted white with a stout pole lashed to a corner to support the loudspeaker to call the faithful to prayer.

At Bab al Mandab, the road turned north. We had effectively come to the end of Yemen's long southern shore line and had begun to follow the eastern edge of the Red Sea. And, at such a strategic point in the country there was a checkpoint and nearby a small military outpost. On a hill inland from the sea and above us were the sturdy remains of an old Turkish fort. The guard on duty told us we had an hour or so still to go before we reached Mocha. He was friendly. We thanked him and were rewarded with a shy smile and a cheerful unmilitary wave. Half an hour later we spotted the beached and rusted hull of a small freighter, lying in the surf to our left. A little later, we encountered droves of hump-backed, horned cattle – several hundred – being driven down the main road – newly arrived, we learned later, from Somalia and destined for sale in Aden or Taiz, Yemen's second city, an hour's drive inland from Mocha.

Soon afterwards the town itself straggled into view. On its edge a new petrol station was under construction. Away in the distance, on a mound beyond the town, was the thick minaret of what looked like a very ancient mosque. In the middle ground was the promised palm-lined boulevard of the guidebook - leading down to the sea. The palms that there were looked like the rest of Mocha - very windswept - and in the long spaces between them we noticed the sad stumps of others that had been roughly hacked down. We turned onto the boulevard and headed towards the sea. The paved road quickly gave way to a rough, bumpy dirt one and ran out altogether in a cluster of tiny shops, a tea house and the inevitable and necessary tyre repair yard. We stopped and went into one of the small shops - not much more than a shed with a tin roof and a rough counter and half a dozen sparsely stocked shelves. We bought a box of cheese wedges, a tin of local tuna and some flat bread and returned to the car.

We drove down a narrow alley doing our best to avoid well laden Chinese motorcycles and their riders who buzzed around us. The old part of the city through which we drove looked like the set for a Second World War movie. We skirted large mounds of baked earth, rubbish and timber that sprawled across the narrow streets where walls of buildings had simply collapsed into the road and been left where they had fallen. Elegant balconies hung precariously over the roads from long, roofless houses, while a few remaining wooden shutters banged incessantly in the wind against the walls of old, once-beautiful villas. It was hard to imagine Mocha in its heyday - its port crammed with vessels from Europe, Persia and India - not only the world's principal port for the export of coffee but itself, 'a centre for general trade with Sanaa, Mecca, Cairo, Alexandria, and India'. Mrs Katherine Edward, a British passenger on board ship to India with her husband in the 1820s noted of Mocha, 'that many of the houses were richly ornamented with highly finished cornices, fretwork, and other Arabesque minarets, from whence the muezzin call the faithful to prayer and are extremely handsome'.[1]

We did go down to the beach. It was sandy, and a dozen dogs lay in the shallows, cooling their flanks in the gentle waves. Further along we noticed little fibreglass fishing boats skimming the waves fast to land a catch beside a waiting fish truck. We drove past the harbour. We smelt and then we saw the cattle ship - still offloading cattle from Somalia. On its stern, below many layers of chipped green paint, we saw it had once been registered in Bremen. Beside it were two small, partially submerged, grey Soviet era navy patrol boats.

In the early afternoon we headed home. The journey back to Aden was uneventful.

[1] Yemen Engraved, *Leila Ingrams*, Stacey, page 127

A week after our visit to Mocha we were informed that the 'security' had, the night after our visit to Mocha, caught, arrested and put in prison a man whom they had spotted trying to climb over the wall opposite our apartment.

(CHAPTER TWO)
INCENSE, LETTERBOXES AND LADAS

Yemen is a big country with a long and fascinating history and a daunting future.

It is the size of France. It has a population which is fast approaching twenty five million.

It occupies the south-west corner of the vast Arabian Peninsula. It is bounded by Saudi Arabia to the north and by Oman in the east. Its southern shore runs half way across the Arabian Peninsula. Its western shore is bounded by the Red Sea and extends a fifth of the way up its coast.

It is a country of great natural beauty and extraordinary variety: from the wide wadis of Hadramaut in the east with their great swathes of cultivated date palms and cities of stunning, colourfully painted 'high rise' mud brick buildings, to the rugged central mountains – many of their sides meticulously terraced and irrigated, and overlooked by stone houses perched precariously on rocky peaks above them. Many of the terraces are centuries old and some as little as a metre wide.

On the far west, running down the shore of the Red Sea, is the Tihama – a fearsomely hot coastal strip where the stone or cinder block buildings of the rest of Yemen give way to round African-style homes with thatched roofs and the women wear colourful dresses and extraordinary tall straw hats.

Once we took a brief break with friends at the little beach resort of al-Kawka, on the Tihama coast. The place had seen better and busier times but the little thatched bungalows with their thick walls and high windows looked clean and inviting. We were shown inside. They were simply but adequately furnished but stiflingly hot. We turned on the air conditioner. There was no response and the young man who had showed us to our rooms smiled apologetically and explained that, "the electricity, it comes in the night."

Disappointed but not surprised, we changed into as little as was decently possible, dug our books out of our bags and went to read in the shade of some sparse trees. We lay under them on high, wobbly, rope-strung beds, resolved along with our two friends to make the very most of our visit – whatever. We read and we perspired. Our sweat fell to make little dark patches in the dust below us. The buildings of the resort shimmered in the heat. It appeared to have grounded even the most energetic flies. In the late afternoon we decided we might swim in the sea to cool off. It turned out to be a rather forlorn hope. The sea was very warm, the beach muddy, and we had to walk over a hundred metres before its waters even lapped our knees. We made our way back to our little bungalow, hot and sticky from the salt water.

Night came very quickly, as it does in Yemen, and with it, thankfully, the electricity. And not very long afterwards a truly wonderful meal of grilled fish and sheets of hot, newly-baked bread. We tore off hunks of both and ate with relish. A long cool continental beer to accompany it would have been nice but we made do with Fanta.

Early the next morning I walked along the beach. After half a mile I saw what looked like the bleached skeletons of some enormous, prehistoric creatures drawn up on the shore line. When I got closer I found them to be the hulls of nearly thirty, partially completed dhows. Work on all but two of them had long ceased and on the wood of some of them termites had already started to feast. But even in their partially completed and now decaying state they were graceful – with their high sterns and dipping bows – and their ribs made from carefully selected and shaped trees. I learned later that the hulls I had seen had been laid down as fishing dhows but that cheaper, faster and more manoeuvrable fibre-glass fishing boats like those that we had seen off Mocha, had suddenly swamped the market, and that demand for the traditional fishing dhows had all but gone. It was sad.

We did make one other brief sortie into the Tihama, to Zabid – once a very significant centre for Islamic study and learning. It had at one time boasted no fewer than two hundred and thirty mosques, one of which, the Al-Ashair, was built during the lifetime of the Prophet Mohammed. Today the town, which is a UNESCO designated World Heritage Site, has just twenty nine mosques. We visited a few and stayed overnight in a simple hotel that looked as if it had long ago catered for western backpackers and overland adventure tour groups. The walls of the dining area were decorated with murals of blue sea and sandy beaches, its roof supported by the trunks of old palm trees. As we came to leave, I discovered we had a puncture. It was quickly repaired in an oily yard for what amounted to less than the cost of a Mars bar. Then we headed home for Aden. We had found Zabid another very hot place. We also felt its atmosphere oppressive.

Other foreigners in the past had thought the same. In 1836 Lieutenant Charles J Cruttenden travelled to Zabid from Mocha, where the surveying brig Palinarus, on which he was serving, was visiting. He wrote of Zabid that it was, 'not quite so large as Mocha ... and had a peculiarly gloomy appearance, owing to the dark colour of the brick with which the houses are built, and the ruinous state of many of them'.[1]

Over the centuries different foreign powers have sought in turn to extend their authority over all or parts of what today comprises Yemen – amongst them Romans, Turks, Egyptians, British and Russians. All found it to be a hard and bitter experience. A Turkish chronicler, writing of Turkish attempts to assert control over Yemen in 1558, described the harshness of the country. 'There was nothing human or friendly there: the land was lost only to gazelle and camels: behind every rock lurked a pack of monkeys or a pride of lions ... nothing but the howling of jackals, the hooting of owls and the sound of crows.' The Zaydi tribesmen who confronted them, occupied the mountain tops – 'spreading out behind the rocks like cockroaches and beetles', and from the safety of their rocky hideouts rolled huge boulders down on the unfortunate Turks.[2]

Once while travelling with some friends to Sanaa in our little Suzuki bus, we were stopped on a steep gradient overlooked by craggy hills, by some dozen or more severe looking tribesmen with turbans, the traditional skirt or 'futa', tweed jackets, sandals and the ubiquitous Kalashnikov rifles. They had strewn the road with large rocks and set up their own ad hoc road block. They had chosen the place well and effectively closed the main highway between the north and south of the country. In the hills on either side of the road we noticed there were other tribesmen squatting among the rocks, their guns resting easily across their knees.

On leaving Aden earlier in the day we had, at the main customs and security checkpoint on the edge of the city, been assigned a police escort

[1] Leila Ingrams, *Yemen Engraved*, Stacey International, 2006, p.121

[2] Victoria Clark, *YEMEN – Dancing on the Heads of Snakes*, p.18. Printed by permission of Yale University Press, 2010

for our journey north - three smiling young policemen with berets askew, in a blue and white SUV - delighted at the prospect of a day out.

When we had first arrived in Yemen these security measures were not thought necessary. Later, with the kidnapping and occasional murder of foreigners in remote parts of the country, a police escort became mandatory. Now, at the time of writing, with the widespread breakdown of law and order across the country, few foreigners remain and for them inter-city travel is permitted only by plane.

On the day when we ran into our unexpected roadblock the police escort were lagging far behind. By the time they came in sight we had been waved to the edge of the road, ordered to turn off the car engine and told to remain where we were. The driver of the blue and white Hyundai police car, clearly startled at the hastily built checkpoint, braked, and with an impressive squeal of tyres executed a tight u-turn and accelerated back the way he had come. One of the men standing at the checkpoint raised his rifle to fire after the fleeing police. He did not fire but the driver of the retreating car was taking no chances and flung his vehicle into a dramatic weaving pattern. The third policeman, seated in the back of the car, was thrown out of it by the motion. He was pitched gun-less into a rocky culvert from which he scrambled and hobbled anxiously after the departing police car.

The gunman lowered his weapon and turned to examine the papers of the driver of a large white bus. Neither he nor his fellows seemed in the slightest bit interested in us. After what I considered a reasonable and respectful period of waiting, I turned on our car engine, caught the eye of one of the tribesmen and indicated, with gesture and smile, our desire to be on our way. He scowled, strode over to us, told me to turn off the engine immediately and waved a grubby finger at us severely. Rebuked, we settled down for a long wait, draping a scarf across the windshield to keep out the sun and opening as many windows as we could to let in the breeze. Peter, our resident volunteer at the time, continued to read a weighty book, Nancy opened her drawing pad and sketched, Maggie, who had been leading a much appreciated retreat at Christ Church for a few days, had her morning devotions, while Gabriel, a visiting ordinand, thought what a great story the experience would make when he got back to seminary. I managed, like ET, to 'phone home' to Mansour and alert him to our plight. I did wonder whether we were all about to be kidnapped.

The bus mentioned earlier was allowed to continue its journey. A number of other vehicles were also permitted to pass. After an hour, a very new twin cab pick-up appeared and was firmly waved in behind us. The passengers were all pale foreigners like us. I got down to say hello. They looked even more serious than the tribesmen. I discovered they were from Moscow. Conversation was hard and after a little while I returned to the others.

After a further hour's waiting, an old Peugeot police car drove up accompanied by two blue and white SUVs, all with their blue roof lights turning. A tall, smiling officer got smartly out of the Peugeot, joined in moments by eight or nine policemen in blue with guns slung over their shoulders. The officer walked up to the oldest man on the checkpoint, whom he rightly guessed to be in charge, put a friendly arm around his shoulder and very probably asked after his family and the quality of the qat. I had noticed it being delivered to him and his fellow tribesmen in little pink plastic bags. (Qat is a mild narcotic chewed for up to six hours every day by most Yemeni men and increasing numbers of women.) All was smiles and good natured bonhomie. Under the old man's direction the boulders that had blocked the road were lifted and tossed aside. The officer then came across to us - still beaming. "Do you still want to go to Sanaa?" he asked. When we said yes he replied expansively that the way was now clear.

He apologised for the hold-up and explained that in the town just ahead of us, Dhala, there had been lots of fighting that morning which the tribesmen had not wanted us to get caught up in. We did get to Sanaa without further incident and had a happy visit. On our return to Aden, we waited in line to be cleared through the main police check point on the edge of the city. We rarely had to wait long and on this occasion were spotted by the cheerful, handsome young officer who had arranged our flighty escort a few days earlier. He immediately left the truck driver to whom he had been talking and walked over to us - a huge, knowing smile on his face. When I protested to him at our being abandoned by his three policemen, his smile grew wider still, and he replied disarmingly, "But you are here and everything is fine. Smile, you are in Yemen." It was hard not to.

We had certainly fared much better than the Turks on whom, long before, tribesmen had rained down boulders.

The Romans called Yemen, 'Arabia Felix' - happy or blessed Arabia - on account presumably, of its rainfall which in parts is very heavy, providing ample water for agriculture - happy also, by way of contrast with the rest of Arabia where rainfall was sparse.

The Romans, like the Egyptians and the Greeks, looked to Yemen for the frankincense and myrrh which they needed to accompany the worship in their temples. At the height of the incense trade, over one thousand camels regularly set out from Yemen laden with their precious merchandise for Rome and Athens over two thousand miles away. It came largely from the Hadramaut, Mahra - at the far eastern end of Yemen - and the island of Socotra.

Plutarch, biographer and philosopher, recalls in his life of Alexander the Second, the Greek, how the young Alexander heaped frankincense on the altars so extravagantly that his tutor, Leonides, told him he could worship the gods that way when he had conquered the frankincense races. He took the words to heart and sent an admiral, one Anaxicrates, down through Bab al Mandab to explore the southern coast of Arabia. However, Alexander's sudden death of a fever in Babylon in 323 BC ended all ideas of conquest.

Some centuries later, in 24 BC, the Emperor Augustus appointed his Prefect of Egypt, Marcus Aelius Gallus, to lead the Tenth Legion into south west Arabia with a view to strengthening the empire's hold on the incense trade. It was not a success. The expedition was dogged by hardship, hunger, disease and the duplicity of their guides and aborted. Aelius Gallus and the expedition's survivors returned to Egypt.

Much earlier, around 1500 BC, Egypt's famed Queen Hatshepsut is recorded as sending an expedition to the land of Punt to bring back incense for her temples. Punt has been variously thought to have been Upper Egypt, Eritrea - and possibly Yemen.

In Old Testament times, the land today designated 'Yemen' was the land of Sheba from where its wisdom-seeking Queen journeyed for an audience in Jerusalem with King Solomon. 'She came,' we are told (1 Kings chapter 10) to Jerusalem, 'with a very great retinue - with camels bearing spices and very much gold, and precious stones', and when she came to Solomon, she told him everything that was on her mind. The Queen was overwhelmed by all she had heard and seen and readily admitted that while the reports she had heard at home of the King's achievements and wisdom were true, not even half had been told - his wisdom and prosperity far surpassed the reports she had heard.

Sadly, the wisdom that so impressed the Queen of Sheba has not been a quality much displayed in her successors down the centuries.

The courageous and long-suffering Old Testament prophet Jeremiah clearly knew the origins of the incense burned in Jerusalem's Temple in his time, and in one of his very fierce tirades against his fellow Jews exclaimed on God's behalf, 'Of what use to me is frankincense that comes from Sheba or sweet cane from a distant land? Your blood offerings are not acceptable.' (Jeremiah chapter 6)

Incense was, for many centuries, an enormously important and valuable commodity in the life of Yemen. The Roman writer, Pliny, noted the huge wealth that the incense trade brought to the tribes of south west Arabia, and protested that they were the richest people in the world, because 'the vast wealth from Rome and Parthia accumulates in their hands, as they sell the produce they obtain from the sea or their forests, and buy nothing in return'. Perhaps Pliny was referring to the people of Hadramaut who have a reputation for being financially astute and tight fisted.

I saw no evidence of the latter, but all Yemenis, Hadramis included, love to tell jokes about the people of Hadramaut and their perceived miserliness. Once we had a fine lady doctor working with us. She was from the Hadramaut. She told us a joke about a rich businessman from her home town who had invited a number of friends to his house for lunch. His hospitable wife bustled in and out bringing in many plates of food. First she brought in little bowls of nuts for them to nibble, then dishes of rice and vegetables. After a little while a voice called from the kitchen, 'Shall I bring you the chicken?' 'Not yet,' was the reply. Some minutes later she asked the same question and received the same answer. The guests continued to eat enthusiastically though some slowed – in anticipation of the chicken. Later the husband shouted in the direction of the kitchen, 'Bring in the chicken!' His wife brought in a hungry, noisy chicken who strutted around the room vigorously pecking at what was left.

Frankincense is still exported from Yemen – the best coming from Hadramaut itself. About five hundred tons are exported annually but it still remains in demand in Yemen too. Figures for the amount burned are hard to come by.

It is burnt in little clay bowls in many homes and the smoke is wafted on to clothes to make them smell pleasant. It is also used to cover up domestic smells that are not pleasant. Whenever the neighbourhood drains backed up and flooded the clinic courtyard, we burned incense. Incense was also an integral part of the beautifully choreographed Ethiopian coffee ceremony put on sometimes in place of our regular mid-morning tea break. The significant birthday of a member of staff or the visit of the Bishop or a foreign surgeon would be a ready reason to hold the ceremony. Coffee beans would be roasted and ground, a special loaf of bread baked and the area around strewn with grass - real or artificial. These were beautiful occasions, the smell of the incense mingling with newly roasted coffee. Sometimes, on special days, we burned incense in the church too.

As mentioned already, Yemen's incense trade flourished for centuries, and for much of that time it was the Sabean Kingdom that held sway. It came to prominence around 1000 BC, about the time when it is reckoned that the Queen of Sheba set off on her visit to King Solomon. The Kingdom lasted some 1300 years and the height of its influence and power was in the seventh century BC. It was during that time that the great dam of Marib was built.

The dam, or rather its remains, were a popular item on the itinerary of foreign tour groups venturing to Yemen until July 2007 when a suicide bomber drove his vehicle, filled with explosives, into a group of Spanish tourists, tragically killing seven of them along with their dedicated Yemeni guides. The attack was attributed to Al Qaeda and came after the group had threatened to take action against foreign interests in Yemen if members of the organisation held in prison in Yemen were not released.

The dam must have been impressive in its day. It was over 650 metres long and 16 metres high. It was constructed of earth and stone. It was built to catch the water of the flash floods that rushed down Wadi Dhana - a river bed that makes its way towards the Desert Sabtayn from the northern highlands. The water caught by the dam was then used to irrigate two huge oases which together supported over 50,000 people. The dam required frequent repair but in 570 AD it collapsed, an event described in the Koran, and for which it judged the people of Marib responsible. 'There was a sign for the Sabeans in their homeland: two gardens, on the right and on the left. And they were told, 'Eat of what the Lord has given you and be thankful, for fair is your land and forgiving is your land.' But they turned away. So we released the flood from the dams, replacing their gardens with two others which bore only bitter fruit and tamarisk and a few spare date trees.' (Sura 34)

We would have liked to have visited Marib but travel to the area, even before the death of the Spanish tourists, was discouraged and our commitments in Aden did not leave us a lot of time for extended visits across the country. Besides, we had, like the Victorian traveller quoted earlier, grown fond of Aden. A New Zealand friend, Jon, who also shared our affection for the city, once commented wryly, "Back home in New Zealand there is lots to do but nothing much happens, while here there is not much to do but there is always something happening!"

Our previous contacts with Aden were slight, but they were enough to catch our interest whenever Aden or Yemen impinged upon the world news. Nancy was born and grew up in India. When the family returned home to America they did so in a leisurely manner by ship, pausing briefly at one point to take on fuel in Aden. Her only memory is of the terrible heat. The vessel they travelled on was one of the last to pass through the Suez Canal before General Nasser seized it, provoking the 1956 Suez Crisis. A year later my father, a career soldier, was sent to Cyprus to take up a new posting there. A few months later, when our prefabricated, red-roofed accommodation had been assembled at Episkopi (the British military base where he was stationed) we sailed as a family on a troopship to join him. During our last year, my father was sent on a special assignment to Aden for several months. When he returned to Cyprus he showed us black and white photos he had taken. Many of the buildings which he photographed still stand today. He also brought us postcards, one of which showed camels being raced on the old RAF airfield at Khormaksar - long since the city's civilian airport. I can still remember looking at the pictures and pronouncing that it looked 'a terrible place'.

Many years later and soon after Nancy and I first met, she was invited by a wealthy Yemeni student, whom she was then teaching in Beirut, to accompany her to the family home in Sanaa for the summer vacation. It was a remarkable experience. The student's family lived in a very old house in the old part of Sanaa. Years later we searched in vain for that house. In a long and welcome letter written to me by Nancy from Sanaa during that summer she described making a journey with the family to Wadi Dhar - a famous valley outside Sanaa - for a picnic. At the time it was quite an expedition, but now the city of Sanaa reaches almost to the lip of the Wadi. Then, the wadi was covered with grape vines but now with qat. Today the cultivation of qat in the area is estimated to consume over sixty percent of the available and rapidly diminishing water resources of the Sanaa basin, while some reckon the daily consumption of qat in Yemen accounts for a million hours of wasted labour every day. The advocates of qat extol its energising power. 'Much better than Red Bull energy drink', a young student told me when he was revising for his exams. Its detractors protest its dire effect on the country's water reserves, the economy and people's health. Our doctor from Hadramaut, referred to earlier, described it once to me as 'the devil's tree'. The current head of Yemen's water resources agency once volunteered, with remarkable candour, that the nation's problems looked much less serious after an extended qat session.

During the brief era of Soviet control in Yemen that followed the departure of the British, qat consumption was limited and very closely controlled. Those whom we know in Aden who disapprove of it, blame its widespread and destructive use, like so much else that they consider wrong in the country, on 'the North' with whom they were hastily and reluctantly united in 1990. In the days immediately preceding reunification there had been a separate North and South Yemen. It was in that time that Nancy had visited.

A question to an older member of staff, soon after our arrival, about shrapnel scars I had noticed on the walls of buildings around the clinic elicited a painful account of the brief and bloody civil war of 1994, which followed reunification and left many thousands dead in Aden. I had, I admitted, scarcely been aware of it, and of Egypt's painful forays into Yemen some years earlier, been completely unaware.

During the 1950s the star of Egypt's Gamal Abdul Nasser was in the ascendancy and enthusiasm for non-aligned nationalism captured the imagination of many across the Middle East. In 1958, Yemen became the third Arab state to join Egypt and Syria in Nasser's vision of a United Arab Republic. But less than four years later, exasperated by Nasser's overbearing sway, Syria bailed out of the arrangement, followed by Yemen. Though Yemenis may have been disillusioned with Nasser himself, they nonetheless remained impressed by what Egypt had achieved under his leadership and had begun to make unfavourable comparison between Egypt and the pathetic state of their own country and the eccentric, often cruel, and unenlightened rule of their leader Imam Yahya. There were numerous plots against the Imam and in 1961 no less than seven attempts were apparently made on his life. In the last of these he was shot three times at close range but survived to die peacefully a year later in Taiz from where he had ruled . He left to his son and heir, Imam

Badr, the desperate legacy of a country no longer able to feed itself, with only one paved road, no factories and just a handful of secular schools for boys and one for girls, run by the wife of a foreign diplomat.

On the evening of the 26th September 1962, only one week after his father's death, Imam Badr and the centuries-old rule of the imams was overturned in a military coup d'état, led by one Colonel Abdullah al Sallal, who promptly became President of the new Yemen Arab Republic.[3] After the coup, rumours circulated that Imam Badr had died in the fighting that had briefly engulfed his palace on the night of the coup. He had not. He had in fact made his way northwards accompanied by 250 loyal followers and crossed over into Saudi Arabia. It had been a hard journey.

In Saudi Arabia, however, his fortunes looked up. The Saudi royals, convinced that their arch enemy Egypt had had a hand in Colonel Abdullah al Sallal's sudden rise to power gave financial and substantial support to Badr, while many of Yemen's highland tribes, encouraged by Saudi financial enticements, came over to his side. Imam Badr, along with his uncle Hassan, who had once been Yemen's Ambassador to the United Nations in New York, and a bunch of his younger relatives, based themselves in some of Yemen's highest and most remote mountains from where they planned to embark on a guerrilla war in the hope that they might overthrow the revolutionaries and return the Imam to power.

Meanwhile, as feared and anticipated by both Saudi Arabia and Britain, Nasser increased dramatically – and as it proved, disastrously – his country's involvement in Yemen. Through support of the new fledgling republic Nasser was determined to extend his control on to the Arabian Peninsula.

Over the next few years Britain, France, Saudi Arabia, Iran and even Israel resolved to thwart Nasser's ambitions in Yemen. They did their best to bolster the position of the Imam and of the royalists by supplying them with funds, arms and military advisers. David Stirling of SAS-renown was at one time involved in recruiting and sending ex-SAS personnel to train the Imam's forces. Those sent caused considerable alarm among the Egyptians, but were not actually very effective.

Nasser's venture into Yemen began modestly but grew rapidly. It was

[3] Not to be confused with President Ali Abdullah Salih, who seized power in 1978 and was driven from office in 2012

not long before hundreds of Egyptian teachers, doctors and technicians were despatched to the new Republic where it had been quickly realised by General Nasser that the project of modernising Yemen 'was about creation rather than reform'.[4] Large numbers of troops accompanied the civilians. By the end of 1965 there were over 55,000 Egyptian troops in the Yemen and when, the Six Day War erupted in 1967, roughly half of all Egypt's troops were still entangled there, some thousand miles or more from where they were then needed. The Egyptian presence in the country was bitterly resented and their troops paid heavily for their generals' incompetence. Between 1962 and 1967 Egypt's military suffered 20,000 casualties. Years later, in the time of the rise of Bin Laden and Al Qaeda, rivalry between his Egyptian and Yemeni followers was common – the latter calling the Egyptians, 'Pharoahs', because of their arrogant involvement in General Nasser's time in Yemen.

Nasser was to call Yemen his 'Vietnam'. The commander of his forces in the country, one Field Marshall Al Amer, wrote poignantly of his nation's last adventure into Yemen. 'We did not bother to study the local, Arab and international implications or the political and military questions involved. After years of experience we realised it was a war between tribes and that we entered it without knowing the nature of the land, and their traditions and their ideas.'

The very same sad epitaph could surely be written over far too many military adventures in the Middle East in the fifty years since the Field Marshal wrote.

At around the same time as the Egyptian forces were pulling out of Yemen – bloodied and disillusioned – the British were struggling to keep order, hand over power and leave Aden. It proved a messy and unhappy exit. In 1966 the British Government had announced its intention to remove all military installations east of Suez, and the last British forces were withdrawn from Aden in late November 1967. A good friend and neighbour of ours was, at the time, a Royal Marine officer, and flew the last helicopter out of Aden to the waiting assault ship, HMS Fearless, at anchor in the harbour. The chaos that ensued after the abrupt departure of the British ushered in the birth of the People's Republic of South Yemen, and twenty or so more years when the South came under Soviet influence and control. Three years later, in 1970, the name of the new state was changed to The People's Democratic Republic of Yemen (PDYR).

[4] Ibid, p.94

In 1968, the year after the British departed, 'the Soviet Union discovered to its delight that, without having to lift so much as a finger, let alone mount a military expedition, it had made the first (and only, as it turned out) Arab convert to its ideology, expanded its sphere of influence to the Arabian Peninsula, and gained a useful port from which to conduct its Indian Ocean manoeuvres.'[5]

Aden had been taken by force by the British in a brief skirmish lasting only a few hours, 139 years earlier, on 19th January 1859. Eager to acquire somewhere to refuel their new and speedy steam ships, Britain tried first to acquire the island of Socotra. When this plan foundered, attention was turned to Aden. At the time Aden was described as a sort of 'international colony for Indian Ocean pirates' – which some may think it is reverting to today. The task of acquiring Aden was entrusted to Captain Stafford Bettesworth Haines of Britain's Indian Navy. He was resolute and tenacious. He needed to be. The negotiations to purchase the port from the sheikh of the Abdali tribe, who nominally owned it, were to prove protracted.

In the end, exasperated at the length and course of negotiations, and stung by what the Captain and his superiors called, 'the tone of arrogant superiority' of those with whom the negotiations were being conducted, it was decided to turn to force. Five hundred heavily armed Indian soldiers were despatched from India to take the port town – which they did, as mentioned earlier, on 19th January 1859. Resistance to the troops was spirited but chaotic. A sergeant major of the Artillery was stabbed and twelve Arabs killed. Three artillery pieces were captured and sent off promptly to Britain as a gift for the young Queen Victoria. One still stands on the river front outside the Tower of London.

Over the long years that followed the Indian sepoys' taking of Aden, British influence and control over the hinterland was gradually extended and consolidated through numerous treaties with different tribes and their leaders. In 1937 Aden's tribal hinterland was divided into the Eastern Protectorate extending through the Hadramaut to Mahra and including Socotra, and the Western Protectorate stretching across to the Red Sea and some twenty miles north towards the city of Taiz. By 1954 there would be a total of ninety treaties in place for a population of less than half a million people extending across an area almost as big as Britain.

[5] Ibid p.113

Keeping Aden was a costly exercise and one which would, in the end, be given up with unseemly haste and little concern or provision for those locals who had served it most faithfully. The last thousand British troops left in the early afternoon of 29th November 1967. In the brief, bleak words of one British official in Aden at the time, 'It was not a moment to bring tears to any eyes, or lumps to any throats unless you happened to be one of Aden's thousands of middle-class Indians, for example, or a sultan of one of the former protectorates, humiliated and furious at Britain's betrayal of their treaties.'[6]

Over our years in Aden we got to know well the Consul of the Russian Federation. We often met him on the beach at Elephant Bay where we tried to swim at least once or twice a week, usually in the late afternoon when it was cooler. Ruslan was normally in the water before we arrived. With his broad shoulders, short neck, close cropped hair and steady stroke he was easily spotted and would always wave and often alter course to greet us. If we found him on the beach itself he would be reading - philosophy or a substantial classic novel. He was thoughtful, kind, observant and mischievous, frequently teasing us with his observations and ready criticism of British and American foreign policy in the Middle East. But he was sometimes a little disappointed to discover how closely our views on the matter coincided with his own.

One day a delightful young, energetic friend of his, Milan, who was training Yemeni fighter pilots to fly very new and sophisticated Mig fighters, asked if they could study the Bible with me. It was a request as unexpected as it was welcome. Milan had had devout Christian grandparents, but he had never opened a Bible in his life. His parents had been staunch Communists. Ruslan had heard it read on his occasional visits to a Russian Orthodox Cathedral near his home. Over the succeeding weeks, we met regularly and worked our way through the Gospel of John. Ruslan and Milan were conscientious students and spiritually perceptive. Their questions were always searching. In the course of our sessions Milan asked for baptism and in a joyful service with all our congregation present, he was baptised. The little stone font which we used had been rescued some years earlier from a long abandoned British garrison church near Silent Valley, while the simple, elegant metal stand on which it stood had been made, at my request, by a local blacksmith whom one of our guards told me confidentially was a Yemeni Christian and 'a very good man'. I had not known.

[6] Ibid p.88

One day, in conversation with Ruslan, our talk turned to a consideration of the legacies that Britain and the Soviet Union had left respectively to Yemen. Ruslan was in a melancholy, reflective mood. "What did we leave?" he asked earnestly. He gave me no time to reply, answering his own question with a disarming chuckle – "the British gave Yemen letterboxes and we gave them Lada cars." I did not say which I considered the more enduring legacy.

A year or so later, when we were seated together on the beach, Ruslan informed me that he would be leaving Aden for good in two days' time. His four year stint was up, and he was returning home to Moscow. He said that he'd enjoyed the simplicity of Aden, read a lot and done his best to look out for the interests of his country and those of the 120 Russians – mostly women – who had, in the Soviet era, married Yemeni husbands. But he also conceded that it would be nice, once again, to have a proper social life and the chance, perhaps, to find an attractive new partner. He had had two short and unhappy marriages.

After a while, he suggested I take a final swim with him. We swam out beyond where the shark nets had once hung when British and, later, Russian swimmers were more common – and the sharks more troublesome. We swam steadily back and forth parallel to the beach. And then my companion slowed, trod water and asked quietly if I would bless him – before he went home. I told him that it would be a privilege. We both trod water. I prayed, and raised my hand to make the sign of the cross over him. Ruslan bowed his head. Little waves lapped at his chin. A great red fireball of sun settled lower into the horizon behind us. We were embraced in its glow.

(CHAPTER THREE)
STRANGER IN THE NIGHT

We were at home on the evening the call came. We did not often go out at night, but that was not because of fear for our security. In fact, in Aden, we felt more relaxed and at ease than in any other Middle Eastern capital city where we had lived. Beirut, where we had been as a family during the last terrible convulsions of Lebanon's civil war, was often dangerous. Car bombs, random shelling, violent and bloody turf wars between rival militias and kidnapping were then commonplace. In Tehran where we lived more recently, we considered that the greatest hazard to life was the traffic and crossing six lane highways on foot a perilous if sometimes unavoidable adventure. The BBC's one-time correspondent there, John Simpson, once wrote dryly, 'in Tehran, traffic lights are purely advisory!' It seemed so.

In Aden, we were usually home in the evenings, quite simply because we were tired. The hours that we worked were not long compared with what we had worked in parishes in England or Wales. But they were full – often of the un-predictable, sometimes of the tragic, frequently of the exasperating and many times, the comic.

On a morning surprisingly devoid of distractions, a wide-eyed, highly excitable Sameera, our Eritrean cleaner, appeared suddenly, shouting, "Emergency, emergency!" It was quite a common cry on the lips of Sameera. And while it usually denoted something serious – like the flooding of the church when the waste pipe on the overworked washing machine fell off – there were others when it was used to describe lesser problems – like the discovery of a trail of muddy feet across her newly swept and washed floors. I always tried to remain calm and to elicit the cause of the emergency before declaring an official state of emergency. On this occasion there was no holding her back as she dramatically disclosed the reason for her outburst – 'Terminites!' I left my desk immediately and followed the small, bustling, black robed figure into the little library at the end of the hall where I knew she had been dusting. I used it for small staff meetings, occasional counselling and the storage of Bibles, which we held in some twenty languages, for distribution largely, but by no means exclusively, to seafarers passing through the Port of Aden. Bibles in Tagalog, Russian and Chinese and various languages of India were most commonly in demand. The Bible Society of the Gulf diligently kept us supplied with whatever we asked for, while the Yemeni customs department readily cleared them. They would permit the import of Bibles in any language except Arabic.

On the table in the library lay a dozen Bibles – Hindi ones with the edges of several pages nibbled by hungry, wriggling white termites. A state of emergency was officially declared. Dereje and Elias, Ethiopians who then comprised our versatile maintenance team, were summoned. They removed, shook out and dusted every Bible. No more 'terminites' were found. The point of their entry into the wall of the library was detected, injected with a dark potion and sealed. Later, over our staff tea break, there was lots of laughter about the termites preferring 'spicy' Hindi Bibles.

The other reason why we rarely ventured out at night was that there was not a lot to go out for. We enjoyed taking visitors to eat delicious fresh fish in any of a number of scruffy, cheerful restaurants. Sometimes we would go to the Ching Sing Chinese restaurant – the closest thing in Aden approaching a foreigners' club, where neither the decor nor the music have changed much since the sixties when it opened. At that time there were over 40,000 British living in Aden. At the time of writing I believe we are five. It is still possible to drink beer in the Ching Sing and until very recently a gin and tonic too, in almost equal proportions. It remains, even in these straitened times, a convivial and welcoming place and the food a unique blend of Chinese and Yemeni cuisine – and good.

Sometimes in the evening we would shop in Crater, which is just that, and the oldest part of the city. The streets are narrow, the heat in summer awesome, and the shops – whether of spices, cloth, perfume, honey or kitchenware – fascinating. At some point on these expeditions, we would usually try to squeeze into a tiny crowded teashop, order glasses of sweet milky tea and freshly cooked, greasy but delicious pancakes cooked in a wok over a huge roaring single gas burner flame.

A few years ago, an enormous mall was built on the edge of Crater beside the sea. The more well-to-do shop there in Lulu – part of a chain of Gulf supermarkets. A young man told us that he and his friends liked to sit and chat and text in the cool of the Mall hopeful that the flowing black robes of young women might just brush against them. We found shopping in old Crater more interesting – and exciting.

In a city where, to western eyes at least, much was unpredictable, ad hoc, and dreadfully untidy, there were some constants. The call to prayer was one of them. When we arrived in Aden, there was just one mosque near us, and a very small one five hundred yards away beside the sea. Occasionally, we were told that the imam there would preach against Christians. This happened once, I recall, when pictures of the abuse of Iraqi prisoners by American service men and women were shown repeatedly on Arab TV channels across the Middle East.

Later during our time in Aden, another mosque was built – significantly larger – a quarter of a mile away towards Maala. And, as we were leaving, yet another was built, this one within a short stone's throw of Christ Church, overlooking our compound and, to the disgust of many of our neighbours, their bedrooms and balconies. 'More hospitals not mosques', was a common cry from Muslim friends. Fortunately, our main act of worship was on Fridays, before Friday Prayers at our neighbouring mosques when, with the volume turned up, possibly for our benefit, the sound of the various preachers was deafening.

The other constant in our lives was the daily routine of our friend and colleague, Gashu. Gashu is one of the longest standing members of staff. Like several others he is a refugee from Ethiopia, and is held in deep affection and respect by all. Part-time gardener, guard, self-appointed sweeper of the grounds, for many years the devoted keeper of the late, fierce guard dog, Millie, and trusted cashier for the patients' fees, he is also a man of deep faith and Christian prayerfulness. We could set our watches by the time we heard his steps on the staircase outside as he left his apartment above us to sweep the courtyard outside the clinics, an hour before they opened each morning. He locked his door every Tuesday evening at seven before setting out for the Ethiopian Fellowship meeting near the airport, where he and friends would gather to study, worship, and pray. If we met him on his way there he would always be smartly dressed in a white, freshly ironed shirt, well polished shoes, a substantial Bible in hand – and fragrant with aftershave. His was usually the last ring at the gate at night, returning from the Fellowship or shopping in Tawahi.

On the night in question the bell on the gate rang long after Gashu had returned. Millie, the guard dog, barked loudly. After some moments the duty guard phoned, "Sorry to disturb you," he apologised, "but there is man who want to see you. He has dead body – a lady – Russian." I put on my shoes and went to investigate. Outside the gate there was a dusty Toyota Hi-Lux pick-up. Beside it stood the driver, whom I took to be about my age, dressed in a futa and sandals. He spoke English, and quietly explained his presence and that of the small body, which I was shown wrapped in cloth and lying under a cover in the back of his vehicle. "She was," he informed me, "eighty years old, and from Moscow and visiting her daughter in Sanaa who is married to a Yemeni. There she die. She is Christian so I bring her to you now, in Aden." It was, I thought, an extraordinarily generous undertaking. I asked him how he had got involved with the burial of a Russian Christian. He replied simply, "I am a Christian. My name is Peter Nathaniel." He delved into his shirt pocket to produce a much-folded identity card in which his Christian names were clearly printed.

We brought the pick-up into the courtyard, made tea, looked through the official papers of the deceased, contacted Mansour to ask him to get a grave dug and transferred the very little body into one of two spare coffins we had at the time. Revisiting Aden recently, I found Dereje making a coffin in the workshop for a young Ethiopian man who had died. It was, he said, the twenty-second one he had made during his eight years of working with us in Yemen. At the time of Peter Nathaniel's appearance we actually had two spare coffins because two of our local doctors had had relatives die outside the country. The relatives had been flown home in coffins which were then thoughtfully given to the church for Christian burials and their relatives buried in the Muslim tradition, in simple cloth shrouds. When all the arrangements had been made, Peter Nathaniel made to go, and as he did so, said with embarrassment, "There is problem. I am sorry. It is two days now and she smell. I am sorry."

At ten the next morning, we buried the little Russian grandmother from Moscow in the dusty, sprawling, lovingly maintained Maala cemetery. I spoke about Jesus and the resurrection. And, at what I thought significant moments, the three barefooted grave diggers nodded sympathetically. When the ceremony was over they filled the grave enthusiastically and dust blew everywhere.

Later, Peter Nathaniel came to the office. Only the diggers, myself and the Ethiopian friend who had translated for me, had been at the graveside. Peter Nathaniel had come to ask Mansour how much money he owed to the church. He told him, "Nothing", and I was glad. After he had gone Mansour asked me his name. He had clearly been impressed by Peter's politeness and concern, and admitted his astonishment that a Sanaani could behave so decently. Generally, Adenis and Sanaanis have as little to do with each other as possible and miss no opportunity to malign the other. We did have reason to visit Sanaa every few months, and when asked by our staff in Aden on our return how we had found it, enjoyed teasing them by saying that it was wonderful, whether it was or not. They could never resist the bait, and someone would inevitably snort, 'Impossible!' Northerners were known as 'dahbashi' disparagingly after one 'Dahbashi' who featured in a popular television series made in Taiz before the reunification of the country in 1990. The series was called Tales of Dahbash. Dahbash was portrayed as an unreliable, lazy rascal with a strong nasal accent like the northern president. 'Dahbash' became synonymous with typically northern behaviour, for anything that was underhand or shabby, 'from the chaotic way in which Northerners navigated Aden's British-built roundabouts to the unjust and opaque way in which [then President] Saleh was seen to be running the country.' [1]

I told Mansour the name of our kind acquaintance who had made such an impression on him - giving the family name as well. His eyes lit up and immediately he said, "This is a famous family. There were two families in Aden who became Christians in the time of the Scottish hospital in Sheikh. This man is from one family. The other family were more famous - and the hospital was later called the Affara Hospital after the fine Yemeni surgeon from this family, who became Christian." Mansour seemed thrilled, and if he was also relieved to discover that our visitor was not from Sanaa after all but a fellow Adeni, he did not say so. Later he was to take us and others to show us the remains of the old hospital, part of which is now a court house. A faded sign on the wall read, 'Admissions', and another, 'Female Nurses Quarters'. Neighbours, who remembered the hospital functioning, readily told us all about it. One pointed out the building that had been the chapel, 'where they prayed every day'.

Tradition suggests that the Christian faith was brought to Yemen in the time of the Apostles. Some think that Frumentius, apostle of Ethiopia, visited south west Arabia in the fourth century. What is sure is that in the reign of Constantius II, Theophilus Indus, a sort of combined ambassador and bishop, took charge of newly formed churches in Ethiopia, south west Arabia, and on the large island of Socotra. He also founded a church in Aden and was given permission to build others in the city of Zafar near Yarim, due north of Aden and roughly half way between the port city and Sanaa. Someone also told us that there had once been a cathedral in Sanaa, and that remains of it still existed, but we did not go in search of them.

[1] Victoria Clark, YEMEN – *Dancing on the Heads of Snakes*, Yale University Press, 2010, p.40

The Christian faith must have made significant inroads in to the region for records exist of the vigorous persecution of Christians instigated by the last Hamyarite King of Yemen, Dhu Nuwas, who reigned from AD490 until AD525. He was a convert to Judaism and zealous. He was eager that his subjects – particularly those who were Christian – embrace his new found faith. Within his kingdom, in what is now Saudi Arabia, there was a predominantly Christian settlement at a place called Najran. The Christian population were invited to convert to Judaism or be killed. 20,000 people opted for death, rather than deny their Christian faith. They died by the sword and also in great pits filled with inflammable material into which they were hurled. Amongst those who died was the head man of Najran and a young mother with her seven-month old baby. The Quran commends the fidelity of the martyrs or rather, 'brethren of the pit', as it calls them.

Peter Nathaniel slipped out of our life as quietly and as unobtrusively as he had entered. I did, however, follow up on the life of Dr Ahmad Sa'id Affara. He came from the Aqrabi tribe and was born in Hiswa, just west of Aden. He came from a strict Muslim family and was himself deeply suspicious of Christian missionaries. Nonetheless, it was to their school at the Scottish mission in Sheikh Othman, started in the 1920s, that his father sent him in preference to a government school, to learn English. Sheikh has long been part of the sprawling city of Aden. But in 1909, when the Scottish hospital was opened there, it was relatively remote, quite undeveloped and, as hospital expatriate staff were to discover, unhealthy. Its location was in part chosen quite deliberately to distance the new work from what was perceived as the unhelpful European influences around Tawahi and Steamer Point where most foreigners then lived.

Today, Sheikh is the bustling hub for bus and communal taxi travel to every part of the country. Beggars – some very young – ragged and bare footed, abound. So do sellers of sweets, locally made sesame seed bars, and polythene bags of iced water. And invariably out of the jostling crowds will emerge, on sight of a foreigner, a tired, veiled woman waving a tattered prescription paper from a pharmacy asking for, or more often demanding, money.

We never took a communal inter-city taxi – usually old Peugeot 504 estates. We were warned off doing so by our local staff. 'Flying coffins' they called them and sadly, on several occasions, we saw the reason why. We did take the national coaches, which were reliable and comfortable, though at the end of a long journey – and few are short – the aisle between the seats looked like the result of the conscientious strimming of a privet hedge, deep with discarded leaves of qat.

At school the young Ahmad Affara joined in a weekly discussion group. He recounts, 'We met on Sunday mornings on the veranda of the nurses' house. The meetings were open to all who wished to come. I was keen on going to them, and did that without my father's knowledge. The thing that appealed to me in those discussions was that the subjects which were chosen were both from Christianity and Islam. We usually chose our subject a week beforehand. During the week we would read our Quran and traditions for reference, the Gospels, anti-Christian publications, and anything we thought might be of help to us in our discussions. A friend of mine became a subscriber to two anti-Christian periodicals, The Light and The Islamic Review. Both are organs of the Ahmediyya sect and published in Lahore and Woking, London, respectively. Armed with arguments acquired from these sources, we met and expressed our views. The Christians were never baffled as far as I can remember and our arguments were answered, sympathetically, although not always to our satisfaction.'[2]

Ahmad and others of his friends sought out their own religious teachers and raised with them the subjects discussed in the Sunday meetings. They were roundly criticised for indulging in dangerous liberal thinking. Aware of the opposition his curiosity had aroused, yet clearly drawn by what he had heard from his Christian teachers, he wrote that, 'to accept the very personal quality which Jesus brings to religion is therefore a very costly thing'. Nonetheless he accepted 'the very personal quality Jesus brings', and, despite very fierce opposition and criticism from some, asked for baptism. He was baptised in the home of Dr Petrie, who had led the discussions which he had attended, in the presence of about forty of his friends. It was to prove, as he had anticipated, a costly decision.

There were threats to his life. Dr Petrie got him out of the country. He went briefly to Wilson College in Bombay, and later to Scotland, and the University of Edinburgh, where he studied medicine. Later he took a diploma in tropical medicine in Liverpool. During his time in Edinburgh he was a valued member of a congregation pastored by Dr Petrie's father, the Rev James Petrie. In 1940, he returned to Aden as a missionary of the Church of Scotland. He worked with the Mission, and later had his own private practice in Sheikh Othman. He was made mayor of Sheikh Othman in

[2] James McLaren Ritchie, *The Church of Scotland South Arabia Mission 1885-1978*, Tentmaker Publications, 2006, p.193

recognition by its people of his outstanding service as a doctor to the community. And at some time, the Scottish hospital came to be known as 'The Affara Hospital'. He resigned from his practice in 1961 and returned with his family to Scotland, where he died of a heart attack in 1968.

He was an outstanding character who came to be held in enormous respect and affection by the people of Sheikh Othman. He was a person of great professional competence and integrity and quite open about his Christian faith. Deeply impressed by the atmosphere of the discussion groups he attended at school, and by the readiness of those who led them to engage in serious debate with attentiveness and courtesy, he wrote later of his understanding of the nature of Christian mission, drawing on those early encounters of his with dedicated, foreign missionaries. 'The Christian missionary enterprise is not a declaration of war by the Christian church on other religions or beliefs, or an attempt to impose the Christian viewpoint on others in a fanatical way. It is a grave misunderstanding of the missionary aim to regard it as such. It is not a question of forcing our views on peoples of other religions, but it is a question of deep love and regard for them, and real concern with their spiritual and temporal welfare.'[3]

These words, written seventy years ago, are as appropriate today as they were then. There are many adherents, both of Islam and of Christianity who, zealous to swell the ranks of their respective faiths, force their views on others.

One evening we were eating in our favourite fish restaurant on the edge of Crater. The family room where we ate was a flimsy lean-to structure with a corrugated iron roof tacked on to the main restaurant. It overlooked many small fishing boats moored below us, and was screened off from the main restaurant with a torn black curtain. We had gone there with a number of friends and had eaten well. Already, half a dozen scraggy cats were circling under our table awaiting our departure and the moment when they could jump up and fight over the remains of our meal. Nancy had gone to the wash room to wash the fish scales from her hands. (Most food is eaten with hands in Yemen.) The tables were substantial and wooden, topped with Formica; the chairs, the white moulded plastic ones with arms that stack easily, blow away in a strong wind and buckle if you lean back on them. When we first arrived in Aden, the Formica tables wherever you ate would first be 'laid' with open pages

[3] Ibid, p.195

of Singapore's Straits Times. Apparently, whole containers of pc
of the paper were shipped into Yemen and used to cover the i
customers in thousands of little restaurants across the country. They were
sometimes the only English language paper, we saw. Latterly, sadly, they
were replaced with long strips of filmy blue and white plastic torn from a
roll and spread across the table. It was a dull, if rather practical, substi-
tute for the Times.

On this occasion Nancy was a long time in the wash room, and when
she did emerge it was clear that she was not amused. Later, on the way
home, she explained the reason. While washing her hands she had been
accosted by a young, veiled Yemeni woman who asked, without introduction or preamble, if she was a Muslim. She told her that she was not,
but that she was nonetheless, a believer in God. The woman urged her
to become a Muslim then and there in the wash room and she explained
how Nancy could do that. Stirred, Nancy told the woman that she was
a Christian and would gladly remain one.

Our Ethiopian staff, travelling as they did daily on public transport, would
be frequently subjected to similar interrogation and exhortation by fellow
passengers, who were Muslim.

At one time we had worshipping with us a senior European diplomat. He
had actually taken a year out from his career to work with a foreign relief
agency in Yemen. He had at one time worked in North Korea. One day
he confided, to our surprise, that Yemen reminded him of North Korea.
There, he said, he was subject to the unrelenting, predictable and repetitive propaganda of the regime. He felt himself under similar daily assault, he told us, from some of his fervent Muslim colleagues wanting him
to convert. He may, by his honesty, have laid himself open to their approaches. He was not, he had told us (and probably told his colleagues)
'very religious', but came to the church for the quiet, and the chance to
speak English - and we were very happy to have him.

As a priest I was not immune from such approaches, but it only happened
once and then in an intriguing and indirect way.

I was seated at my desk one morning in the office. Mansour and I had
dealt together with the most pressing business and in a lull he told me
that he had something for me from a friend of his with whom he prayed
each evening in the mosque. He handed me a large white plastic carrier
bag turned inside out so that the face depicted on the outside could not

be seen. Islam does not approve of the depiction of the human form. The inversion of the bag suggested that the gift came from a devout and observant Muslim. "It is not a bomb," said Mansour, with a naughty smile, "I have checked." Intrigued, I peered inside. There were eight books; some were quite substantial, two, little more than pamphlets. One, I noticed, was written by someone who had been an Anglican, and that another had been printed in Parson's Green in West London. All were written to recommend the Muslim faith and to suggest the reasonableness of adopting it.

I asked my watching colleague if I might send back some Christian reading material - in Arabic. "As you like," he replied with a smile.

Often we were visited by little groups of Christians, mostly from Europe or North America, concerned for the evangelisation of the Muslim world and of Yemen in particular. We were grateful that they took the trouble to seek us out and we appreciated their interest in the work of the clinics and the church. They asked lots of questions, and I think that some of our answers surprised and even shocked them, as indeed it was sometimes our intention. They seemed surprised that we employed so many Muslim staff and that we spoke so readily and openly with them about issues relating to faith and life.

Inter-faith dialogue, something I had long associated with learned, structured debate and discussion between religious intellectuals was a normal, natural and happy part of daily life around Christ Church and the clinics. Ramadan invariably provoked lively conversation about the merits and difficulties of fasting and the searching question to us, "Do Christians fast also?" Once toward the end of Ramadan, when the spirits and energy of our Muslim staff were clearly flagging, an older lady member of staff said wistfully, "It's very hard to purify the soul." As our first Christmas in Aden drew near, another asked eagerly when I would, "put up Bethlehem". In her mind, Bethlehem was the traditional Christmas nativity scene and I learned from my enquirer that in previous years an attractive crib with the appropriate figures had always been put up in a prominent place in the community centre before Christmas.

I had not known and had, with the help of two of the guards, already constructed a small life-size stable in the church the previous day. I took my colleague who had asked after Bethlehem to see it. It looked, as was intended, a little bit like a hut in one of Aden's teeming refugee camps. She gasped, put her hand to her mouth and exclaimed in excited wonder, "It is a real Bethlehem!" Later, having walked all around it and peered inside, she said thoughtfully, "I think the prophet Jesus would come to somewhere like this today."

Some years ago, and long before I took up my position in Aden, a foreign employee at Christ Church was advised to leave the country having, as I gleaned, been rather over-enthusiastic in sharing the Christian faith with a local. Then, when I was in Aden, the same person wrote to me asking if it would be possible to return to work with us. I thought it would be unwise as I knew that, whatever had happened, it had not been forgotten by the authorities in Aden. Still, I thought I would run the request past one of our older staff members who had worked closely with the person in question.

She recalled the person immediately - and warmly. "Of course," she volunteered, "she was a missionary", and added, "Every Christian is a missionary. It was bad luck, she gave a Bible to a long beard" - the local rather disparaging shorthand for a seriously fervent Muslim man. It was my turn to be surprised. The person whose advice I had asked is a devout Muslim. There was no hint of disapproval of her past colleague; it was rather - 'this is what Christians do and she had the misfortune to give a Bible to the wrong person'.

Years earlier, living in Damascus, I met regularly with a local Syrian Muslim friend to discuss issues of belief. One day I apologised to him for being, as I thought, 'too pushy'. He rebuked me, "Do not apologise; if you did not speak this way, your faith truly would not be important to you. And a man without faith in God is only a quarter of a man; no," he hesitated, "just a tenth of a man."

If my colleague's opening comments surprised me, her closing words on the matter were remarkable. "Anyway," she said, "there is no need now for our friend to return to us. If we want to become Christian we just look it up on the Internet." Her lovely local colleague looked at me, smiled, and nodded in agreement.

(CHAPTER FOUR)

NOT AN ORDINARY CHURCH

There was a gentle tap on the half-open door, and the bright, hopeful, white faces of a man and woman - in their early fifties - peered round and enquired cheerfully, "What time's the service?" I must have looked quite blank for they continued helpfully, "We thought it would be at ten, but perhaps we are just too late. We looked up Anglican Churches in the Middle East and were so pleased when we discovered Christ Church, Aden, and here we all are." The 'all' was slipped in to explain the presence of another couple of similar age and equally full of hopeful anticipation, who had by this time squeezed, with the first, into the crowded office. I cannot have looked much more comprehending for with a flicker of apprehension, the little group's spokeswoman said, "It is Sunday, isn't it?"

I reassured them that it was indeed Sunday, and that while they had every right to expect there to be a service of Christian worship in an Anglican church on a Sunday, it was common for Christian congregations across much of the Middle East to worship on Fridays, when all employees, local and foreign, had the day off. This explanation was received with glad sighs of relief, knowing nods and exclamations of, "Of course," and, "Silly not to have remembered that!" They were English. I told them that we did have a simple informal meeting on Sunday nights in the church for worship and Bible study to which they would be very welcome. But they pointed out, regretfully, that it would be a long journey back from where they were staying - and at that moment I spied Sameera hovering outside the door, mimicking tea drinking, and looking at me enquiringly. I nodded assent and she bustled off to the kitchen.

I discovered that our visitors were on a ten-day tour of Yemen. This was some time before the British Foreign Office issued a travel warning to their nationals cautioning against unnecessary travel to Yemen - and before the tragic killing of the Spanish tourists which occurred while we were still living in Aden. While we waited for tea the visitors plied us with further questions. What kind of service did we hold usually on Fridays? Did we have a choir and, most searching of all, did we by any chance have a Flower Guild? We ducked the last question but did our best to answer the others. We did not know what our friends would think of us if we told them that the plastic palms and lilies in the church were dusted

44

weekly, washed quarterly and replaced altogether when they looked tired and brittle. On special occasions we did cut flowers from the garden, but cut in the early morning, they had always wilted by dusk even in the relative cool of our lofty Victorian building. I told them a little of the history of Christ Church and did my best to explain its present day ministry.

It was constructed in 1864 and built to accommodate several hundred worshippers. An old framed photograph on the office wall shows the main doors of the church open to the sea - barely one hundred yards away, while behind it on a steep rocky crag is the old signalling fort, its great masthead decked out with flags run up to give instructions and commands to waiting ships. It is still there - accessible to the nimble and energetic - but showing evidence of the ravages of weather and war. The massive metal securing rungs for the mast's ropes are pitted with rust and the fort's walls dented and broken from artillery shelling in the civil war of 1994. By the time we had pored over the old photo and looked at a faded colour photograph of the congregation leaving the church after Sunday worship, as it was then, in the early sixties - the women in floral dresses and wide hats, the children sporting shorts or skirts, and all with sandals and white socks - tea had arrived. It was received enthusiastically along with the digestive biscuits - a happy reminder of past British influence. I continued with my brief resumé of the history of Christ Church.

In 1970, three years after the formal departure of the British, the church building was requisitioned by the navy of the newly-formed Marxist-leaning People's Democratic Republic of Yemen. It was used as a store for ropes and chandlery and also as a gymnasium. One long-term British resident of Aden enjoyed telling me that he had played squash more frequently in the church than he had prayed in it. In the early nineties, however, the church building, largely intact but somewhat scarred and filled with rubbish, was returned to the Diocese of Cyprus and the Gulf within whose far flung responsibility it lay.

The story of the building's return is a remarkable and inspiring one. A fatwa was formally issued authorising the return of the building to the Diocese. The late Bishop John Brown - at the time the Bishop of the Diocese of Cyprus and the Gulf - worked tirelessly and enthusiastically for the restoration of Christ Church and for a renewed ministry through it. In a little book which he wrote called, A Way in the Wilderness, he describes how the fatwa came to be delivered, helpfully explaining first the meaning of the word fatwa. 'The word means a 'formal legal opinion' relating to the Muslim religion and it may be delivered by a Muslim religious leader qualified to deliver legal opinions. These opinions are delivered, not only against someone or something, as in Rushdie's case, but they may also be delivered in support of a person or project.'[1]

In his book the Bishop describes how he formed a friendship with the Grand Mufti of the Yemen, His Excellency Grand Mufti Zabarah, who lived in one of the wonderful tower houses of the Old City of Sanaa. And it was he, who in due course delivered to Bishop John the fatwa. Translated it read as follows,

In the name of Allah
I hereby issue my formal religious rule stating
that there is no objection for the church in the city of Tawahi,
Aden, to continue conducting religious services,
and to allow it to be renovated. It is our duty to allow members
of the Christian community to exercise their religious rights,
and to worship in their churches, as it is the case in
our mosques and Islamic centres all over the United Kingdom
and the rest of the Christian world.

(signed) Grand Mufti Zabarah of the Yemen[2]

The title deeds relating to the founding and building of the original church, drawn up 140 years earlier, had also to be found - no small challenge given the long and often tumultuous intervening years. But they were found, and by a blind employee in a government office in Aden, who knew where they lay. The text of the crucial document had been somewhat eaten by termites, but Queen Victoria's seal and signature were still attached.

In the course of earlier discussions with the then governor of Aden, Bishop John had asked how the newly opened church and the Diocese of Cyprus and the Gulf could best serve the people of Aden, while at the same time providing a spiritual home for expatriate Christians of any nationality and background. He was told that a primary health care clinic for mothers and children would be a great contribution to the neighbour-

[1] John Brown, *A Way in the Wilderness – A Bishop's Prayer Journey through the Arabian Peninsula*, Christians Aware, 2008, pp. 90, 92
[2] Ibid.

hood. This proposal was welcomed by Aden's health authority and over the years the clinic has become a respected and valued part of the city's health services. The clinic quickly came to cater for more than just mothers and children and after a few years a specialist eye clinic emerged beside the original clinic. In recent years the two clinics have handled between them nearly 20,000 patients a year, the majority of them very poor. Generally only those living in our immediate area can be seen in the general clinic. Eye patients can come from almost any corner of the country and do.

I recounted all of this to our four visitors. We then did a brief tour of the clinics, meeting the staff who readily and ably answered their questions. When our new-made friends came to leave, one said reflectively, "It's not a normal sort of church really, is it?" A few weeks later we received a thoughtful e-mail on behalf of the four saying that their trip to Yemen had been wonderful and the visit to Christ Church one of the highlights. We were touched and grateful.

On a normal working morning interruptions could be many – the occasional tour group, officials from the Ministry of Health or the city's security services, salesmen from local drug companies, Somali refugees wanting help, students from Aden's University School of Architecture wanting to see the interior of the church – and many more. On entering the compound all would be screened by one of our uniformed Group 4 guards. Foreigners wanting the director were usually led straight to my office. Of the presence of local officials I would be informed and they would be shown to a comfortable lounge area beside the office, while refugees would be asked to sit in the shade in the courtyard, where I would see them as soon as I could. Our own staff, whether from the clinics or the maintenance team, could see me at any time. Most days brought their share of heartbreak and generous bouts of frustration – but no day passed without laughter.

One day Wonderson, husband of Sameera referred to earlier, and one of several Ethiopian refugees on the staff, came to the office door. His head was slightly bowed, his smile wide and his eyes – hopeful. I tried to guess what it was he wanted. I knew the look. Wonderson was our official gardener. His duties were not onerous for the garden was hardly begun. He watered it absentmindedly, over-generously and, to my exasperation, in the hottest part of the day. He also tidied the compound and swept up the eucalyptus leaves very vigorously if I happened to be passing, bagged them and tossed them into the neighbourhood garbage skip. He was also quite adept at selecting plants that would survive and grow in our very salty patch. Jasmine thrived, spread quickly and, in the evenings, smelt lovely. Hibiscus did well too and a white lily that only came out at night and closed up coyly at the approach of dawn. During the previous week, we had gone together to one of Aden's street-side nurseries, where plants - mostly tumbling, gorgeous bougainvillea in rusting square, milk powder tins - stood on display. We had bought two. I had also bought, to Wonderson's evident concern, a small lemon tree. I expected that on this occasion he had come to tell me with mingled grief and satisfaction that it had, as he had anticipated, expired.

I was wrong. "I need," he said, very slowly in a gentle voice and with his large appealing eyes, "fertilisation". I was aghast. Nancy and I had, in the short time we had been in the Aden clinic, learnt about cataracts, visual fields, refractometers, malaria and the prevalence of diabetes - and much else, but not this.

At that moment, I remembered that he and his wife were expecting their first child and so I suggested, as best as I could, that in that area all was surely well. Wonderson understood, and giggled, and attempted to clarify his unexpected request. "I need," he repeated, "fer-ti-li-sation". My heart sank. He continued, "I need what comes from the back of the sheep." He paused to explain visually. He raised one arm and with his other hand indicated little things falling from the arm pit of his up-raised arm. "It is," he concluded momentously, "for the lemon tree." I under-stood. At the end of the morning Sahil took the staff to the minibus rank in Tawahi, deviated slightly on his return and presented me a little later with four warm black bags of sheep droppings for the ailing lemon tree.

We had four and a half very happy years living in Aden. When we re-turned home to Wales people would occasionally ask what we had been doing there. Once or twice we replied mischievously, but truth-fully, "making a garden". We had talked from time to time about doing something with the piece of empty land between the church and the accommodation block in which we lived. A conscientious predecessor had planted fast growing trees around the edge of the compound and on one side of the church there was a very small patch of fenced off grass, onto which Wonderson frequently turned the hose and forgot to turn it off. The inspiration to create a garden came through the unexpected visit of a group of Korean students. There were thirteen of them - students and young graduates - a number of whom were medics.

By the time they arrived the clinics had already closed and the staff and patients gone. We lingered on in the office, tidying up ends and noting tasks to be done the next day. Just when we had finished and were about to go home to satisfy the rumbling demands of two hungry stomachs, they appeared. We had heard the bell on the gate ring but we had assumed that it was one of the two ladies - Nadia or Boosie - who came to clean the clinics every afternoon.

The duty guard who had brought them into the hall beside the office told me who they were and where they were from. He was himself the holder of Yemen's gold medal for tae kwon do, had had a trainer from South Korea and was clearly excited and pleased to meet other Koreans. They were very deferential and profusely apologetic for turning up out of hours. We were hungry, but they were delightful and we walked them through the hall into the church where we gathered chairs into a circle and listened to their story. The church is a long, simple, barn-like structure with neither spire nor tower. It was very creatively re-developed when handed back to the diocese. A partition wall was built, dividing it in half across its middle. The sea-facing end was made into an attractive hall, off which there was a small open lounge area, a library, kitchen, toilets and the office. A mezzanine floor was constructed above it and five very comfortable bedrooms with bathrooms, kitchen and a large sitting room made. The front half of the church was retained as a church, and it is beautiful. The Victorian stained glass windows have long since gone. Instead, there are stunning Yemeni-style ones. The church was restored just before the 1994 civil war, ransacked during it and lovingly restored after it.

Instrumental, and indeed central to that remarkable work were Tom and Edna Hamblin, who are remembered still with deep affection and gratitude by many in Aden. Tom once described to me his grief – and resolve – on seeing the damage wreaked on the newly restored church in the civil war.

> "When I finally arrived in September, I was shocked at seeing the destruction to the church and stood weeping. The roof, which had been repaired just before the war, had fortunately escaped serious damage, but the interior had been wrecked. The lovely wooden staircase to the upper guest room floor was gone, also all the individual partitions, doors to the bedrooms, all toilets, showers, electrical

fittings, even wiring in the walls had been removed. The communion table, which was originally from the Church of Scotland's chapel, beautifully carved oak, with the words carved around, Do This in Remembrance of Me, was also taken with other church items, as well as all our own personal effects.

John Spracken, our good contractor, had just received a container, days before the outbreak of the war, which was packed with all the beautiful tiles for the church and clinic's floors. Everything was gone ... an empty container stood forlornly in the church grounds. Of course my bicycle had gone too!

It was all such a sorry sight and my heart sank. I telephoned Bishop John in Cyprus explaining the devastation. 60,000 plus pounds spent had been wiped out; that money was mostly from church fellowships and individuals from the UK and Singapore, little money was left in the Bank, nowhere to live to start again ... was it worth it? The Bishop's reply after a pause was, "Dear Tom, you haven't lost your vision have you?" That was what I needed to hear at such a time, for Edna and I knew God had opened the door to Aden and had given us a vision.

I got temporary accommodation, then rented a villa – Edna joined me and we commenced again."

The visitors explained that they were on vacation, came from a variety of churches and were touring Yemen – some of them with a view to returning after graduating to work in the country. They asked lots of questions about the nature and scope of the ministry of Christ Church and about living in a Muslim country. One of them asked Nancy, if she 'covered up' in public. She always did, but not excessively – wearing a scarf over her head which fell easily across her shoulders. The local Muslim staff appreciated the gesture, though I never heard a whisper of disapproval of one or two of our foreign female staff who worked with us with heads uncovered. Once, when visiting Sanaa, a man beat on our car window and remonstrated angrily that Nancy should cover up her head. We had just arrived in the city and it had been a very long, hot drive up from Aden and she had shed her headscarf on the way. This was the only encounter of its kind that we had during our entire stay in Yemen. Aden, however, has always had more experience of foreigners and a cheerful, laid-back accepting hospitality.

The Koreans were warm-hearted, dedicated, missionary-minded young Christians. Our spirits, which had been flagging, revived in the company of our young friends. They asked if they could sing. We assured them that it would be absolutely fine. One of the young women produced a flute, another a guitar and the rest – from their pockets or back packs – little travelling song books. Their singing was lovely and we were familiar with the tunes of several songs. Afterwards, they asked if they might pray for us and the work in Aden. We gladly accepted their offer. So they all prayed – at once – and the sound was very great. We prayed in turn for them, their travels and their future. As they left, one of the young women drew Nancy aside and told her that God had shown her some Bible verses, which she in turn was to give to us. Later at home we read the verses in English. They struck us as being both appropriate and very timely. They became the closest thing we had to a 'mission statement' and were from a chapter of the prophet Isaiah. They were,

'If you do away with the yoke of oppression,
with the pointing finger and malicious talk
and if you spend yourself on behalf of the
hungry and satisfy the needs of the oppressed,
then your light will rise in the darkness
and your night will become like the noon day.
The Lord will guide you always, he will satisfy your needs
in a sun-scorched land and will strengthen your frame.
You will be like a well watered garden,
like a spring whose waters never fail.
Your people will rebuild the ancient ruins
and will raise up the age old foundations.
You will be called, 'Repairer of Broken Walls',
'Restorer of Streets with Dwellings'.'
(chapter 58 verses 9-12)

Slowly a garden evolved. Early one morning before it got really hot and on a day when the clinics were closed for one of Yemen's many national holidays, I began scratching in the earth the course of a path to run diagonally across the area we had decided on for a garden. I did not want a straight path; I wanted it to meander from one corner to another. And I thought the path could be laid after the style of 'crazy paving' and edged with some stone. I had driven past many stone yards on the outskirts of the city and had seen the piles of rock off-casts after stone had been cut for the floors or the facing of the homes of the rich. As I stood back admiring the gentle curves of my scratchings, I was aware of a presence. I looked over my shoulder to see the solid figure of Gashu, "It is not straight," he said. Ethiopians can be very direct. I explained that it was to be a winding English path alongside which I hoped, in time, to plant flowers and bushes. "It would be quicker and easier, Mr Peter, if it went straight and was concrete," replied Gashu, unimpressed. "I don't want a straight, quick concrete path like the others," I responded peevishly. "I made all the other paths," Gashu replied stolidly. I extolled the merits of his concrete paths - their usefulness, durability and straightness, but begged indulgence of my eccentric and sentimental wish to make a winding, English path. He did not look convinced.

It was getting warm, and I did not want to be caught up in a protracted discussion about the merits of straight or meandering paths. I retreated to the cool of our apartment for a late breakfast of coffee, mangos and fresh rolls. A little later I looked down from our small balcony onto the site of our future garden. To my astonishment there was Gashu, shovelling earth into a wheelbarrow and making a wide shallow trench along the line of my scratchings. The guard walked over to ask what he was doing. I would have loved to have heard his explanation.

A few days later, with the two other Ethiopian staff members, we hired a Toyota Stout - a very elderly hand-painted green pick-up - which nonetheless still lived up to its name. We went to a stone yard where Elias, one of the two, had worked when he had first arrived in Yemen. He explained our business to a distinguished looking gentleman with a red beard and a flowing white robe. He waved to a heap of discarded flat stone off-cuts and invited Elias and Dereje to help themselves. As the truck was being loaded I spoke to the man and told him that my father had been in Aden in the 60s with the British Army. His eyes twinkled, "Maybe," he said, "I shot at him." "Maybe my father shot at you," I retorted. He roared with laughter, slapped his thigh and said, "Anytime you want stone, come and take it without money - for your father!" Amongst older Yemeni men and women the British seem, despite everything, to be remembered with deep affection and their return, hoped for. One patient, on hearing that a very small group of Royal Naval personnel were to be stationed in Aden to train the Yemeni Coast Guard, hobbled across the courtyard to tell me excitedly, "the British - they're coming back!"

The garden progressed. Spurs were added to the original path and

Dereje and Elias became professional and speedy path layers. Plants were planted. A bamboo hut was built for children to play in, and the jasmine trained to romp over it. At one time, when we gave refuge to some twenty stranded Nigerian seafarers, they laid little cobbled court-yards under the growing trees. Mansour produced a small aviary and we bought songbirds for it from the market. On the 10th anniversary of the re-opening of the church, Dereje and Elias created a pool and a waterfall. The pump was brought out from a garden centre in Dorking, in England. We even worked out a primitive drip system with black plastic pipe and an unreliable timer. If it was not quite the Garden of Eden, we thought it was not a bad attempt. It had become the 'watered garden' of our Isaiah reading and was to be enjoyed by many, many people.

Not all our visitors were foreigners. One morning the phone in the office rang and a woman, who told me that she was calling from Sanaa, asked for the director. She sounded Yemeni and had excellent English. I told her that she was speaking to the director. With little small talk or preamble she asked what we did at the clinics. I told her. When I had finished she asked, to my surprise, "Is that all?" I filled in a few more details, of-fered clarification of some things I had mentioned rather hastily, but all in all I reflected that we actually did quite a lot - and I had said nothing about our work with either refugees or seafarers. She thanked me for the information and said that she might visit after the feast at the end of Ramadan. It was still some months away and although I had been a little puzzled by her call, thought no more about it.

Some months later and after the Eid, a guard told me that there was a Yemeni woman who wanted to see me. I suggested that he show her into the little open lounge area beside the office. A few minutes later I went out to greet her. She was veiled and all in black and she spoke excellent English. She told me that she had travelled down by bus from Sanaa the previous day. She asked if I was the director and, when I as-sured her that I was, asked me what we did at the clinic. A question from me confirmed that she was the telephone caller of a few months earlier. The conversation followed the same course as before. It was strange. When I had repeated my pitch she thanked me and made to leave. I asked if there was anything else we could do for her. She hesitated and then asked suddenly if I believed in evil spirits. I told her that I did. She explained that her family thought her possessed and were doing some unpleasant things to her to drive away the spirits. She was calm, clear and very matter-of-fact about it. At that point Nancy slipped in to join us and quickly picked up the story. After a while I told her that, though I was the director, I was also a priest and pastor and that in that context had sometimes prayed for people in the name of Jesus, and that troubled and anxious people had, as a result, found peace and strength. I asked if she would like me to pray a prayer in the name of Jesus for her, her home and her family. She said that that would be fine. Afterwards, as she rose to go, I asked why she had come down to the clinics. She explained simply, "My friend in Sanaa had an operation here eighteen months ago, and she told me that the people she saw were kind."

CHAPTER FIVE

PART OF THE COURSE

Omar leant forward in the chair opposite me. His hands were loosely clasped and he had a scarf wrapped around his head. He had at least two days of stubble on his chin. He spoke very slowly and deliberately in English, and his dark eyes were fixed intently on my own. "Will you baptise us?" he asked searchingly. I had had a hunch that this was where the conversation with he and his friend Mustafa was headed. I hesitated briefly and replied cautiously that to do so might prove a dangerous and costly step for us all. "We have read the Bible," he responded. "We have studied the words of Jesus. He talked about the cross. We are ready to take up the cross. Do not stop us."

I thought about that meeting with the two men and their burning question when, a week later, we were invited to attend a reception on a French naval warship, part of the anti-pirate international coalition, which was then visiting port. Visits from ships of the coalition were infrequent, but when the French came they always made a point of holding a party and welcoming aboard both locals and the few expatriates who remained in the city. It was an unlikely but congenial setting for the lively conversation that unexpectedly opened up onboard between myself and senior members of Aden's security and police services, who had also been invited to the reception, about Yemeni Christians. I cannot remember how the subject arose, but the questioning was friendly, and the interest in the matter, evidenced in the faces of the dozen or more smartly dressed men around me, considerable. I knew many of them already; some from my regular visits to the port, others from meetings related to the church, dealing with the provision of extra security over Christmas or at the annual Remembrance Day services in the different cemeteries. I had found them unfailingly helpful.

"Are there many Yemeni Christians?" came the first question. "Yes," I replied. No-one asked me how many, and I would have been hard pressed to give a figure if I had been asked to. If I had been, I would have ventured several hundred at least, and it could well be several thousand. "Where are they?" asked another officer. "Everywhere," I said. It was perhaps a slight exaggeration, but I thought of the two young men with their question, whom I had met in a noisy restaurant on the other side of the city, both of whom came from towns some hours' distance from Aden.

I thought of a young student who had made the long bus journey down from Hodeida to Christ Church to ask for a Bible and who, after receiving it, asked for some 'Christian teaching', before he took the afternoon bus back home! I had actually heard of groups of Yemeni Christians, men and women, meeting in or near to all the country's major cities. And I thought of the soldier, whom we had met at a lonely checkpoint on the long road to Mukalla whose face, on reading our papers, had suddenly lit up. He had then spoken enthusiastically of one of our predecessors, and with a knowing wink, radiant smile and other gestures indicated that he was a Christian too. There were no other soldiers in sight. I did not tell my attentive audience about any of these people. It was not necessary.

The officer, who had asked the whereabouts of Yemeni Christians, was quick to follow on my reply with a final sharp, if predictable question, "How do these people become Christians?" My questioner was clearly very interested to know. "How long do you have?" I joked. I did not wait for an answer, but told them that I had met young men who had read the Gospels with the help of the Internet, and through that had become convinced that they should become followers of Jesus. I told them that I had also heard of both men and women having visions of Jesus, or dreams, which proved significant in their becoming Christians. I could have given them many examples. Amongst them might have been Ahmad. He had, on his own initiative, acquired a Bible and read it in a fitful, half-interested way on and off over a period of years and had enjoyed discussing its content from time to time whenever he had come across foreigners of Christian conviction. Then one day, while taking a shower, he found himself unexpectedly, profoundly convinced of the truth of the Christian faith. A few days later he had a dream: he was in a neighbouring country, with local Christians, whom he had once met while visiting there. While Ahmad was understandably reluctant to dwell upon the immediate circumstances in which his conviction about Jesus and the Christian faith had come to him, he had no hesitation in saying that together they had awoken in him a desire to follow Jesus. I could have mentioned the young Yemeni father, whose wife had died of cancer only weeks after giving birth to their first child. The man came to see me, and told me that not long after she had died he had been sitting one night on the beach not far from the church, wondering what the future held for him and his baby. As he sat, he told me, he became aware of a presence. He looked up and into the face of one whom he knew was Jesus, who told him not to be frightened, and who assured him that he would always be with him. As soon as he had spoken, Jesus disappeared. I only met the young father on the occasion he came to tell me the story. In the course of recounting it he spoke gratefully of the kindness and faith of a Christian Filipino work colleague who had actually told him to come and see me. The people whom I have met and spoken to, or heard of, who have had visions or dreams of Jesus were almost all in difficult circumstances. Jesus appeared to them in their grief, perplexity, fear and pain, just as he is reported to have done in his ministry, as recorded in the Gospels.

Again, I did not tell my listeners all this. I concluded by saying that I had heard of Yemeni people becoming Christians also through listening to Christian radio broadcasts from other Middle Eastern countries. I thanked them for their questions, and we dispersed easily to talk with our naval hosts and other friends. It had been an interesting encounter without, I thought, a trace of animosity or awkwardness.

Each year we would be invited, with other clergy and their spouses and representatives of their congregations, to Cyprus to attend the annual Synod of the Diocese of Cyprus and the Gulf. We enjoyed these occasions. They provided a chance to catch up with old friends, to make new ones, to listen to reports from across our far-flung and wonderfully diverse Diocese, to be stimulated, provoked and inspired by the conference addresses and seminars, and often to be moved by our times of worship and prayer together. It was also nice to enjoy a glass or more of wine – Yemen is a very dry country. We were present at the last Synod presided over by Bishop Clive Handford, the bishop before the present one – Bishop Michael Lewis. In his conference address, Bishop Clive looked back over his decade in office and shared with us some of the significant changes and developments he had witnessed in that time. He spoke appreciatively of the increasing financial sufficiency of chaplaincies and of the phenomenal growth and variety of other Christian congregations using Anglican facilities for their worship, especially in our Gulf churches – their congregations drawn from the vast numbers of Christian migrant workers from India and the Asian subcontinent in the region. The Annual Report that year from St Andrew's, Abu Dhabi, was just one of several church reports that spoke of the size and diversity of these congregations to whom they offered hospitality: 'The compound teems with hundreds and thousands of worshippers throughout Friday from 5am until nearly midnight, and every weekday evening, some 60 congregations. Often several different worship services can be heard in full swing at the same time – the ecstatic exuberance of Pentecostal groups competing with the measured chanting of Orthodox congregations or the drums and ululating of Ethiopian house maids.'

Bishop Clive also mentioned the greatly increased number of Christian missionary groups, largely Western-based and funded, working for the evangelisation of Muslims across the region; "their presence," he said, "is an important reminder of the missionary dimension of our Christian faith." From time to time we were invited by these groups to attend their conferences, seminars and consultations in the region. We were glad to be included by them and grateful too, especially when we knew that some of their number regarded Anglicans with considerable suspicion.

The programme at these events was invariably full, policy and strategy papers numerous, and debate, when encouraged, lively. I am indebted to the work of several of these groups, especially those producing materials in Arabic suitable for putting into the hands of Muslim friends curious to know what Christians believe, and why.

Years ago, I read a book, Temple Gairdner of Cairo, by one Constance Padwick. I read it again recently. It is an enthusiastic portrait of a most attractive, intelligent, far-sighted and passionate missionary to Islam. Temple Gairdner was a dedicated Anglican priest who lived and worked in Cairo from the 1890s until 1928 when he died after a short illness. He felt in his day the inappropriateness of a lot of literature produced by Christian presses and intended for Muslim readers. Its tone he thought far too strident and contentious. I think that some of the material produced today for the same readership still is. But while he did not for a moment believe that difficult issues should be avoided, he appealed for more warmth and humanity in what was written. There needed, he thought, to be an apologetic literature unafraid of controversial points. Silence, he felt, was tantamount to a denial of the truth he knew and lived. But the literature must be humanised, written, 'for fellow men, not only for the defeat of argufiers … stories, history, drama, music, poetry, pictures – all that would bear the impress of the Spirit of Christ was a reasonable part of the Christian apologetic to the whole man'.[1]

A hundred years later all those things – stories, history, drama, music, poetry – and much more, are creatively deployed by Christians of the Middle East eager to make known to others the meaning of their faith. Temple Gairdner would, I think, be pleased. He once wrote memorably of the need of, 'the song note in our message to the Muslims – not the dry cracked note of disputation, but the song note of joyous witness, of tender invitation …' I have heard that note as I have watched some

---

[1] Constance Padwick, Temple Gairdner of Cairo, SPCK London 1929, pp. 148, 149

excellent Christian television programmes out of Cyprus and Lebanon.

We appreciated, as mentioned already, the invitations we received from different missionary-minded groups to attend some of their consultations and meetings. We admired the dedication of these groups and their people to the cause of evangelism. We were impressed at the number of people coming forward to work with these groups in often difficult and demanding situations, and we were impressed too, at the sacrificial and generous support many had from their congregations and friends back home. We continue to count many of their personnel our good friends and remain in contact with them. But I have to confess that we rarely left their gatherings without some niggles of concern. It was not just that we sometimes felt rather unzealous in the company of these friends! It was more than that. I could not help feeling that in their circles Muslims were, first of all, the 'target audience or target people', or something like that, before they were fellow human beings with very similar hopes, fears and anxieties to ourselves. An Egyptian co-worker with Temple Gairdner, one Yousef Effendi Tadras, once paid him this striking tribute, "No one taught us as he did. Others taught us to refute Islam – he taught us how to love Muslims."[2]

Some years ago Nancy and I were able to spend a few very useful and happy months at the college in Selly Oak on the edge of Birmingham in England which the Church Mission Society then ran to prepare people for Christian mission in Britain and abroad. One day, and I think it was at a moment's notice, the Anglican Bishop of Egypt, the Most Reverend Doctor Mouneer Anis, was asked to address the students. We were a marvellously mixed international group from all sorts of backgrounds, experiences and professions. The Bishop gave us two pieces of advice: first, he warned us against the danger of negativism. Then, secondly, he spoke of the imperative of love. He was very down to earth.

He began by telling us of his own experience of coming from his home in Egypt to study medicine in London. At first, he said he and his fellow Egyptians would get together to extol the merits of England. Then, as time passed and perhaps as autumn and winter encroached, they found themselves running it down. "We became," he said, "negative about everything British." He warned us all against doing the same when we went abroad and got together with other foreigners. He then spoke about the need to love the people whom we were sent to serve. He said,

[2] Ibid, p.302

"they will forgive you your cultural insensitivity, and they will overlook your awful Arabic if they believe that you really love them. But they will very quickly sense it if you do not." Having delivered these succinct exhortations, the Bishop concluded by urging us, nonetheless, to be good language students. To his wise words of advice to aspiring missionaries I would dare to add two more of my own.

The first is a caution not to underestimate, still less to ignore or belittle, the work and witness of other Christians in the country where they find themselves working who come from a different background - whether social, national or theological. One might think that such a warning would be unnecessary, but I recall the grief that Nancy and I felt when, in one small congregation in which we served, a young Pakistani family confided that none of the westerners in it, almost all of them mission-focussed people, had made any effort to befriend them in the six weeks since they had joined us. We were saddened and ashamed, and all the more so because the congregation was not large. By contrast, when a new family from a similar missionary background to their own had arrived and joined the church some months earlier, there had been loud applause and clapping after I had interviewed and welcomed them into the congregation. I had given the same welcome to the Pakistani family when they had first arrived in the country. They were greeted with smiles, but not applause. Ironically, I learned recently that those who were so quick to clap and had made it known that they were in the country for the long term, were amongst the first to leave the country when the first winds of the Arab Spring blew into it. At the time of writing, the Pakistani family remain - devout in their faith, brave in their witness and faithful week by week in helping to lead worship in a church long since bereft of a pastor. They could not leave the country if they wanted to. The husband has not been paid by the company he works with for several months. When one day they do come to leave, a few hours will suffice for them to do their packing. They live simply and travel light.

Ramon Lull, who lived seven hundred years ago, was a truly remarkable man who felt compelled to give his life to the task of taking the Christian gospel to the Muslim world. He was born in Majorca in 1235. Like Saint Francis, with whom he had much in common, he came from a wealthy family. He was rich, popular and gifted. He was a poet, musician, scholar, philosopher and nobleman courtier. He underwent a dramatic life-transforming and enduring conversion to Christ. It came through a vision of the crucified Christ. At the time, Ramon Lull was composing a romantic ballad. The vision was repeated three times. His conversion was followed by an extended period of retreat and study. It lasted nine years, and much of it was devoted to the study of Arabic. The call to be a missionary to Islam came early on. It was, in the atmosphere of his time, an extraordinary, undreamed of vocation to embark upon. Saracens were loathed as conquerors in the East and hated as the partially conquered in the West. Christendom was smarting over the loss of Jerusalem and the Holy Lands. Lull shared their loss but was grieved at the way in which the conquest had, in the first place, been attempted. He wrote movingly, 'I see many knights going to the Holy Land beyond the seas, and thinking they can acquire it by force of arms, but in the end all are destroyed before they attain what they think to have. Whence it seems to me that the conquest of the Holy Land ought not to be attempted except in the way in which thou and thine Apostles conquered it, namely, by love and prayers and the pouring out of tears and blood.'[3]

He spared no effort to win a hearing in universities and in the ecclesiastical corridors of power for the cause of taking the Gospel to Muslim lands. He envisaged training colleges for mission and drew up the most rigorous and demanding curriculum, which not only included a thorough training in Christian theology, but also in philosophy, Arabic literature and language. He also cherished the dream of a great Christian missionary movement in which monks, aflame with love for Christ, played a significant role. 'I find scarcely anyone, Lord, who out of love for thee is ready to suffer martyrdom, as thou hast suffered for us. It appears to me agreeable to reason, if an ordinance to that effect could be obtained, that thy monks would learn the various languages, that they might be able to go out and surrender their lives in love to Thee ... O Lord of glory – if that blessed day should ever be, in which I might see thy holy monks so influenced by zeal to glorify thee and to go to foreign lands to testify to thy holy ministry – of thy blessed incarnation and of thy bitter sufferings that would be a glorious day.'[4]

His dreams of the training colleges and missionary monks were not realised. He was stoned to death outside the walls of the town of Bugia in Algeria in 1315. He was eighty years old. In the years immediately preceding his death he had preached to both Jews and Muslims in his native Majorca and in Cyprus. After this, he returned to North Africa where he had laboured extensively before. There he won fresh converts

[3] Temple Gairdner, *The Reproach of Islam, The Foreign Mission Committee of the Church of Scotland*, Edinburgh, 1909, pp.228, 229

[4] Ibid, p.233

to Christ and cared for them diligently until thrown into prison. In prison he was urged, over many months, to renounce his faith. He was eventually released and deported, only to return to spend a final year back in Bugia, encouraging his converts. It was at the end of this time that he was stoned to death by an angry mob.

Today across the Middle East, and in the countries where Lull visited and laboured, Christian monks are scarce. But there are tens of thousands of men and women – migrant workers from Africa, India, Pakistan, Sri Lanka, the Philippines and elsewhere, forced to live lives of almost monkish simplicity, Christians, many of them incidental missionaries amongst whom I know are those who bear a good witness, in often very hard circumstances in these Muslim lands. One day, when I lay paralysed in intensive care in a hospital in Dubai, the nurse looking after me said something which made me enquire whether she was a believer. I cannot now remember what it was that she said, but it made me think that she was either a very sincere Christian or a very sincere Muslim. She came from a neighbouring Arab country and told me that she had become a Christian, like a number of her friends, while working in a hospital in Saudi Arabia. I would have loved to have known more but supper intervened. I expect that 'incidental missionaries', like those to whom I have just referred, had a part to play in the story.

In Damascus and in Aden we have encountered, to some degree worked with, and enormously admired, the tough, practical and profoundly prayerful work of the Missionary Sisters of Charity – the Mother Theresa sisters. There are 4,500 sisters active in 133 countries around the world. All take a vow of poverty, chastity, and obedience – and a fourth, to give wholehearted and free service to the poorest of the poor. In their founder's own words, their work is 'to care for the hungry, the naked, the homeless, the crippled, the blind, the lepers – all those people who feel unwanted, unloved, uncared for throughout society – people that have become a burden to society and are shunned by everyone'. A sister's possessions include three saris – one to wash, one to mend, and one to wear. They also have a pair of sandals, a crucifix and a rosary, a plate, a metal spoon, a canvas bag and a prayer book. And in Damascus, where it is sometimes cold, but not in Aden, where it is always hot, they can have a woollen cardigan.

In four of Yemen's cities – Aden, Taiz, Hodeideh and Sanaa – they have homes for the destitute and the abandoned. All are bright, clean, cheerful places, and the work done in them, held in the greatest respect across the country. We always enjoyed visiting the Sisters. They seemed unfailingly happy and delighted to see us and any friends whom we brought with us. They were as ready to laugh as they were to pray. Some were from Africa, others from India, and nearly always there were one or two from the Philippines. They were often moved around within the country from one centre to another and every year each one of them had a month's retreat – in Jordan or Lebanon. In Aden they cared for over fifty people, men and women, most diligently. The first time I visited the Sisters I asked one of our guards to go with me to show me the way. He had been there several times on different errands, the last time with the eye team, who had been invited to check the eyes of those in the Sisters' care.

As we drove he told me that a few months earlier one of Aden's daily newspapers had run a double page spread about the work of the Sisters in Aden. I was impressed. I was also amazed when my companion told me that he had read the article with a good friend of his, whom I knew, and that what they read had made them both cry. I was curious to know what had provoked such a response in them, especially as both of them were athletic, rather macho and not given to ready displays of emotion. I asked him why they had been so moved by the article. "Because," he replied, "they have come here from all over the world. They have nothing and they give everything for our people whom we cannot be troubled to look after ourselves." He went on to remind me that three of the Sisters, whose names I later learned were Lillian, Anetta and Michael, had been murdered in 1998 in their centre in Hodeideh by a twenty-five year-old man who was in their care. "Their deaths," said my friend, "made people in the Yemen angry and sad."

Sometimes we joined the sisters for prayer in their chapel beside the Centre. We appreciated these times. Mother Theresa once said, "The more we receive in our silent prayer, the more we can give in our active life." We shared their prayer, and we admired their active life. Once after prayers and over biscuits and a Fanta in the kitchen, one sister from Tanzania, asked almost the same question as the young Yemeni officer at the French naval reception, "Do you know of any Yemeni people becoming Christians?" I assured her that I did. "I am so glad," she replied, "I pray every day that God will open the eyes of our people here to see the beauty of Jesus."

My next word to aspiring missionaries is this: Put your trust more in the Holy Spirit than in the newest, fashionable strategy for reaching unreached peoples out of the latest international conference on the subject. And before expanding more fully on that plea I would be bold to add: Trust more in God's protection and in the conviction of your calling than in the doubtful protection of coded messages beloved of some Christian organisations, secure e-mails considered essential by others and in anxiously observed security protocols which I believe are little defence against those really determined to cause us harm, and which provoke bewilderment and sometimes suspicion amongst those who do not. Where, I sometimes wondered as I listened to these friends preoccupied with security, was the spirit of the apostle Paul who, confronted with danger at every turn, nonetheless wrote, 'by the open declaration of the truth we commend ourselves to the conscience of everyone in the sight of God'.(2 Corinthians, chapter 5 verse 2)

Temple Gairdner, referred to gratefully earlier, was a terrific one for thinking big plans for reaching the Muslim world. He was a great strategist, but faced with the enormity of the task wrote sombrely; some might feel a little harshly, but I think realistically, 'If Islam's forces are indeed nature, the world and the flesh, then Islam has left us one weapon in taking away all others - it has abandoned to us the Sword of the Spirit. The Spirit of Jesus is the only asset of the Church.'[5]

One day I was visited by a young Yemeni man from Aden who sought me out and told me that he wanted to become a Christian. There was something about him that made me cautious, even a little sceptical. I decided to seek the advice of a fine Yemeni Christian, widely known and respected as a man of integrity and unafraid to be known as a Christian. I made contact and asked, a little apprehensively, whether he might be willing sometime to meet with my visitor. I shared with him my doubts about the genuineness of his inquiry. My friend replied readily, "I'm not afraid. We have the Holy Spirit. If the man is not a serious enquirer but from the police, maybe he will learn something new!" I was impressed. His cheerful confidence and willingness to help spoke eloquently of his claim to have the Spirit.

Renowned Christian evangelist and statesman, Billy Graham, wrote once of the unpredictability and independence of the Holy Spirit, something I have tried to illustrate in the stories and incidents described in this chapter. He wrote, 'The Bible teaches that the Holy Spirit is like the wind and who can tell the wind what to do? Another symbol is the dove, and

[5] Constance Padwick, p.185

who can tell a dove when it can fly into the sky, and where it should? Water, living water that shall be poured out in a mighty torrent – all these symbols express the sovereignty of God. We dig our little trenches, and we say, O God, you're going to work this way and only in this way. But God breaks out, and does it his own way.'[6]

In more than thirty five years of serving widely differing congregations in different parts of Britain and the Middle East, I have found that it has often been through crises – painful, unsought and unexpected – the sudden death of friends, unforeseen political upheaval, our own physical sickness and occasional bouts of dark depression, fractured relationships and other hard things – that the Spirit of God has brought us deeper insights into our faith and new experience of the grace of God – as much as through the regular worship, prayer, study, teaching and service that make up the life of a church.

I was blessed for an all too brief time with a remarkable father-in-law. He was possessed of a quick and very dry sense of humour and a deep and warm faith in Christ. Once, when climbing in the Cascade Mountains near Seattle with three of his sons, who were up ahead of him on a slope, the oldest, Dave, shouted down, "How are you doing, Dad?" The reply was as surprising as it was memorable. "Pulse so and so, breath coming in G-strings ..." "What?" asked Dave in astonishment. "Well," came the gasping response, "that's one worse than short pants, isn't it?"

Prayer, shared together around the kitchen table, usually after supper, was an important part of my wife's upbringing and family life. Prayers were for the world and the neighbour next door. Sometimes the praying was a bit stilted and Dad seemed to do most of it. Occasionally it degenerated into uncontrollable giggles. It's hard not to laugh when someone prays fervently for the people of Turkey with the words, "God bless those turkeys". Personal problems and individual dilemmas were offered up in prayer, along with the state of nations, and when in discussion a situation seemed more than usually perplexing, my wife's father would say, with a note of quiet expectancy and trust, "We must allow God to do something we never thought of."

Something rarely thought of amongst Western Christians and never seen in the curriculum of any missionary training college I have visited, is raised pertinently in an excellent book, The Message of Mission, jointly

[6] David Watson, *One in the Spirit*, Hodder Christian Paperbacks, 1973, p.20

written by Howard Peskett and a friend and one-time colleague, Vinoth Ramachandra of Sri Lanka. In a chapter penned by Vinoth, he writes, 'ever since the church's first great conflict with the power of Rome, the victory of the Gospel has been won, not by the efficiency of its mission strategies, the effectiveness of its fundraisers, or even the cleverness of its preachers, but by the blood of its martyrs.'[7]

It came as no surprise to me to learn from Muslim friends in Yemen that numbers of their fellow countrymen had become Christians around the town of Jibla, near to Yemen's second largest city of Taiz. There, for thirty five years, American Baptists ran a fine hospital caring for over 40,000 patients every year, and where tragically, in December 2002, three of their staff, William Koehn, Martha Myers, and Kathy Gariety were gunned down and killed. Ironically, they were killed just two days before the hospital was due to be handed over to the government of Yemen after approaches to other Christian groups to take it on had failed. The gunman responsible for the murders apparently slipped past the hospital security guards with a concealed gun, posing as a father seeking treat-ment for a sick child. He murdered the Americans to, 'cleanse his religion and get closer to Allah'. And today as I write, I have learned with great sadness of the death of another American in Yemen – a fine teacher, a dedicated Christian and father of two young children – killed for his obedience to Jesus' great and unrevoked commission, 'to go and make disciples of all nations'. After his death his students took to the streets to denounce his murder and sing his praise. 'He was,' they said, 'a good man'.

At the height of the Iranian revolution of 1979, two young men posing as enquirers asked for a meeting with the Anglican Iranian priest for Shiraz, in his home. I describe the circumstances more fully in a later chapter. They murdered him there in his study. The Anglican Church in Iran, its membership made up almost entirely of converts out of Islam and Juda-ism, suffered grievously through that time but continues today, in the face of great difficulties, to bear faithful and courageous witness to its Lord. Just a few years ago, we listened in England to an elderly and lively Iranian Christian lady who had just made an extended visit back to her home city, which she had left many years earlier. She told us of the phe-nomenal growth of small Christian home meetings right across the city. A young man whom she met, told her that there were over 600 small groups meeting. She did not believe him and thought the figure a wild

---

[7] Howard Peskett & Vinoth Ramachandra, *The Message of Mission*, Inter-Varsity Press, 2001, p. 197

exaggeration. The young man in question invited her to go along to one of those meetings. There were over forty people present of all different ages, and the meeting was actually held on a hillside on a Friday morning. She was impressed at the enthusiasm and commitment of those with whom she worshipped, and while I think she thought the figure of 600 still a little extravagant, she was nonetheless confident that there were many groups like the one she had attended, and far more than she could have ever imagined.

While the persecution of Christians has at times completely eradicated their presence and the witness in some parts of the world, it has also watered the ground out of which new Christian life has wonderfully sprung. That this should be so should not surprise us. The symbol of our faith is a cross, not a cushion. It was through his death on the cross that Jesus defeated the power of death and sin. It was through the resurrection that God raised him to life, and it is through participation in his death and resurrection that his followers are given new life through the power of the Holy Spirit. Jesus, speaking in the shadow of the cross, told his followers and would-be followers of the necessity of a seed falling into the ground if it is to bear fruit. 'Very truly I tell you, unless a grain of wheat falls into the earth and dies, it remains just a single grain but if it dies, it bears much grain.' (The Gospel of John, chapter 12 verse 24)

At the time when Temple Gairdner was an undergraduate at Oxford, confident Christian evangelical missionary fervour, especially for foreign missions, ran high. This interest was stimulated by visits to the university from missionaries returning from, or heading out to the mission field. It was nurtured in prayer groups in colleges of the university, and it was a prominent feature of the great annual Christian Convention held at Keswick in the English Lake District. Constance Padwick, in her biography of Gairdner, describes her subject relaxing in a boat on Derwent Water at the end of a Keswick week. 'Suddenly,' she writes, 'a tall, rather majestic figure standing bareheaded at the prow of one of the boats uttered an unforgettable call. His hands outstretched, his face with a shining on it Gairdner never forgot, he cried to that company of happy youth, "AGONIA is the measure of success".' ('It was,' she explained, 'someone called Robert Stewart, shortly before going out to meet martyrdom in China'). "Christ suffered in agony, so must we. Christ died, so perhaps, may we. Our life must be hard, cruel, wearisome, unknown. So was his." The words made a deep impact on the young Gairdner. He wrote, 'Those words and thoughts will, I hope, be with me all my life.'[8] His friends knew that they were.

While in Britain today hostility to orthodox Christian beliefs, values and behaviour grows more aggressive, I have thankfully yet to hear of martyrdom for holding the Christian faith. And yet for very many Christians, nationals and expatriate, in many parts of the world today, as in the past, martyrdom is a real possibility. It is, one might say, part of the course, and pretty much what Jesus told his followers from the start.

[8] Constance Padwick, p.31

(CHAPTER SIX)
GANGPLANKS
AND GLASSES

Moammar Singh wore, as expected, a turban. It was a very deep red colour. He was tall, thin, and very polite. He was dressed in a clean white shirt, blue canvas trousers and wore chappals on his feet. His top shirt pocket bulged with well-thumbed papers. He was an anxious man and wasted little time telling me the reason for his concern.

He was, he informed me, the second officer of a Dubai-owned salvage tug, the Numo, that had been at anchor in Aden's harbour for the previous seven months. During that time neither he nor his six fellow crew members had received any wages, despite almost weekly assurances from the company's Indian manager in Dubai that the money had been paid into an account of a large and well known bank in Maala - the main commercial area of Aden. Sadly, the story he told is a very familiar one and at any time in almost any port around the world it could be repeated.

Aden, blessed with its vast harbour and strategic position on the corner of the Arabian Peninsula, was once the world's second busiest port after New York. Sadly it is now just the palest shadow of her former self, its reputation tarnished by greed, incompetence and corruption – its big container port running at far less than its considerable potential.

Much of the business of the container port is transit business - the off-loading in Aden of containers destined for shipment up through the Red Sea and Suez Canal to the Mediterranean, or from there to Aden and onward shipping to anywhere in the world. Many of the ships speeding in and out of the container port bear boldly on their hulls and super-structure the names of the companies - Maersk and Evergreen - to name but two. Their silhouettes against a setting sun as they steam in and out of Aden, are ungainly and unmistakable - like shoe boxes on half submerged logs with slivers of smoke trailing behind them.

During our time in Aden I was honorary Mission to Seafarers Chaplain for the Port of Aden. It was a new role for me, one I enjoyed and fitted in as best I could around my other responsibilities. I rarely got to the container terminal, still less into the oil refinery port beyond it. Both were on the far side of Aden's vast harbour bay – almost opposite us in Tawahi – the refinery being nearly an hour's drive away. There was a fine young Indian Christian, a junior officer on a small oil tanker who visited us at Christ Church whenever he was in port; to attend worship if he could, to borrow books and to chat. He was hoping to study in Liverpool and was all set to do so when the vessel that he was on was taken by Somali pirates. He spent several months as a hostage before being released. He had been put in touch with me by my energetic and thoughtful colleague, Stephen Miller, then port chaplain in Dubai, on whose wisdom and experience I was from time to time most gratefully to call.

Once, some time after leaving Aden and when we were settled home in Wales, I received an unexpected call from Stephen asking if I could phone the captain of a large container vessel who was in hospital in Hong Kong having, like myself, been suddenly struck down with Guillain Barré syndrome and paralysed. I phoned immediately and was quickly put through to the phone beside the captain's bed in the Hong Kong hospital. He was frightened and tearful. One day he had been manoeuvring a huge container ship into port and the next evening had been carried on a stretcher down the gang plank, hardly able to move a limb. I briefly told him my story and assured him, on strong evidence, that he would probably make a very good recovery. I had, and I was twenty years older than he when I had been similarly paralysed just a few years earlier. He asked many questions and seemed calmer and more resolved having listened to my answers. I believe he made a good recovery.

The Mission to Seafarers is a remarkable organisation, with outposts in 230 ports around the world. It was founded in 1856. The initiative for its founding came through the labours of an energetic and big-hearted Anglican priest, the Reverend John Ashley, who lived near Bristol. Living there he became aware of the sad and pathetic conditions of hundreds of seafarers on ships at anchor for weeks on end nearby in the Bristol Channel. They were wretchedly accommodated, poorly fed and frequently unpaid. Determined to alleviate their conditions he began a ministry of visiting ships, urging owners to improve conditions, providing what physical help he could, and conducting services on board the vessel which he had specially built for the purpose. It was called the Eirene.

These three concerns of the Reverend Ashley over 150 years ago continue to be very much the staple business of the Mission today. In the many larger ports there are attractive, modern seafarers' centres offering recreational facilities, from gymnasiums to pool tables, restaurants, a chapel, a library and access, of course, to the Internet which increasing numbers of vessels now offer their crews. In Dubai, as one might anticipate, there is a large and very well appointed seafarers' centre with excellent facilities and good accommodation. But there is also The Angel, a thirty foot launch which visits ships at anchor. There can be over 200 at any time waiting to discharge their cargo or containers. The Angel has her own crew, a communications hub for crews visited, simple medical facilities and usually the chaplain. She might visit twelve or fifteen ships a day. It is, to quote a phrase of St Paul, 'a work of faith and a labour of love', appreciated by thousands and follows in the wake of the pioneering work of the Reverend John Ashley.

In the course of my brief involvement with the Mission I learned – amongst other things – that there are, at any moment on any day, well over a million seafarers at sea, and that one third of them are from the Philippines. I also learned that every major airline has a department dedicated to flying seafarers around the world. For the airlines it is a significant and valuable business. Strikes by cabin crews or air traffic controllers or the eruption of volcanoes can cause havoc to tightly scheduled timetables for crews joining their ships.

While the ships slipping in and out of the Aden container port were of reasonable size, relatively new and owned by well-known international companies, those coming in to the main Maala port, for which I felt more particularly responsible, were more disparate. There was, for example, the Jameel – which means beautiful – which she was no longer. Those parts of her hull which still bore paint were dark green. Jameel, I noticed, was only one of a number of names which she had carried. Her displacement was a mere nine hundred tonnes. She had begun life carrying cattle in Norwegian fjords. When I first went aboard she was carrying grain. The owner and crew of five were from Djibouti. They were very welcoming and plied me with sweet black tea in a glass which we drank at a tiny table in the mess room. The portholes were open and a welcome breeze blew through them. At one moment the captain looked down at my dusty shoes and his eyes lit up. Enthusiastically he told me the name of their American manufacturer – correctly – and went on to tell me that he had bought a similar pair in Seattle the previous year. We discussed matters of the sea also.

Many months later I spotted the Jameel again and went on board. One

71

of the crew, an unusually stout one, had just slipped and fallen down a companion-way, badly cutting his leg as he fell against a piece of protruding metal. I have a tendency to faint at the sight of my own blood but I can cope quite well with that of others. I offered to take the injured man to the church clinic just ten minutes' drive away. He quickly agreed and one of our lady doctors washed, stitched and covered the wound. She and her colleagues got used to my bringing in seafarers for treatment. The seafarers were always grateful and I think it increased our standing with the port authorities and security who observed my comings and goings carefully. On another occasion, I happened to appear on the deck of a general cargo vessel immediately after a Filipino crew member had raised his goggles while sanding a rusty bulkhead. As he did so, a splinter of metal flew into one eye. Fortunately we had with us a visiting eye surgeon at the time and half an hour later the splinter was deftly removed by him with no significant damage to the eye.

Actually offering eye appointments – for which we often waived the fee – to port employees and their families was something which Mansour and I did often. It was an easy way of expressing our thanks to helpful police, other officials and friends, and I expect spared us from being asked for bribes for small favours. On one occasion, one of the staff in our eye department gave me a box of spectacle frames for one of the guards on the main gate at the port to try out. It was not a busy morning for port traffic, a few ancient, over-laden Russian trucks ground to a noisy halt behind me as I stopped and explained to the guard, who conveniently happened to be the one for whom I had been given the box of glasses, that I had them with me. He was delighted and insisted on trying them on then and there. He was quite unconcerned for the drivers behind me. This was his moment and he made the most of it. Each pair of frames was tried on and, in turn, discarded. Spectators, always on hand in Yemen, gathered to watch – guards, stevedores and minor officials – and to pronounce on the suitability of the frames on trial. (There were probably ten or a dozen.) "No," said one bright bystander, "those are Harry Potter glasses," while of another pair the same person said, "no, he looks like an owl." All were rejected. The box was returned. I drove on, and port traffic resumed.

Each year the Aden Port Authority issued me with a port pass, which I showed whenever I entered the port and when I boarded a ship. When we first arrived in the city I tried to spend at least two full mornings every week visiting ships. As time went by and other commitments grew, I did less. I was also forced to do less after recovering from Guillain Barré which left me with diminished energy levels and a slightly impaired sense of balance. Gangplanks, especially of large vessels, were a great challenge. Sometimes I chickened out altogether, especially when getting on to the gangplank involved a small jump from the quayside onto its lowest rung or step. There were many ways in which I thought one might die in Yemen, but falling and being squeezed between a rusting cement carrier and the quayside was not one that I wished to risk.

Once I had ascended the gangplank, I would be greeted by a Yemeni watchman, who would in turn take me to a crew member who would ask for my pass, enquire of my business, record my details, issue me with a visitor tag, phone the captain or chief officer and escort me to them. It was a protocol carefully observed whenever I went on a ship. And the vessels varied; from the aged and scruffy Jameel to brand new, smaller container ships of the Maersk line, with state of the art galleys, compact but well-equipped exercise facilities, and smartly dressed crew members serving attractively short contracts of three or six months. It was the first officer of one of their vessels who, learning of my business, greeted me warmly with the words, "Wonderful - you people from Seafarers are the only people who come aboard not wanting to sell us anything or to collect dues from us." He had had a wide and very happy experience of the Mission to Seafarers. And when he learned that at that particular moment we were giving refuge at the church to 22 Nigerian seafarers stranded in Aden without pay for many months, he pulled out his wallet and gave me a handful of dollar notes, "for their food", he explained adding simply, "I was once without money in the port of Rotterdam and the Mission helped me."

Most chief officers and captains to whom I was shown were hospitable, courteous, and curious too - especially if they had had previous experience of Mission to Seafarers - to know what we had to offer them in Aden. Unfortunately, it was much less than most had been used to elsewhere, something I said I hoped we could rectify. One of my predecessors had drawn up plans for a seafarers' centre on the Christ Church compound - while I had explored tentatively the idea of having a grand portakabin inside the port itself.

I would often be invited to join a crew for breakfast or lunch in the mess, an offer I rarely declined, and not only for the sake of the food, which was always plentiful and often delicious. I always enjoyed talking to crew members. Once I was asked to see the ship's cook. He had asked, on hearing that there was a priest on board, if he could meet me. He looked very young. He told me that he was from Myanmar and that this was his first voyage. More important, he told me enthusiastically, was that he was a new Christian and had been baptised in his home church just before joining the ship. His joy was contagious, and with his new and curious ship-mates looking on, asked if I would bless him and his kitchen. It was a wonderful moment in a busy morning.

Once, I was asked by the captain of a large container ship if I would hold a service of Holy Communion on the bridge for the ship's new crew before they sailed the following evening. I gladly agreed. The liturgy was simple and the singing of the crew - almost all Filipino -in Tagalog and English, rousing. The chart table served us well for Communion. It seemed a good way to begin a voyage.

A recent survey carried out by the Mission to Seafarers on seafarers' needs revealed that the vast majority considered provision for their spiritual needs every bit as important as care for their physical wellbeing. One vessel I visited, with the crew made up mostly of Christians from Kerala in South India, had a small room set aside as a chapel. There were small rugs on the floor; a little wooden trellis was attached to one wall up which the tendrils of a plastic plant were climbing, on another was a cross and on yet another, a picture of Jesus with carefully positioned candles below. Crew members were happy to show it to me and told me that they visited it, 'quite often'. It looked well used.

Once, the port was visited by two diminutive Royal Navy mine chasers. Informed that they were in the main port, I took it upon myself to visit them. They were not easy to find. They were tiny and hidden from prying eyes by some well positioned old ships' containers. Armed Marines in desert camouflage fatigues stood guarding the gangplanks - smiling, alert and turning quickly pink in the searing sun. I was welcomed aboard and shown around. It did not take long. I learned that the two little ships had set out from Plymouth in the South West of England a few weeks earlier and were headed for Salalah on the coast of Oman. Amongst the crew was a friendly, blond-haired young officer, who introduced himself as Tim. When he heard that the church was attached to a clinic he asked if he could come over for a check-up. I phoned ahead to tell Doctor Nada we were coming and informed her that the person I was bringing was a handsome young English naval officer. Nada was in brusque practical mode, "It doesn't matter what he looks like - see if he can bring us extra drugs!"

The young officer was duly checked out and pronounced healthy. Later Doctor Nada conceded, with a hint of a smile, that the patient was nice and spoke very good English. I showed him around the church and introduced him to the clinic staff. A little later Tim suddenly asked if I could help him with writing sermons. He explained that at the start of the voyage the senior officer had asked if any of either of the ships' companies was a church-goer. Tim put up his hand and was promptly made chaplain of the fleet for the duration, with responsibility for arranging the weekly church parade. It sounded as if he had coped well but he clearly thought he was running dry, and with three more Sundays still to get through, eager for any help. I gave him some popular books dealing in a lively way with different aspects of the Christian faith. He was grateful.

His request was more easily and speedily dealt with than that brought to me by the anxious second officer of the stranded salvage tug, the Numo.

After listening to his story, I promised to visit him and his crew just as soon as I could, and to make contact immediately with the tug's owner in Dubai. An hour later I was talking to the owner who explained, without elaboration, that his company had had some 'bad problems' but that these were now resolved and that the crew would receive their wages, in full, very soon. I thanked him for the assurance and a few days later managed to get a ride on the harbour master's launch out to the Numo. She was an impressive old ship, at least forty years old, with a high bridge set well forward with a great open expanse behind, dominated by an enormous winch. I met all the crew in a spacious wood-panelled room, with brass portholes and faded black and white framed photographs of other vessels of similar age and type. I was served chai and listened to the difficulties of crew members and their families – all in India. They included stories of school fees unpaid, rent arrears, long-awaited hospital operations postponed. They made light of their own privations, which were considerable. They were running the ship's generator as little as possible to conserve fuel and sleeping at night under the sky, rather than under their fans. The ship's agent responsible for overseeing their welfare had not supplied them with fresh vegetables, meat or fruit for many weeks. They could catch fish, and did so easily to supplement a staple diet of dahl and rice. Several of the crew had earlier on been sick and had been taken by the agent to see local doctors. I was shown the receipts, purportedly for the payment of doctors' bills, paid by the agent, which he hoped to recoup in due course from the owner. The cost of two very ordinary laboratory tests came to over fifty dollars – more than a week's wage for very many Yemenis. It was not the first, nor the last time that I found local agents and other port related officials benefiting from the plight of stranded seafarers.

Over the following weeks I contacted and sought the advice of the Mission to Seafarers' office in London, conferred with my colleague Stephen in Dubai and was put in contact with an energetic and resourceful representative of the ITF (The International Transport Workers Federation) in Australia. We discovered that the owner had indeed had problems - that contracts for salvage, in particular for towing vessels to India's great ship-breaking yards, had fallen through. But I also learned that authority could be obtained to have any of the company's other vessels impounded and, in theory, sold to meet outstanding wages and other debts.

I resolved on a policy of prayer and polite but persistent harassment of the company's owner in Dubai, reminding him on every opportunity of the pathetic condition of the Numo's crew, and their families. At the same time, the ITF in Australia added their own steady pressure, along with regular warnings of the potentially awkward consequences of constantly putting off payment of the overdue wages. On a number of occasions I was told by the owner himself that the payment had been made and that the agent would shortly be calling the crews to come and get their wages. It was complete nonsense. I continued to phone the Dubai office at least once a week. I was surprised at how often I was put through to the manager himself. I had expected to be put off and simply told that he was unavailable. After some six weeks, I phoned the company and was connected once again with the owner, who remonstrated with me, "I am very much fed up with your pestering, and the pestering also of your Australian friends - you give me no peace. I will pay the wages as soon as I can."

Three days later, at four in the morning, I received a phone call from the Numo's agent asking me to go immediately to Aden's International Airport to witness the full payment of the crew's wages prior to their flying home to India later in the morning. I dressed quickly, told the guard on the gate where I was going and drove through empty streets to a largely empty airport. It was rarely bustling with life. I was greeted with a warm handshake from Moammer Singh and with shy smiles from the rest of the crew. They looked smart and very happy. The agent was businesslike and not unfriendly. We sat and he opened his briefcase. Inside were seven large envelopes, each with the name of a crew member written on it. They were handed to each of them in turn. Inside were many hundred dollar bills, which each crew member counted and signed for. We said our farewells and I returned home. Later in the day I phoned Dubai to thank the company owner and wish him well. The crew were all Hindus. At Christmas that year, several months later, our first Christmas card was from the Numo's second officer. Sadly, five years on, there are still ships' crews stranded in Aden, waiting for their wages. Some crew members are Somalis, and a number of these have grown tired of waiting and gone off to become pirates.

(CHAPTER SEVEN)

OUR ISLAND STORY

The plane was old. It was a Boeing 727, and we had boarded it by climbing up a little flight of steps that descended from under the plane's tail and lifted up into the fuselage for take-off. We followed the flight attendant's instructions for take-off. We dutifully fastened our seat belts and pulled our seats into the upright position. But they did not remain in the position for long. As the elderly aircraft trundled down the runway and eventually gathered momentum, our seats reclined. There was noth-ing we could do about it. The lady flight attendant, belted and seated upright against a bulkhead opposite us smiled sympathetically, shrugged her shoulders and mouthed quietly, "Yemenia" - the name of the national carrier on whose plane we were flying - by way of explanation and apology for our predicament. Once properly airborne, we were able to pull the seats upright and to turn around and apologise to those behind us for lying in their laps at take-off, like dental patients awaiting a filling.

We were on the weekly flight from Aden to Socotra - the large rectan-gular island in the Indian Ocean situated some 400 kilometres south of the Yemeni port of Mukalla. We were accompanied on the flight by John Sandford Smith, an eye surgeon of some renown, a good friend to the eye clinic and a regular and valued visitor. He was from Leicester in England and had come to us over a period of years for intense stints of surgery and the training of our local staff and other eye specialists working in the city. He was to head up a week's outreach on the island. Two of our own local Adeni staff, Qaid, our very able male technician and Rana, our lovely theatre nurse, had already gone ahead to screen patients and select those needing surgery, and to prepare the island's little hospital for our visit. While they had been busy on the island, lining up patients, Mansour had been busy back in Aden, preparing all the equipment we were to take with us to Socotra. Almost everything had to be taken - microscopes, lenses, sutures, drugs, instruments, drapes - and more. Getting all the necessary equipment together was one thing, and Mansour did it superbly - getting the necessary signatures from numerous junior officials in customs and other departments was another. It got him down. Towards the end of that very full week he gave rare vent to his frustration, "twenty four signatures to do for the poor people on Socotra what no one else will do - and for free - and all my week just getting signatures - for charity work." Though this week's outreach was to be funded retrospectively and generously by the British Embassy, we decided that in the future it would be easier to travel to conduct outreach on the mainland and in parts of it as remote from medical care as Socotra. It was this decision that led us to the desperately neglected and needy town of Mocha which we have visited at least twice every year since.

Mansour had been at Aden's airport long before we arrived to take the early morning flight to the island – checking and re-checking all the equipment and making sure, as best he could, of its safe and secure passage out to the waiting plane. A couple of years earlier an expensive, high quality microscope given by one of our chief supporting agencies disappeared in the airport. We had been notified of its arrival and phoned and asked to come and collect it. By the time we arrived just a few hours later, all trace of it had vanished and no-one could throw light on its disappearance.

Although the outreach had been planned for several months to coincide with one of Dr John's regular visits, Nancy and I had not planned to be a part of it. Return tickets to Socotra were, for foreigners, notoriously expensive, and we did not think we had much to contribute, as non-medical personnel, to the venture. But expatriate friends in Aden extolled the island's beauty – its lovely beaches, mountains and extraordinary plants. John also assured us that we would not be in the way and that he could find employment for us – preparing patients, taking them in and out of the theatre and, if we had a steady hand, learning to give them injections. I was not enthusiastic about the last suggestion but was eager to see how our team functioned away from home. We were also quite interested in seeing the island after all that we had been told about it! Little did we know that it would prove to be a week that would change our lives.

Socotra is described in one new guidebook to Yemen as an, 'earthly paradise' – a slightly extravagant claim I think, for what is nonetheless a very remarkable island. It is part of the Socotran Archipelago, which is made up of four islands, of which Socotra, over fifty miles long, is the largest. The other islands are Abd al Kuri, which for tragic reasons to be explained later, will long be etched in our minds, and the islands of Samhah and Darsah. The climate is pretty arid, though subject to monsoons which occur between March and May. Access to the islands during that time, by sea, is hazardous and, we were to learn, rarely attempted.

Plant life on Socotra is amazingly varied. There are over 900 known plant species on the island, a full third of which are unique to the island.

Most famous and most photographed is probably the Socotra Desert Rose – known more commonly as the 'bottle tree' for its thick, distinctively bottle-shaped trunk. It grows, along with frankincense and myrrh, on the foothills of the mountains of Socotra. Amongst other plants of particular interest are the Socotran begonia, the Persian violet and a relative of the pomegranate. I was consciously only aware of the bottle tree. It would have been hard not to be. The trees are truly remarkable. On the one day when we took off from the hospital to explore the island we saw falcon, some Socotra buzzards circling far above us, and on a long and lonely silver beach noted the trails of numerous busy crabs. Turtles apparently lay their eggs on the island's beaches, but we saw none when we were there. But we had not come to the island to study the wildlife.

Rana and Qaid and a young man called Ali met us at the island's little airport, and we quickly loaded ourselves and all the equipment in the back of a white Toyota twin cab pick-up. We were dropped off with John at the modest but clean Taj Hotel, and the others went on to unload all that had been so carefully packed, packaged and labelled back in Aden.

Word of our arrival had spread quickly across the island and the next morning Hadibu's hospital yard was full of jostling, pushing figures – from young children in arms to little, shrunken, wizened, barefooted women in black, their headscarves wrapped over their heads with the ends held between their remaining dark teeth to prevent them being blown away in the constant, tugging, dusty wind. Hands, young and old, reached out to grasp our shirt sleeves, and we were all greeted as 'doctor'. Qaid did his best to bring the unruly crowd into line, but they took little notice of his gently voiced directions and many may not have understood him anyway, for the people of the island have their own language – unique, like the bottle tree, to Socotra. In the end, and I expect for a small fee, a soldier was found who did get the patients into the semblance of a line and without too much berating or bullying. The scene made me think of the Gospel accounts of Jesus being pressed hard by surging, clamouring crowds desperate for his attention. Those who had been seen in the preceding days by our little advance party were called forward first and asked to present the cards they had been given already with all their personal details written on them. John checked each of the patients in turn and assigned the day on which those needing an operation should come. Many complaints could be readily treated with the presentation of a tube of ointment and some clear and often repeated instructions. By then we had a local interpreter to help us. Some of these patients were clearly disappointed that they were not to have a status-enhancing operation at the hands of the tall 'doctor inglisi'. Many more did actually need a cataract operation, but for some there was nothing at all that could be done to restore or save sight – or even life – as in the case of a handsome young nine year-old boy, whom John diagnosed with retina blastoma. The boy's father, intelligent and deeply concerned, listened attentively and without difficulty to the translation of Dr John's sombre prognosis. He thanked John, and said that he would try to take his son to see another specialist, perhaps in the capital, Sanaa. "Of course", replied John graciously – "as you like."

Sometimes – and especially when we had a visiting surgeon from abroad with us – families who had often spent hundreds of scarce dollars traipsing around Yemen's private eye clinics on behalf of relatives with failing sight, would come to us as a last resort. Sadly, a moment's fleeting examination would all too often be enough to confirm that the patient's condition was beyond help, something that would have been obvious to even the most inept private practitioner, who would nonetheless suggest treatment – even operations – for their personal financial benefit, and the patient's certain disappointment. We did not hear what happened to the young nine year-old. John did not think that he would live very long.

The first day of operations went well and as the system improved, so the numbers handled increased day by day. The operating theatre was rudimentary. There was an operating table, the floor was bare concrete and the walls were painted dark green. There was a wheelchair for patients, but both its pneumatic tyres were flat. With the use of the theatre came the grudging and surly services of a local male nurse whom I found smoking in the theatre between operations on the first day. Later in the week, when I complained about his attitude, I was told that I should overlook it because of his problems at home! The duties given to Nancy and myself were simple; we washed the patients' faces, we trimmed their eyelashes, we administered the drops at the appropriate moment to dilate the pupils, we led them in and out of theatre, and after operations, gathered up the discarded drapes and gowns. Much of the time we spent squatting on the floor beside the patients as there was nowhere else for them to sit. It was a simple, happy and rewarding routine. We also took it upon ourselves to provide lunch each day for the team. That too was simple – flat bread, processed cheese wedges, tomatoes, a tin of tuna and fruit. Surprisingly, almost all fruit and vegetables were flown across from the mainland, and consequently expensive, and after a few days very tired-looking indeed. Sometimes we opted for 'takeaway'. This consisted of a large plastic bag of rice, chunks of grilled fish wrapped in newspaper and a smaller, invariably leaking, polythene bag of hot, red spicy sauce. For some reason we always opted to eat our lunch and scatter our meal on the floor of Rana's room. Afterwards, we returned to our respective rooms to nap before resuming operations.

I was also appointed 'minister of transport'. After a brief altercation with the hospital's delightful but less than pro-active manager we were given, for the duration of our stay, the island's Land Cruiser ambulance for our own personal transport. John, whose patience is considerable and skill and dedication legendary, asks little when 'on the job' - a swim and transport to get to the beach, and a can of chilled beer with his supper. We did not enquire too closely how the necessary beverage was supplied but it was always there, and I think that the one who had so carefully prepared and packed the equipment for our island outreach had slipped in a case of Amstel in a black bag, along with the drugs. Both were very important to the mission in hand.

On our first day - a long and demanding one - we found that we had to track down and hire a taxi to get to our lodgings, and then find another to take us to the beach. John was upset. We did not expect the hospital director to provide us with a chauffeur-driven, air-conditioned limo but we thought some transport a very minimal provision, particularly in view of the fact that the hospital's sole contribution to this venture was the use of its theatre and a generous supply of patients. We even paid for the surly nurse and his reluctant help. We made our case to the director for transport, and as a result were given the dusty ambulance which we promised, like the theatre, to return in an emergency. I enjoyed turning on a siren to stir Rana and Qaid from their lodgings in the early mornings. Ironically, the only emergency in the course of the week requiring the use of the ambulance, was one I provoked. When it came I relinquished the steering wheel and was laid in the back on the stretcher.

It all began on the Friday, which we had set aside for doing some sightseeing - the hospital being closed. We went up into the mountains and then down to a small village with a gorgeous aquamarine blue lagoon edged with silvery sand. Nancy and I had made up sandwiches and bought fruit and fizzy drinks. Qaid went off to the village mosque in the ambulance for Friday prayers and returned later with an enormous round tin tray heaped with a mountain of rice and broiled fish - a present from grateful islanders - 'for the doctors'. We abandoned the sandwiches in the ambulance, sat ourselves around the tray on the ground and tucked in enthusiastically. It was absolutely delicious. The suppliers of the meal had considerately even sent along some spoons for the foreign doctors. Afterwards, Rana, John and Qaid stretched out under the trees and dozed. Nancy sketched, while I set out to climb the gentle hillside behind us to get some decent photographs. I did not get far. Where the slope began, my legs simply refused to carry me. I stumbled, but did not fall. I struggled to go on, but could not without losing my balance. I turned around and sat down for some minutes and then returned slowly and without a problem to the ambulance, telling Nancy that I had decided to take a nap after all. It was a puzzling predicament. I continued to drive, though cautiously, and said nothing to the rest of the company. Later in the day, we drove through some impressively elegant plantations of soaring palm trees. The road out of the plantation was deeply rutted and very muddy. Although the vehicle was in four-wheel-drive, the tyres were almost completely bald and spun hopelessly. I struggled to control the clutch properly. Qaid's friend, Ali, was with us and kindly offered to help. I gladly accepted and he quickly drove us out of the mud and safely home. That night we ate in the open air restaurant attached to the Taj. I found that I had to concentrate very hard to will my feet up the few steps to get there. It was still harder going up the same steps to breakfast the following morning. Then I discovered, to my dismay, that I needed both hands even to lift the cup of tea to my lips, and that the effort was exhausting. More tea splashed over the table than went down my throat. It was with some difficulty that Nancy and John got me back to our little room and onto the bed. The hotel staff observed us with puzzlement and concern. John slipped off to the hospital to brief the team and get them started on the day's work, promising to return as soon as he could to make contact, as best he could, on the hotel's land line with medical friends in Leicester on my behalf.

After a while, I thought I would try and take a shower. Nancy helped me in to the shower - just off our little bedroom and turned to tidy our room. Moments later my legs folded completely. I had no control over them at all. It was as if a great puppeteer had suddenly laid down the controls of a puppet, whose limbs then suddenly went limp in every direction. I slipped down the shower wall, one leg going awkwardly into the hole in the floor that doubled both as toilet and drain hole. Nancy heard me exclaim as I slithered and crumpled onto the tile floor, and came quickly to investigate. With some effort she dragged me out of the shower room and onto the thin, stained carpet of the bedroom, where I lay with my head resting sideways on the carpet looking under the gap below the bedroom door, down the corridor, wondering where help might come from. I was not frightened. Neither Nancy nor I were frightened. We were bemused and anxious, but from the first onset of the rapidly spreading paralysis we had shared our confidence that our lives were in God's hands and that into them we could entrust what lay ahead. And I know that we prayed that in some way good might come for all caught up in our unexpected drama. These lofty thoughts were not the ones, though, that passed through my mind as I lay on the floor, looking down the corridor. As I lay, and Nancy paused for breath, I was conscious of a pungent odour right under my nose and said, "I think a cat has peed where I am lying."

We knew of the presence of a few other foreigners on the island, working with different agencies on agricultural, environmental and educational projects, and had met one - a fine, older Australian man, who was to prove a most practical and patient friend in those difficult days. It was he, Len, who providentially appeared in the corridor outside our bedroom door just when we needed him. He helped me on to the bed and, amongst many other things, later requisitioned a plastic armchair from the hotel and cut a hole in its seat for purposes which I do not think require further explanation.

Later John returned, having spoken to a neurologist friend in the Leicester Royal Infirmary in England, who confirmed what he had suspected, namely that I had Guillain Barré Syndrome, which attacks the nerve endings and from which he assured me most patients made, in time, a full recovery. He did not tell me everything and expressed some concern, lest my breathing get difficult. Fortunately it did not, but later I was to meet somebody who had had the same condition and had spent many weeks on a life support system, before eventually making a complete recovery. The following hours seemed filled with the sound of a constantly ringing phone in reception followed, on nearly every occasion, by a tap on the door and a kindly summons to Nancy to answer the call. There were calls from the Diocesan Office in Nicosia, from the health insurance company in London, from the Mission to Seafarers' offices in both London and Dubai, from Mansour in Aden, desperate to 'do something', and from friends and family in England, Austria and America. Nancy kept a diary of those days.

'The Socotran idyll has become lost in a web of phone calls about Peter's medical condition. John has been very helpful and has suggested that we try to medivac Peter out - probably to Dubai. Calls have been going to various parts of the world, and we seem finally to have connected with somebody re air charters and insurance ... my head has been spinning. Different details - can they get a plane here by dusk? Actually it is too late now. So it must be at first light tomorrow. I said Jordan at one point, but now I think Dubai. Suddenly the phone has gone completely quiet, and I'm worried that things are in a muddle. Lord, I am so stupid; please help me to get things clear. Dr John has just talked to the insurance people, and they are working on getting us out to Dubai tomorrow. It seems like my muddle has been cleared.'

The next day's entry in the diary is headed, 'Last morning on Socotra'. It was not. The entry began,

'This morning John ordered breakfast and they (Rana and Qaid and others) all came after the post-op clinic to chat and say goodbye. John made some helpful suggestions about how the work back in the eye clinic in Aden could be improved. They have gone off now, and a Swiss-German medic called Stefan, and his son, have come to escort us to the airport and see us off. It is a strange ending to a wonderful week. It doesn't do to wonder too much what it's all about. God is with us and we'll go with him through the next phase of this adventure.'

Just before John left us to follow Qaid and Rana out to the waiting car he paused to pray for us. It meant a lot.

We were to make two return trips to the airstrip that day. On the first we were told on our arrival by an official that the plane would be coming three hours later than expected. We returned to the hotel, waited there for a couple of hours and then returned to the airport. There, we did some more waiting. After an hour or more, a man in a white shirt sauntered over from the control tower to inform us that the plane had broken down in Mukalla. During our wait I had been lying comfortably on the stretcher in the shade of the ambulance. Nancy had once again taken up a sketch pad. We were told that the plane had left Nairobi early in the day, but no-one had informed us, and perhaps not even the control tower until then, that the plane was not going to make it to the island. Stefan drove us back to the hotel. It was a low moment. Dr John and the others had taken the weekly flight back to Aden earlier in the day, confident that we would soon have been safely en route to Dubai.

The hotel staff, shocked at what had happened, brought meals to our room for which we later learned they refused to take any payment. There were more phone calls, and we were informed that another plane - this time coming from Jordan - would be with us the next morning. The arrival time was put back throughout the day. It was a long flight from Amman but the changes in schedule were not due this time to mechanical, but rather diplomatic problems. It required the intervention of the British Ambassador in Sanaa for the little plane to over-fly Yemen and recover us.

Once again, Stefan proved unflappable and wonderfully, reassuringly, competent. When we judged that the plane was getting near to the island, he loaded us back into the ambulance to drive us once more to the little airport. We were accompanied by the male nurse from the hospital and his utterly delightful ten year-old son, who had adopted me and sat on the jump seat in the back of the ambulance by my head. Just as the light was fading a tiny speck appeared in the sky, grew rapidly larger and dropped neatly on to the runway. It was a very small twin-engine jet. As soon as it stopped, the emergency door in the fuselage was opened and removed and I was handed up onto the wing and passed through it. There were two doctors, a nurse and two crew members aboard, and room just for myself and Nancy. Moments later we were airborne. In the course of the flight I learned that the little plane had once been the private jet of King Hussein of Jordan. It now did regular ambulance flights, often to Afghanistan.

We refuelled in Mukalla and flew on to Dubai, where all the landing formalities were quickly dealt with before we were taken in another ambulance to the Welcare Hospital which was, effectively, to be our home for the next three weeks. The hospital staff - Filipino, Jordanian, Iraqi and Indian - were diligent, kind and conscientious. The clergy from our congregations in Dubai visited. John Weir from Holy Trinity brought us communion and anointed us on Palm Sunday. Stephen, of Mission to Seafarers, and his wife Catherine, called, as did Steve Wright of Jebal Ali. Nancy struggled to cope with all the well-wishers, the phone calls and others who were eager to visit. Initially she stayed with Tim and Anthea Fawdry, who ran the Resource Centre at Holy Trinity and who, amongst many other wonderful things, cooked an Easter Day Sunday lunch and brought it hot and inviting to the little room to which I had been transferred after the early days in Intensive Care. There was a little pullout bed in it too for Nancy, which was great.

Progress was slow but sure, and the staff, family and friends very patient and encouraging. There were two Indian physiotherapists who took me in hand from the first day I left Intensive Care. They started by helping me move my fingers and great was my excitement when I discovered I could make my thumb touch each of the fingers on my hand in turn. About two weeks later, one of them stunned me by saying with a smile "Today, you walk." I managed a few very wobbly and uncertain steps, and just as I reached out to grasp the hands of the nice physiotherapist he took two steps back. I protested. He smiled mischievously and said, "I am the boss – just two steps more." By this stage things were looking up. The days before had not been so easy and I know that at times I was grumpy, difficult and unappreciative. Then, and for months afterwards, my legs twitched constantly. During the time in hospital I found it impossible to lie in one position for very long. It just seemed to hurt and I asked frequently to be moved to a more comfortable position. Later I was hoisted, with a lift, into an armchair where I sometimes managed to doze. Once, when being wheeled around the hospital, I suggested churlishly I be tipped down a long staircase; I felt so frustrated and useless. But those moments were rare, and there were many more times when laughter prevailed and a deep joy crept up, surprised and enfolded us.

Our son Tim came out to visit, bringing with him an outrageous present from one of my brothers of 'Pope on a Rope' shower soap with which, the attached label suggested, I wash away my sins! As the Pope was then dying in Rome, and many of the hospital staff were devout Roman Catholics, the Pope on the Rope was quickly banished to the back of the bedside cabinet. Tim and Andrea Fawdry had given us a slender book of Christian hymns and choruses and in the evenings after supper, and with anyone present, we sang. It was wonderful for our spirits and we hoped not too troublesome for the spirits of others around. The lines of some well-known hymns took on deeper meaning and relevance in the circumstances: 'Through all the changing scenes of life, in trouble and in joy, the praises of our God shall still our hearts and tongues employ'.

After I was discharged from hospital, a kind and resourceful friend, Andy Thompson, found us a ground floor apartment where we spent a further week before flying home to recuperate more in Britain. While back in the UK we received an e-mail from Sahil, then the senior guard at Christ Church. Attached was a beautiful photograph of the black, weather-beaten, lined face of his mother. Her eyes were closed and her hands raised in supplication. Beneath the picture was the simple caption, 'My mum – she pray for you.' We knew that she was not the only one. We felt overwhelmed and grateful and undeserving of so much attention. Five months later we returned to work in Aden.

(CHAPTER EIGHT)
FOOTPRINTS IN THE SAND

It had been a wretched meeting in a long line of wretched, futile and frustrating meetings in the office for Maritime Affairs. We knew every undulation and pothole in the narrow, unpaved road that led past the little car body repair shops under faded tarpaulins, to the office. Over the weeks we had watched the work progress on individual cars. We had seen them dismembered, beaten, welded, sanded, primed, resprayed and restored. Most of them were over twenty five years old – the majority Toyota Corollas with long bonnets and traditional boots. Sometimes they blocked our way and we had to wait as young teenage workers pushed them back out of the road. Sometimes the pot holes were filled with water, and the road awash with grey, creamy mud. Tiny bare–bottomed children played delightedly in the water – the result of the generous washing down of the cars between paint coats.

We knew the gateman in his plywood shelter below the Maritime Affairs office. He had a beautiful, toothless smile. His dog had got used to us too and no longer barked at the Englishman with his grey beard and his five sturdy black companions. We knew the two young veiled receptionists, who enjoyed practising their English and who, I think, regarded us with both amusement and sympathy. With amusement, because we were an unusual group; with sympathy – because I am sure that they considered the plight of the five Nigerian captains and the crews of the five vessels quite hopeless.

At first we met with Captain Ahmad with whom I had had a run in a year or so earlier when a Panamanian registered cement carrier, the 'Marion IV', had sunk in a gale off the island of Socotra. It was an extraordinary story.

The ship had bunkered two days earlier in Aden and had then set sail for Zanzibar with a full cargo of cement. Some hours into the voyage the ship encountered gale force winds and huge seas and began taking in water. The crew started pumping out the water but the volume was too great and it began to flow into the engine room, quickly flooding the generator. There was an explosion and the generator went out. Attempts to close the steel bulkhead doors throughout the ship to contain the sea flowing in proved impossible. Many were rusted hard onto their hinges.

The captain was a well respected Somali from Aden. He ordered his crew to abandon ship in the early hours of the morning. The ship was listing seriously, making it impossible to launch the lifeboat but they did get a life raft into the sea and most of the crew managed to scramble aboard. It was carried by the wind and great waves towards Abd al Kuri Island (mentioned in a previous chapter) lying between Somalia and Socotra, but it overturned some way from the beach when it hit a reef. One young crew member, who had just joined the ship, had a thumb severed and torn off as he struggled to leave the sinking ship. His family had paid many dollars to secure him the training position on the ship. Sixteen of the crew made it safely to shore but three drowned, including the captain. He and the chief officer jumped into the sea after casting off the crew's life raft.

Some hours after being washed up on the island, a crew member spotted footprints in the sand which led to tyre tracks and later to a small encampment of Yemeni soldiers. The soldiers gave them food but were extraordinarily suspicious, and only after the crew had gone on hunger strike did they allow them – four days after their struggling out of the foaming sea – to radio their situation to the wider world. A week after landing on the island a helicopter from a passing German Navy frigate airlifted them off the island to the warship. An Indian crew member, whose arm had been badly injured when coming ashore, was promptly operated on. The waves had been terrific and the rocks against which they had dashed him, very sharp. The arm had turned gangrenous and had to be amputated. The operation appeared to have gone well and sometime later, after recovering, he had joined his fellow crew members to watch television in a lounge. But sadly, he was to die later, only a few hours after being admitted to Aden's main government hospital. Almost all the rest of the crew, who came from Tanzania, India and Pakistan, were repatriated with two months' wages within a week of being landed in Aden.

We saw them several times, and on the last day went on a memorable shopping expedition with them to Crater to buy clothes and kit bags. Most of them had been washed ashore barefooted with their clothes ripped and torn in the struggle to leave the sinking ship and make landfall. The crew of the German frigate had given each of them a bright red, skin hugging, lycra tracksuit and sneakers or flip-flops. It was a generous gesture but it made all the crew more prominent than any would have wished. They seemed well pleased with the purchases made with us in Crater – two shirts each and a pair of trousers and a bag. The patient

Sahil, our guide and driver, negotiated prices cheerfully on their behalf and pacified the shop owner when crew members suddenly decided that they wanted a different coloured shirt or a smaller pair of jeans after all.

The ship's chief engineer, the gentle spoken Julian from Sri Lanka, did not, however, fly out of Aden with his friends. He was detained by Maritime Affairs and held effectively as a hostage in a downtown hotel in Aden in the hope that the owners of the ship that had gone down could be persuaded to pay the Maritime Affairs generous compensation for polluting Yemen's waters with the ship's fuel oil. It was a cruel, outrageous and completely illegal step and the cause of my first run-in with Captain Ahmad. The accusation of pollution was also ridiculous for the amount of fuel oil would, in the storm in which the 'Marian IV' foundered, have been rapidly dispersed. After two weeks, the Authority relented and sent him on his way. At the time I wrote, 'whether it was the admission of the futility of this hope – getting compensation – the prayers of Julian's many friends or pressure from the International Maritime Organisation in London, or all three, Julian was released in late July and, praise God, is now home in Sri Lanka with his young family.'

What none of us realised at the time when the survivors were flown home, was that there was another survivor, the ship's Chief Officer, Lin Zaw from Myanmar, who had been swept by the wind and waves way beyond all the others to land on an even remoter corner of Abd al Kuri Island. We learned that he was alive during the time when Julian was still being held in Aden. Much later we heard how he had actually seen the German Navy helicopter land but had been too weak even to wave. The chances that anyone would have been able to see him if he had been able to wave were remote, for the helicopter landed a long way from him. A day after the rescue of his friends, 'Sunny', as he liked commonly to be called, had, in his own words, been 'miraculously found' by two simple islanders who housed, fed and cared for him very tenderly over the long weeks that he remained on the island. Their home was no more than a flimsy shack made of driftwood. Asked how he had survived until he had been found, he said by licking wet patches on a small cliff and eating the leaves of a scrubby plant, which he had seen a goat nibbling.

When I heard of the Chief Officer's presence on the island, and at the time knew none of the details just mentioned, I drove straight to the office of Maritime Affairs, which was then situated in a much more accessible place only a few minutes' walk from the clinics. I was already full of righteous indignation at the treatment of Julian, and I am thoroughly ashamed to admit that I strode straight into a meeting chaired by Captain Ahmad, which was in desultory progress, to demand loudly what was being done for the shipwrecked Chief Officer of the 'Marian IV'. I did not behave well. Captain Ahmad did. He gestured towards an empty chair and very politely invited me to sit and assured me at the same time that the condition of the Chief Officer was being investigated. I was sceptical and my face probably showed it. The others around the table glanced at me with suspicion and disapproval. The business of the meeting was resumed and within half an hour, concluded. Papers were tidied into briefcases and laptops stowed while I sat like a naughty child on my chair in the corner. After everyone else had departed, the captain patiently explained in Arabic that the sea was then far too stormy for any attempt to be made to rescue the Chief Officer. I did not believe him.

Later the same day I consulted with Captain Roy Facey – delightful, resourceful, enormously knowledgeable on all matters maritime – a long-standing resident of Aden and a keen supporter of Christ Church and the work there. He breezily endorsed Captain Ahmad's opinion about the state of the sea at that time and thought that any attempt to rescue the Chief Officer by sea was impossible. He did, however, volunteer to contact those overseeing the movement of foreign coalition navy vessels in the area to enquire whether any of them could be diverted to the island to carry out a rescue mission as the German Navy had done. He was as good as his word, but reported that there were simply no ships near the islands nor likely to be in the foreseeable future.

Many months elapsed before I reappeared in the office of Captain Ahmad and when I did, accompanied by the five Nigerian captains, his welcome was not effusive.

Our visit had been precipitated by a phone call I had received late one night the previous week from a Nigerian crew member of a shrimp boat moored in Aden's fish port, not far from where we lived. Jimmo, who phoned me, we knew well. He was one of a number of Nigerian fishermen who worshipped with us whenever the little fleet of five locally-owned shrimpers were back in port. They were a happy gang and had among them some wonderful names – Wisdom, Ommonia and Pascal, to name but a few. From time to time when in port, I visited them aboard their vessels. I did not have an official pass covering the fish port but the captain of one of the five had negotiated my way in for visits, explaining to the relevant authority that I was their 'Christian imam', which seemed both to amuse and satisfy everybody. On one occasion, I had been asked to visit a young Nigerian, Benjamin, on his boat where I found him stripping down the boat's big Caterpillar engine. I joined him in the engine room to talk. The temperature below was a little over 50°C. We did not talk very long. Before I left, he asked if Nancy and I would like to share some shrimps. When I said yes, he led me into the boat's freeze-room. My glasses fogged up immediately and my sweat froze. A few minutes later I left, laden with four kilos of frozen shrimps. Life on those boats was very hard and the conditions, primitive. The boats themselves, originally from the east coast of America, were over forty years old. Those who worked them were well used to danger but, in conversation, made light of it. The clear note of anxiety in Jimmo's phone call was thus quite unexpected, and most unusual.

He reminded me that night that none of the crews, which were made up of both Somali and Yemeni members as well as Nigerian, had received any pay for seven long months. He told me that the ships' owner, a nephew of Yemen's then president, had told them that he had no money to pay them, and wanted them off his boats by the next morning. If they were not off the boats by the morning he said he would send people to kneecap them. Jimmo was understandably agitated. The order to leave 'or else' had been given, not directly by the nephew but by one of his henchmen, accompanied by a couple of well-armed thugs who dem-onstrated with their guns what they could do to knees by shooting off a chunk of the wooden bridge of one of the boats.

I had met the President's nephew eight months earlier when he had come to call. He knew that many of his Nigerian crew members worshipped with us when they were in port. At the time of his unexpected visit they had gone on strike, while at sea off the port of Mukalla. They had been without wages for many months, and they had bravely said that they would not fish again until he paid them. He came to see me at the church and invited me to join him in his shiny, brand-new Toyota Land Cruiser to discuss the problem. He was young - about thirty years old - and arrogant. He wore a traditional Yemeni flowing shirt and nice leather sandals. He wore a wide belt notched to accommodate a generous stomach and a small silver revolver. I told the quick-witted guard on duty what I was doing, got into the car as invited and told him to take note of its number plate just in case my return was unexpectedly delayed. As he drove he asked me what he should do to get his workers back fishing. I told him that as soon as he paid them they would drop their nets again. He replied contemptuously that God could pay them. I told him that in the circumstances he was God's representative, responsible for the welfare and the payment of their overdue and hard-earned wages. He was really most unpleasant, and told me in a rather bored and superior tone of voice that he was 'tired from them'. I was grateful when, after some fifteen minutes of driving and talking together, he stopped back at the front gate. The following day I learned that he had paid all his crews a month's wages, and that they had returned to work. They had received no more over the following months prior to Jimmo's anxious late night phone call.

I thought that we should take the threat that Jimmo had told me about seriously and the following morning, with friend and guard Sahil, hired an enormous high-sided Izuzu truck with which to bring the men to the church. It proved a more difficult and dangerous undertaking than either of us had imagined. The entrance gates to the fish port were closed, padlocked and guarded by at least two dozen armed police. The Nigerian fishermen stood inside the gates, angry and anxious, their kit - a huge mound of it - heaped beside them. The police stood back as we went to ask Jimmo and his friends what had happened. They explained. Apparently the owner, aware that the sudden departure of the crews would leave his vessels totally useless, had suddenly changed his mind, bludgeoned the port police into closing the gates and had a spokesperson order the Nigerians back on the ships. As we spoke, two of the Nigerians began to climb the link fencing. They were shouted down by the officer in charge of the police. A few minutes later, a large military pick-up truck appeared with a heavy machine gun, with a gunner in place at the ready. It looked, as was intended, very intimidating and parked opposite the enraged fishermen. It was then that the shocking thing happened.

One of the Nigerian fishermen - short and stocky - stepped forward from the others to within three or four metres of the gate and slowly and deliberately stripped naked in front of the growing crowd of onlookers. Then he spoke, "This is what has been done to us. We are nothing and we have nothing." And there was more - simple, heart-wrenching and, to all who heard him, patently true. Some soldiers turned away embarrassed, others looked on, curious to get a glimpse of a naked African. The colonel in charge of police told the gate duty to unlock the gates and let the Africans go. He then walked over to me in great distress and apologised for the behaviour of the President's nephew who, he said, had treated 'these good boys like this'. All the Africans were well known in the port and liked. Sahil had stood beside me watching everything with growing apprehension. Months later he confided to me that he had been quite sure the police would open fire on the Nigerians.

We moved the Isuzu nearer to the port gates and the fishermen loaded and stacked their trunks, cases, boxes and bundles with great speed and efficiency. Twenty minutes later we drove through the gates of Christ Church with the crews of the five boats seated on top of all their belongings in the back of the truck. They numbered 22 crew members, all but one of whom was Nigerian – the other was from Ghana. One of them was a Muslim, and all the others Christian. It was for all of us – the clinic staff, our congregation and the fishermen – the beginning of an interesting voyage into hitherto unknown waters. If the removal of the fishermen provoked anger and consternation in one quarter, it elicited from many more great sympathy and unstinting support.

We accommodated the crews in two small staff apartments, which happened to be vacant at the time, and bought 22 foam mattresses from the market for them to sleep on. If their new quarters were cosy they were, at their own admission, much more spacious than they had been accustomed to afloat, had air conditioning and did not roll. Their kit was stacked in the church, a great teasing pyramid – some eight feet high – a daily reminder of our friends' predicament and a constant challenge to our faith.

It was remarkable how quickly and easily our new friends adapted to their circumstances, and our staff and congregation to having them among us. We learned to live together in a way that proved both happy and constructive. While there was nothing outwardly to distinguish the captains from their crews – the use of titles, distinguishing dress or separate or better accommodation – they remained responsible for their own crews. On all practical matters relating to accommodation, daily routine, provision of food and, inevitably and wearily, the ongoing negotiations with the Maritime Affairs office and others, and their employer, we conferred together. After the arrival of the Africans in the compound, we would wake in the morning to what a friend called, 'the sound of Africa'; the vigorous sweeping of the grounds by two or three designated members from the crews. Afterwards, two more would be sent to go and buy hot, fresh bread rolls for everyone for breakfast from a little bakery in Tawahi. Later, most of them would join us for prayers in the church with the Christian members of staff – just before the working day began. When we asked them to teach us songs in their own language we drew a blank. Almost every crew member had a different language to the other. English was the common tongue, and it was their songs in English that they brought us. They were very simple and hard to sing while remaining still. Soon, even our rather formal Ethiopians shuffled, swayed, clapped and smiled as they moved around singing, 'Today today, Jesus will answer me, today, today', and, 'It is a great thing to serve the Lord'. Sometimes one of the Africans would lead our morning prayers and offer a reflection on the Scriptures. One day one of them took us through Psalm 36. It opens with a brief sketch of evil people: 'there is no fear of God before their eyes ... they flatter themselves in their own eyes that their iniquity cannot be found out and hated ... the words of their mouths are mischief and deceit.' Our leader that morning said simply, "we all know people like that," and continued, "but God is not like that," and he read thoughtfully the rest of the psalm – 'your steadfast love, O Lord, extends to the heavens, your faithfulness to the clouds ... Your righteousness is like the mighty mountains, your judgements are like the great deep, you save animals and humans alike, O Lord, how precious is your steadfast love ... All people may take refuge in the shadow of your wings.'

On another occasion, a month or six weeks into their stay at Christ Church, when we were again together in the church and the resolution of their problems seemed more remote than ever and the pyramid still teasingly mocking, two crew members burst spontaneously into singing the stirring hymn, 'Great is thy faithfulness', with which the rest enthusiastically joined in. I watched their upturned trusting faces and listened to them sing 'Great is thy faithfulness, O God, my father. ...Morning by morning new mercies I see, all I have needed thy hand hath provided, great is thy faithfulness, Lord unto me.' I cried.

Not all of the company were fervent Christians – but many were – and their faith and cheerfulness greatly impressed our local staff. Abdul Rahman, the lone Muslim among them, prayed discreetly at the appointed times in the courtyard. He seemed to enjoy an easy and relaxed relationship with the others. All of them were very hard workers. After prayers each morning, tasks were assigned and the work supervised. The tasks ranged from cleaning the apartments to laying concrete, to preparing lunch. This was their main meal of the day – served with an avalanche of green chillies and eaten after the clinics had closed and the local staff had gone home, at about three in the afternoon. In one week, the entire boundary wall surrounding the church and the clinics was repainted – twice. The crews also laid cobbles, or more accurately, rounded stones from a nearby beach, to provide an attractive place for chairs under the palm trees, when we had church or staff parties. One crew member, a carpenter, who opted to live off campus in the refugee camp of Basateen with his girlfriend, came in each day and remodelled the office.

While the five shrimp boats stood idle, the President's nephew told people that the church could not keep the Nigerians very long, and that the crews would soon be back asking for work. He could not have been more wrong.

A week after their arrival at Christ Church, I went with the five captains – all of them very smartly dressed – to make the first of several visits to Captain Ahmad in his office at the end of the bumpy road overlooking the harbour, described earlier. It was a while before we were shown into his presence and when we were he wasted little time in denouncing the shameful behaviour of the Nigerian fisherman who had taken off his clothes in public in the fish port 'in front' he said, 'of men and women'. We had not noticed any women present. The captain seemed obsessed with the conduct of the brother who had felt compelled to bare all. It was not an encouraging meeting. In the end, we were asked to compile a list of all the crew members, giving their names by boat, indicating their position on each vessel, the time they had served and wages which they were due. All this information we were told, would be forwarded to the agent of the company and the nephew of the President. Over the following weeks we met with the company's own solicitor and requested meetings with the President's nephew himself. He was actually known to all the crew, some of whom had worked for him for several years. He never did meet with us, but he was observed driving around the perimeter of the church on two occasions.

Those with whom we met, whether in Maritime Affairs or in the company's main office never gave a reason why the wages could not be paid. They contested the amount that should be paid, on one occasion claiming that the engineers from the boats could not be paid the money they requested because they had produced no certificates vouching for their being marine engineers, even though the company had taken them on as qualified engineers and paid them as such. It was a wretched and protracted business but in every one of our encounters with the various officials and representatives the captains were polite and dignified but no push-over either. Once, one of them asked the company solicitor whether the company's seeming lack of concern in the predicament of he and his fellow fishermen and their suffering families back home was not on account of the fact that they were black. The company solicitor, an enormously fat young man protested, "Islam makes no distinction in its treatment of people because of their colour." It was not a statement any of the captains contested but they could have done so with considerable justification from their experience of working in the region.

Our annual Diocesan Synod fell during what we came to call later, 'the Nigerian time'. We flew to Cyprus. It was a good time and, as always, a great opportunity to relax and catch up with friends and colleagues. However, we returned to Aden with some anxiety for, while in Cyprus, Mansour had reluctantly phoned us to say that bad things had been written about the church in a Saudi Arabian newspaper and in another one published in Sanaa. The latter, he said, featured a double page article with photographs of churches and what purported to be a copy of a letter from the heads all the mosques in Aden demanding that these churches – and there are just four church buildings in Yemen – all of which are in Aden, be demolished immediately.

Our feelings of apprehension were, however, momentarily forgotten in the exuberant welcome we received on our return to the church from the Nigerian brothers. The mighty Ommonia seized me around the thighs and threw me effortlessly over his shoulders, determined to carry me home. The few bags which we carried were taken from us; Ommonia led the procession back to our apartment. He would have carried me upstairs too, had I not protested and insisted he return me to earth. As we were accompanied back to our apartment I heard some of the Nigerians kindly asking 'Mama Nancy' how our time away had been. It was a terrific welcome home.

In the evening after his prayers, Mansour appeared at our door – smiling, solicitous and apologetic. He filled us in with the stories in the newspapers and promised to bring them to the office the following morning. He told us that when they had been published he was called almost immediately to the local police station. There, a kind major from the security services laid the newspapers, with their provocative articles, before him to read. When he had done so, the major asked him what he thought about what he had read. He replied that he thought I had probably made the nephew of the President very angry and that he had probably bribed or bullied the editors of the two papers to write, or to have written, what had been published. The major agreed. By the time of his meeting with Mansour, he had already contacted a selection of Aden's imams about the newspaper articles, and in particular the letter purporting to be written from them. Not only did none of them know anything about it, but they were quick to disassociate themselves entirely from its content and sentiments. The major then folded the papers, gave them to Mansour and thanked him for his time. Later, he translated them for us. They were mischievous and muddled, the very few facts that they had culled for the article being either hopelessly distorted or grossly exaggerated. Mansour advised us to think no more about the matter. But it was hard not to.

However, we took some comfort from the fact that people in Aden generally had little love for Saudi Arabia and even less for Sanaa, the President or his family. Still, I cannot say we did not worry. It needed only one inflamed fanatic to lob a grenade into the courtyard and there had, in the past, been two attacks on the compound. A well-meaning local friend had actually warned me when first we took in the Nigerians that I could easily be killed, "a bullet costs only fifty rials and here accidents are easily arranged". When the clinics were first opened and Mansour invited to join the staff, he went to seek the advice of a young imam to enquire whether he thought it would be good for him to work with foreign Christians. The imam asked for time to think about his question. He thought, and later gave Mansour an answer. He told him that it would be absolutely fine for him to work at the clinic as the people who were running it had travelled from their own countries to serve Yemen's poor. There was some opposition initially to the re-opening of the church, and suspicion about the clinic, but it quickly dissipated as patients came and discovered for themselves, with appreciation, the care and medical help they and their families received through the clinic. Still, there were a few dissenters and one day someone attempted, unsuccessfully, to torch Mansour's car. He told us that he had been very frightened. He had, at that time, a young family and he had just turned down a very well-paid job with an international company to work for us – for a pittance. I asked him what he had done. He replied, "I said to God, if it is your will that I do this job, then please protect me and my family." In our anxiety we prayed the same.

Some months before we took in the Nigerians, we had purchased a new Toyota mini-bus for the work of the clinics, but we had not had it long before some young men threatened to torch that too. Qaid, one of the eye team, had taken the bus home after work and had parked it in the street outside his home. After his lunch and a rest he had gone out intending to go in the bus to purchase drugs for the clinic. He found a crowd of angry men gathered around the bus, pointing at the fresh red lettering on its side. It read in Arabic and in English, 'Serving the people at Christ Church, Tawahi'. Much thought had gone into the simple wording and the staff had been unanimous that, 'at Christ Church', should feature. But it was these words that had incensed the young men. They remonstrated with Qaid. "What is this church? There is no church in Aden. Shame," they cried. "If we see your bus again we will burn it." Qaid did his best to explain the work of the church and the clinics and returned to us later in the evening, a little shaken.

Early the next morning, I carefully cut the offending words in Arabic from the sign which was printed on plastic, with a razorblade. The English wording remained. We never had any objection to them. But if there were occasional, unexpected outbursts against the church, there were also times when we received unexpected support. One day the follow-ing e-mail arrived; it was from a Yemeni living with his family in Chicago. 'I came about your website today and was extremely gratified learning of your good work in Yemen. Being Muslim, I have a great respect for our Christian brothers and sisters, who humbly make other people's troubles their own ... what you are doing is truly Good News.'

The Nigerians, amongst whom we always included in our thinking the lone Ghanian, became not only a part of our lives but also of the whole neighbourhood. We watched them sometimes walking into town and were encouraged to see how often they were stopped by locals eager to talk with them and learn their news. They were always greeted warmly and from time to time local people would bring me money or food for them. A young Nigerian, David, who helped each day with cooking, learned sadly that the girl to whom he had planned to get married had given up waiting and broken off the engagement. All of our Nigerian friends were in debt, and over the previous months had borrowed money to help their families at home - with rent, school fees, or medical ex-penses. I would often find them sitting disconsolate in the garden after making calls home.

It got hard to find work with which to keep them active. One day, almost in desperation, I presented them with two very well used wheelbarrows. Their wheels were wobbly, their tyres flat, and their bodies very dented. Our resident maintenance team had several times urged me to buy new ones. Three days later, after much banging, sanding and a little weld-ing, they were brought to me - totally transformed. Their undercarriages were painted deep red and their wheels the same. Their upper bodies were white, without a dent to be seen. The wheels no longer wobbled, and each was shod with a brand-new Chinese manufactured tyre. I was awed, and reluctant even to consider putting them back into service. Filled with flowers, they would have graced the entrance of an English country pub. The men seemed pleased with their work. It was, said one of them, easier and more enjoyable than scraping down and painting the hulls of the fishing boats.

At one point during their stay with us, I was provoked into writing to the Yemen Observer, the local English-language newspaper, about their situation. One or two people in the Maritime Affairs office had been criticising my role and that of the church in the whole drawn out and unhappy business. I wrote explaining that I was associated with the work of the Mission to Seafarers, which was an international Christian charitable organisation serving seafarers in many ports all around the world – of every background and religion – or none. I mentioned my own regular involvement in the port and the modest help we had been able to give to sick or stranded seafarers in Aden in recent months. I also pointed out that the shameful treatment of the Nigerians reflected very badly on the already dismal reputation of the port with foreign sailors. In the article, which was printed in full and drew appreciative comment from the few local people who read it, I also quoted a well-known Muslim proverb, which says that workers should be paid their wages in full, before the sweat has dried on their foreheads.

I sent a copy of the article to the British Ambassador, soliciting his help in the case. He wrote back, good-naturedly, explaining that in the course of a year he could only make one or two 'big asks' of the President of the country or of those closest to him, and that he had to think carefully and long about how best to use such rare opportunities. It did not sound to me, however, as if he had ruled out the possibility of helping us. At the same time, the Sanaa-based office of the Arabic news channel, Al Jazeera, came across our story and phoned to make an appointment to see myself and, more particularly, the crews and their five captains. The following day their reporters travelled down to Aden to interview us. They filmed the crews lying around in their cramped quarters looking dejected, and they filmed them all worshipping in the church looking radiant. They also interviewed the five captains at length. They visited the office of the fish company as well, and met with the solicitor representing the nephew of the President. They were an impressive little team – conscientious, businesslike and sympathetic. A few days later, the news channel screened the story of the Nigerians five times across the region in twenty-four hours.

Just a little before the story broke, we had made what turned out to be our last visit to the office of Maritime Affairs - the visit, which I described as 'wretched', at the beginning of this chapter. At the conclusion of the meeting we were told bluntly that our only recourse was to take the company to court and to be prepared for the proceedings to take at least two years. As we drove home, one of the captains said loudly and resolutely, "Reverend, we put our trust in no man. Our hope is in God." When we got back to the church, the five went into the church to pray.

It must have been about a week later, and two days after the Al Jazeera screening of the Nigerian story that a call came from the fish company's agent saying that the men would be paid, given their tickets and flown home within thirty-six hours. The news electrified the compound. The rejoicing was great and it was shared by all.

The next day we hired a truck for the baggage and took the crew to the airport in our two buses. They received only half the wages that were due to them, but in the excitement and euphoria of returning home I heard none complain. In the hours after their departure we received phone calls from different crew members in the different airports, where they were in transit on a long and rather circuitous route home. Our lives had been enriched by them, and in the weeks that followed we missed them and spoke often of them.

Later I learned that 'the big ask' had been made to Yemen's Foreign Minister by the British Ambassador after their viewing of the Al Jazeera broadcast of the Nigerian story.

On the night before they left us the Muslim crew member, Abdul, came to see me and asked if he might have the sticker from the back window of my little Suzuki bus. I peeled it off and put it on a little strip of Perspex for him to take home. He wanted very much to put it in the back of his car in Lagos. It read, 'Mission to Seafarers - caring for seafarers around the world'.

The Nigerians had lived with us for a little over two months - almost the same length of time that the Chief Officer of the 'Marion IV' spent on Abd al Kuri Island living with his kind rescuers. He was on the island for ten weeks before a passing dhow picked him up and took him to the island of Socotra, from where he was flown to Aden a week later. The first stage of the journey, he said, was almost as frightening as the last voyage of the 'Marion IV'. It took sixteen hours and the seas were enormous. On his arrival in Aden the company put him up in a hotel from where he came to visit us. While with us he wrote his report of the sinking of the ship. It made for desperately sad reading,

> 'Ship drifted about 5 miles and then Captain ordered crew to abandon ship. The lifeboat could not be lowered, because it was rusted and impossible. The crew threw down the inflatable life raft. I was holding the rope of life raft. The rest of the crew were shouting and confused. I told them not to go away. Some jumped into the sea, and some in the life raft. The captain stayed on the ship with me, because the ship was listing heavily to port side. Situation was very confused. The life raft shot off as the ship sank suddenly. I went down about ten feet, and when I surfaced the life raft was far from me. I saw two other people in the water, and I heard the captain call for help - also the Tanzanian. Life raft had gone. We swam. When I came to the island, the swell was huge and pressed me down. I saw only two lifejackets - but no bodies. Later I learned that their bodies had been washed up elsewhere.'

Afterwards, Lin Zaw Soe, or Sunny, as he told us helpfully we could call him, phoned home to his family in Myanmar. He got through immediately, apologised for the delay in getting home, asked after the children and told his wife that he hoped to be home within a week. Thankfully, he was.

A PERSIAN INTERLUDE

The following chapters were written in the spring of 2002 soon after our return from an unexpected, wonderful and all too short experience of working with the Anglican Church in Iran.

(CHAPTER NINE)
BY BUS TO MASHAD

The bus purred steadily on into the night; snow banks, dirty and mud-spattered, rose on either side of the highway. The red numbers on the thermometer above the driver's head registered a snug 28 degrees centigrade in the cabin, a crisp -5 outside. Nancy, her head swathed in a dark head scarf, dozed beside me. From time to time the bus would swing out to overtake a truck, dimly lit and heavily laden, struggling up a long incline. Occasionally another bus would emerge out of the darkness ahead, dip its lights, sound its powerful horn and continue westward to Teheran. Sometimes I caught sight of a sign beside the road reassuring us that we were still on the road for Mashad – and closing on it. We had left Teheran's enormous 'Argentine' bus terminal late that afternoon. The normal journey time was between fourteen and fifteen hours. We reckoned we would arrive with the dawn. It all seemed a very long way from the rural Warwickshire villages we had left a few weeks earlier.

I had done nine years as a parish priest in six rural parishes. I had never thought I would be a country vicar, nor having become one that we would remain in the villages as long as we did. We suspected that some friends thought we had been put out to pasture; others expressed concern with how we might cope with genteel Warwickshire after ten years of living in the turmoil of the Middle East. The contrasts were certainly sharp. A few days after we moved into an attractive old vicarage, the local hunt rode by. It was a bright, cold winter's day. There were pink coats, steaming hounds, jolly faces and good-natured waves. I actually thought it was part of a film set. I quickly learned that for many it was a way of life. A few days later, the self styled 'squire' of our little hamlet came to request my signature on a petition to keep open a local right of way. As I signed it, I thought wryly of the last petition I had put my hand to – a petition protesting the tear-gassing of children in a school beside our home in Jerusalem.

But we did adjust, and came soon to realise afresh that the human need for love, security, purpose and forgiveness is universal and as strident in the Midlands as the Middle East. Over the years we discerned changes in the congregations (as perhaps they did in us) which encouraged and excited us. There was a discernible movement from a preoccupation, almost obsession, with the preservation of buildings to a recognition of the importance of making known the one for whose worship they were first built. The years in the villages were as demanding as they were rewarding and we remain in close contact with many friends there.

Throughout that time we had continued to follow with keen interest events in the Middle East, returned twice to visit, and corresponded often with friends there. When therefore, at the time when we were thinking about leaving the parishes, an e-mail suddenly came asking us to consider a possible opening to work with the Anglican Church in Iran, our hearts missed a beat and our curiosity was aroused.

It was all rather tentative and vague, and it wasn't a whole lot clearer even after we had met in England with Iraj Mottahedeh, the Anglican Bishop in Iran, who was over from Iran visiting his family. Nonetheless, he bravely encouraged us to visit, to travel the country, meet with his scattered congregations and consider how Nancy and I might in due course work with him, Nancy possibly as his administrator and I with the training of new church leaders.

The timing of this exploratory visit was not auspicious. It fell just one week after '9/11' in America. Foreigners were few on the flight. Some Scottish oil men got off at Baku. When asked by the Dutch flight attendant before landing in Teheran how long we were staying, I replied, "a month". "Oh dear," she said with feeling before recovering herself and wishing us politely a very happy stay.

It proved a happy stay indeed. We travelled the country by bus and train. We visited the congregations and we made friends. In almost every place we were greeted with great kindness and often curiosity. Talk of an imminent allied invasion of Afghanistan was frequently in the news. The popular theory behind the bombing of the Twin Towers was that it was an Israeli conspiracy. Didn't we know, people enquired, that 1000 Jewish employees in those buildings had been instructed to stay at home on 11 September? There was surprise at Mr Blair's unwavering support for the American President. But for the most part, Beckham stirred more interest than Bush, and the cost of rents in Teheran more anxiety than what might happen in Afghanistan.

Towards the end of our visit we met with the Bishop and his wife, whose warm and generous hospitality we had by then enjoyed on several occasions. He asked us to return as soon as possible while he, for his part, would try his best to negotiate approval from the authorities for us to work with the Anglican Church in Iran. We were none of us very hopeful of his success and it came as no great surprise to learn some weeks later in Britain that his gentle overtures on our behalf had been coolly received. Undeterred, we applied, with his encouragement, for visas to return, expressing in the application forms our intention to study Persian in the International Centre for Persian Studies in Teheran, with the hope that it might equip us one day to serve in Iran.

Teheran, which we had left in the pleasant warmth of early autumn, was very cold on our return. Snow lay heaped on the pavements and we were grateful for the radiators in the small apartment loaned to us by one of the Teheran congregation.

Registering at the language centre was not straightforward. We beat a well worn path to the office of its director. He was patient and charming but there always seemed to be something more required by way of identification and verification. It was while our application was being processed that we took the bus to Mashad.

I had passed through it quickly in the early, carefree 1970s, newly graduated from university and working as a volunteer in a school in Jordan. I worked there for two years. In the first summer I travelled to visit a good friend and fellow volunteer, Vanessa, in Isfahan; the next, I went overland to visit another friend, Steve, in India. Crossing the necessary borders then was easier than now but the buses weren't as good! The seats were covered in shiny plastic and the 'air conditioning' as effective as your neighbour would allow the window to be opened. Still, it was a better way to travel than that endured by Dr William McElwee Miller, a distinguished American Presbyterian missionary and scholar, who made the journey as a young man by diligence from Teheran to Mashad in the summer of 1920.

'A diligence was engaged, in which we could ride all the way to Mashed. The four horses, which pulled this vehicle abreast, would be changed at stables situated every 20 or 25 miles along the road. A diligence was a wagon with springs, a roof and open sides. It had no seats, so passengers sat or reclined on the bedding. It was possible to travel both day and night if horses were available. The 560 mile journey to Mashed might be made in eight days and nights.

So I packed my possessions, bade farewell to my dear Teheran friends from whom I would now be separated probably for years, got into the diligence with my luggage and off we went on our pilgrimage to 'Holy Meshed'. We jolted along the dirt road mile after mile, hour after hour. Sometimes we talked, often we dozed, but never got undisturbed sleep. Often fresh horses were not ready at the places where they were changed and we had to wait for them and their driver. We ate food and drank tea at the places where we stopped.'[1]

On this arduous journey, Miller describes meeting a group of Russians in a caravanserai, who had fled the turmoil of the Revolution, as well as losing his hat box which fell off the wagon one night. 'It was,' he wrote, 'a serious loss for the box contained hats for several years.'[2]

Mashad means place of martyrdom, and over the years it has become a very important and popular Muslim shrine. Over 12,000,000 pilgrims flock to it each year. At the centre is the tomb of Imam Reza, the eighth grandson of Prophet Mohammed. Imam Reza died in 817 AD and is widely thought to have been poisoned.

We had originally planned to make the journey there by train. On our earlier exploratory visit to Iran, we had taken the overnight train from Teheran to Isfahan, and had shared our compartment with two young men – students returning home to Isfahan – and a young, married couple and their very new baby. Our companions were polite and deferential but clearly a little apprehensive at the presence of two foreigners among them. A few minutes after leaving Teheran station, there was a roar as the train's air conditioning system was turned on. It was a welcome sound for the carriage was warm but our pleasure turned to dismay when through the air ducts of the compartment came the unmistakable smell of eastern toilets. The two students looked towards us with amusement and apprehension. Nancy and I held our noses, rolled our eyes and with an exaggerated motion of our free hands waved them in an attempt to clear the air. The students laughed and the young couple looked relieved. The smell had made us friends. It was not long before clean, cool air entered the apartment and we settled contentedly into the journey. We managed to exchange some words with our companions in Farsi and in English and shared each others' food. When it came time to sleep, the two young men graciously ushered the rest of us into the corridor while they made up our bunks with sheets and pillows provided by the carriage attendant. The students took the bunks near the ceiling, to myself and the other hus-

[1] William McElwee Miller, *My Persian Pilgrimage*. Pasadena: William Carey Library. 1989, p. 51
[2] Ibid

band they assigned the middle ones, while Nancy and the young mother and her child were given the lower ones. I thought how attractive and at home Nancy looked, her head wrapped in a dark head scarf, asleep as the train rolled on into the night.

We had learned that there were five trains every day from Teheran to Mashad but on this occasion, we discovered that the seats on all of them were already fully booked for several weeks ahead. When a kind friend offered to reserve seats for us on the bus instead, we accepted gratefully, only to find out on arrival at the ticket office that just one seat had been booked, and it took a long time to get to the front of the queue to learn that! Frustrated but still determined to get to Mashad (where friends awaited us) we withdrew into the late afternoon sun to consider what to do next. As we stood, we were approached by a lean, trim, middle-aged man with short greying hair wearing blue mechanic's overalls. When he discovered our nationality he readily volunteered, in excellent English, that he had worked in Coventry for a well known but long since vanished engineering company. He was now the chief air conditioning engineer at the bus terminal. We told him a little of our story and after a few minutes he disappeared to return soon with a tray of tea and the assurance that he would help us get to Mashad. He was as good as his word, and some twenty minutes later, with new tickets in our hands, he ushered us graciously into our seats on a bus for Mashad.

It was just another one of many acts of kindness with which we met on our travels.

Teheran is now a vast city of more than 12,000,000 people. It took well over an hour to clear its sprawling suburbs, the car body shops and brick factories before reaching the main road east to Mashad some 550 miles away.

The bus we had boarded was a new Volvo. It was warm, the seats reclined, and in the course of the evening tea was served and videos – most showing smart Iranian ladies talking on phones, and car chases around north Teheran – were shown. It stopped twice, once around midnight, and again just before dawn, an hour or so short of our destination.

At our first stop the bus drew up to join a park of some thirty others before a stark, steel and glass, partially completed restaurant, illuminated garishly with neon strip lights. Behind it, silhouetted against the skyline, was a ruined, mud brick caravanserai. Inside the restaurant passengers sipped tea, tackled mountains of rice and kebab or just stared and blinked sleepily, resentful at being awoken and forced out of the bus's cosy cocoon. In the shadows, at the side of the restaurant, was the 'Gents'. I balked at the length of the queue of men outside and made off with others to stand before a rapidly melting snowdrift. Meanwhile, Nancy waited her turn, gratefully anonymous in head scarf and overcoat, outside the 'Ladies', whose grim breeze block exterior was decorated with surprisingly suggestive paintings of cherries and pears.

We were not tempted into the restaurant and were content to stay in the yard watching the comings and goings and reading the slogans painted on the sides of the buses. Many were emblazoned with 'God only', which seemed a little exclusive, while several had 'No one', written on their sides, which we later worked out stood for Number One! It was cold outside, though, and we were grateful when the driver unlocked the door of our bus and beckoned us back into its warmth.

We dozed our way fitfully to Mashad, arriving just after dawn, an hour or so earlier than we had originally anticipated and too early, we judged, to rouse our friends. Our fellow passengers dispersed quickly, leaving us exposed to the persistent but good-natured entreaties of circling taxis eager for custom at that early hour and hopeful at the sight of two obvious foreigners. We bought tea and buns and sat bleary-eyed on a desolate, cold, concrete bench. From our stupor we were stirred by a young smiling figure volunteering to 'get a taxi, find hotel – show you WC', at which point he chuckled mischievously, dropped to eastern toilet posture and made a vulgar noise. We had arrived in the holy city of Mashad.

(CHAPTER TEN)
AN ORDINATION
IN ISFAHAN

Breakfast, served at a long table in the newly refurbished Thompson Memorial Hall in the church compound of St Luke's in Isfahan, was a rather sleepy business. This was no surprise as most of those present had travelled through the night by bus, train or car from Kerman, Shiraz and Teheran to attend the hastily convened conference/retreat for the young leaders of the diocese.

In the end we numbered about forty - most were in their twenties, but there was a lively group of children too. Several were the gifted and attractive children of blind parents who had been educated in the church's Blind School, which was taken from the diocese in the wake of the 1979 Revolution. We were impressed by the way the children looked after them, escorted them to meals and looked out for their needs, while the laughter, camaraderie, boundless curiosity and robust Christian faith of their parents was a tonic to many. Several younger people told us that it was the faith and prayers of 'these Blinds', as they were affectionately described to us, that had kept the church through the harsh, uncertain years which followed the revolution. We found out that they could recall easily and describe accurately and warmly the volunteers from England whom they had known in the Blind School over twenty years earlier. I had known some of them myself, and when I told them that I was still in contact with a couple of them they clapped their hands with sheer delight and pressed me hard for news about them.

When, a couple of weeks after the conference, we made a fleeting return visit to see Bishop Iraj, he told us of an intriguing encounter he had had with a visitor to the evening service on the previous Sunday. It had to do with one of the 'Blinds'. When the service had ended and the Bishop was saying goodbye to members of the congregation, a sixteen year-old girl whom he had not seen before, introduced herself and asked if he had a moment to talk. He had, and as they talked it transpired that the girl was a Muslim and had come to church with a friend the previous week when someone else had been conducting the service. The Bishop asked what had drawn her back to worship on this occasion. She told him that she had been surprised and touched to hear an elderly blind woman in the congregation praying with great feeling for the suffering people of Afghanistan. "If," added the young girl, "I had lost my sight, I would be praying for myself, not for people I don't know – thousands of kilometres from here." Before leaving she asked the Bishop if she might return the following Sunday with her mother and another friend. I am sure he agreed. Most church services in Iran draw visitors, amongst whom there are often genuine enquirers wanting to know more about 'the way of Jesus'. Sometimes they are brought by Christian friends.

An older, rather traditional member of the Isfahan congregation expressed to us her admiration for the way in which the new, younger members of the church invite their Muslim friends along. "I'd never think of doing that," she admitted. Others just seem to find their way. On several occasions we found ourselves drawn into conversation with those who had just slipped in, so to speak, off the street, curious to know what went on in a church. I expect that some may have been sent to inform on the church but none whom we met had any anxieties at all about coming. "It is not forbidden," said one young man with a disarming smile.

Interestingly, we did meet a man in his mid-thirties at the conference from Kerman, who had actually been forbidden to attend church by the Anglican priest there. It was a long time ago, and sadly the church building there is now closed. But when he was fifteen, Andreas, as he now likes to be known, was a Muslim. He and a good friend of his, who was also a Muslim, had both somehow been provoked to find out more about Christianity. It seemed obvious to them that they should talk to the local priest. They sought him out and he treated them with grave suspicion. He did not think their interest could be genuine and tried to shake them off. They were not discouraged and did not give up hope that he might help them. Further, in recounting his story, I could detect no trace of resentment in Andreas at the treatment he and his friends had received. In fact, I think he was rather impressed at the pastor's approach. Eventually the priest relented and told them they could come to a church service once a month on a specific Sunday, providing they stayed at the back of the church. "How," Andreas told me, "we counted the days till that first visit and from then until the next." Much later, the genuineness of their quest no longer in question, the two young men received Bibles from the wife of the priest. Andreas began by reading Matthew's Gospel. "The Sermon on the Mount hit me – it was so revolutionary." When we met Andreas and his lovely wife Elisabeth at the conference, they were exercising a valuable and costly ministry in the south of Iran. Sadly they have now left Kerman and are living with their young family in another part of the country.

Friendship with the Bishop and his clergy had, we learnt, been very significant at crucial moments in the lives of a number of individuals in the course of their journey towards faith in Christ.

The conference in Isfahan lasted just four days and culminated in the ordination of two new deacons, Ibrahim and Bahman. Each day began after breakfast with prayers in the church, led thoughtfully by an engaging and somewhat controversial layman, who had once been a medical student in Teheran, but who at the time of the conference was living rough on the streets of the city. He is a mystic, a visionary and a compelling speaker. He put a lot into his preparation of our worship and into his reflections on each day's Bible readings. A little music group led our singing and there was always an extended time for open prayer. It was well used – the youngest present often taking the lead. The shape of the worship followed that of the Anglican Book of Common Prayer and even in Persian it was not difficult to follow. The congregational parts were said with vigour and conviction.

A tea break followed prayers and then usually an address by myself, Ibrahim or the Bishop. I had prepared little before coming for I had been given no idea what was wanted, nor who would be present. And so, with a study Bible and a notepad, I prepared in the early hours of each morning. I felt my talks came together alright. People seemed to appreciate them and Bishop Iraj told me I was easy to translate. Iranians are always polite to foreigners … Ibrahim, who had been asked to speak on the nature of the church, was given a rough ride by some hearers. His Christian nurture and development had been almost entirely within the Roman Catholic Church and Bishop Iraj was keen we hear that perspective. But some were not appreciative, protesting that they had left Islam with its cult of saints and martyrs and they did not want to take on a bunch of new Roman Catholic ones! I am afraid that they thought his addresses confusing. The Bishop spoke about the church constitution, and while I appreciated his generosity in giving me a morning slot for my Bible talks, I thought it unwise of him to opt for the warm and sleepy mid-afternoon slot for his.

It was at the conference that we met the warm-hearted and delightful Dr Farshad, who over tea one evening told Nancy and myself the story of his coming to faith in Christ. He was brought up in a devout Muslim family. When he was about six years old he accompanied his parents to Reading in England, where his father was doing graduate studies at the university. He made some English friends and, with the approval of his parents, attended a children's Sunday school at a well-known Reading church with one of them. "It was," he told us, "a happy memory."

The family then returned to Iran where Farshad continued his schooling and later went on to university. He became, with many of his student contemporaries, bitterly disillusioned with religion, in particular with Islam, through what he considered the excesses of the Revolution. In fact he told us that he came to believe in God no longer until the day when, newly qualified as a doctor, he was summoned to attend a mother in labour. She was young and pretty and sufficiently composed to offer assurance to the anxious-looking doctor attending her. But when the labour pains began in earnest, she apparently swore 'terrifically' up until the moment of her child's birth. And it was then, he told us, that the transformation from pain and struggle, to joy and love was so sudden and so complete that it pierced him right through, provoking within him a restless quest to discover the source of such love. He read a number of religious books but could find none that satisfied his search. Sometime later he got to know an Armenian doctor at the hospital where he was working who gave him an English Bible which he began to read. As he read the Gospels, "Jesus stepped from the pages" and spoke clearly to him. Farshad's faith in God was rekindled and found its focus and joy in Jesus. His parents were pleased that he had 'come back to God'. Not long afterwards he opened a clinic for the poor without charge, one evening every week. He felt it was something God wanted him to do.

Meal times, tea breaks and shady spaces in the heat of the day provided opportunity to talk and learn more of those who had come to the conference. Nancy attracted a solicitous and lively cluster of young mothers and new brides eager to know about our family and to solicit her opinion and views on everything from fashion to prayer.

Each evening after supper (the food was plentiful and delicious), prepared and overseen by Minoo, the Bishop's unflappable and charming wife, we all gathered in the main hall to sing and share. All ages were present, and on one memorable evening it was suggested we take it in turn to introduce and commend the person on our left to the rest of the group. It was a long evening but also a fascinating and revealing one. We were, in particular, very touched by the way in which some of the youngsters, aged only eleven or twelve, participated so fully and spoke so naturally, confidently and thoughtfully about their elders. Sometimes there were games such as Pass the Parcel, with appropriate penalties for the person found holding the parcel when the music stopped. The Bishop reduced some to tears of laughter with his rendering of a poem. When the meeting ended, little groups sat around talking till late. Eventually people made their way to their rooms scattered around the compound.

On one evening I was engaged by two thoughtful men wanting to know whether they should change their names now that they were Christian. One was all for making a definitive break with his past wanting, like the apostle Paul, to take a new name to signify a new beginning. The other expressed his misgivings. "If," he said, "I tell people my name is Andrew or John, they will just assume I am an Armenian. I want people to know I am Mustafa, and a Christian." We did not reach a conclusion. Later I learned that the previous Bishop of Iran had, on his conversion to Christianity, both retained his former name, Hassan, and taken the Christian name Barnabas, thereby acknowledging his past and affirming his new Christian identity.

Despite the busyness of the schedule and the last moment preparations for my talks, we managed a happy afternoon browsing the miles of Isfahan's covered bazaars. I think it was on the same afternoon that the two ordinands were dispatched to purchase black shirts for later 'conversion' by Nancy and Roya, Ibrahim's wife, into 'vicar shirts'. We revelled in the spice stalls, at the colours and smells of all on display and marvelled at how, at the end of the day, it could all be stowed into what looked no more than an alcove in an ancient wall. At one point we emerged suddenly into a bright courtyard edged with shops bulging with electrical goods, washing machines, huge fridges, mixers, blenders and coffee makers. We watched Afghan porters struggling to lift enormous loads onto the backs of battered pick-ups. We negotiated our way between them and back into the bazaar, passing a tiny shop specialising in huge single gas burners – the sort used to heat six foot wide cauldrons of soup or stew for great national festivals or family parties.

No sooner were we back into the bazaar than we had, quite literally, to flatten ourselves into the wall as a great swathe of young mullahs in their flowing robes, dark turbans and black shoes swept past and disappeared through a narrow doorway beyond us. They were a rather awesome sight, very well turned out, and we wondered whether they were hurrying to a graduation ceremony or special event.

We meandered on down smaller, narrower alleys and noticed in a number of places sudden gaps between houses which we learnt later were the legacy of the Iran-Iraq 'War of the Cities'. Isfahan, a notably religious city, had given many volunteers to the war with the result that the city's poorer suburbs, through which we were then walking and from where many of the volunteers had come, were specially targeted by the enemy. It was a sobering thought; Iraq seemed so far away. Later, under quite bizarre circumstances, we found ourselves late one night with Minoo, looking for a galvanized coffin in the dusty basement of the church hall. The reasons for our search are too complicated to explain, but it was during the search in the basement we learnt that the community of St Luke's had spent many, many hours sheltering there during the War of the Cities. Later, I read a letter written by a member of the congregation during those dangerous days. It reminded me vividly of our experience of living and working in Beirut. It reminded me, too, of the way in which our church there, and in Isfahan, had shared so fully in the convulsions of their nations and in the suffering and deprivations of their people.

The letter was written on 21 January 1987:

> I am writing these lines while at any moment we may be disturbed by the noise of sirens. Then we have to find as safe a corner as we can and live in dreadful moments of trepidation and anxiety. It is now more than ten days that the bombing of the cities continues day and night. The sound of terrible explosions heard from far and near makes everyone tremble – fearfully. Every day numbers of our fellow citizens are either killed or wounded as the result of these bombings. Each time the siren sounds everyone thinks that maybe it will be his or her turn to perish this time. It is an awful situation to be in, and yet there are lessons to be learnt: we become intensely aware that we are weak mortals and very vulnerable. Evil rumours abound, adding to the fear of people. Some get to the point of madness and shake as if in a fit of epilepsy, others get heart attacks. The situation is more difficult for children, old people and the disabled, especially the blind, as their mobility is limited.
>
> But there is a positive side to this awful situation. New and precious truths can be learnt by those who are ready to place themselves at the disposal of God whom we call our Deliverer. On the surface, there does not seem to be

117

any occasion for thanksgiving but in the depth, every moment and every relationship can become important and full of meaning. All false things fall to the ground and one can see openly that the only real unshakeable and lasting thing is love. Life becomes full of valuable opportunities for loving service. Ordinary events such as 'separations' and 'meetings' and common-place sayings such as, 'Peace be with you', and 'God protect you', suddenly loom intensely meaningful. Those of us who normally regard others as indebted to us, become aware how much we owe to God and to others – more than ever. And we realise that of ourselves we do not deserve anything, and all we have is through grace.[1]

On our return to the Bishop's house, we found Bahman and Ibrahim in high spirits recounting their afternoon's exploits and eventual successful purchase of black shirts. Nancy settled to adapting the collars while I went with Ibrahim to rummage in the vestry for cassocks and surplices. The ordination service was scheduled for the following evening. The Bishop had decided he wanted to include the ceremony of washing the deacons' feet in the ordination. An e-mail was sent to the Roman Catholic priest, Père Hamblot in Teheran, for a suitable piece of liturgy.

The conference programme continued the next day but there was a festive spirit in the air and in the kitchens of the Bishop's house and hall, as preparations for a mighty feast were underway – and it seemed that everyone was involved in one way or another. A little delegation was despatched to the Armenian Cathedral gift shop to purchase suitable gifts for the ordinands. Others hoovered the church's lovely carpets and with Mourad, the church's accountant and reader, I rehearsed three young 'actors' who were to illustrate my sermon based on some verses from Saint Paul's second letter to Timothy. They were to act out the roles of farmer, craftsman and soldier, whose labour, skill and courage the apostle commended to young Timothy. They were the children of three young church families and entered into their roles wonderfully. Earlier in the day I had found myself plunging blocked drains with the Bishop. We plunged and wriggled drain rods to no good effect for half an hour when, patience exhausted, the Bishop resorted to a mysterious bottle of clear potion whose contents he poured down the drain with dramatic results. Hissing and sizzling followed and before long all that was meant

[1] *Iran Diocese News*, April 1987

to pass down the drains did so – unhindered.

The service held together beautifully. It was deeply moving, power-ful with symbol and hope. The church was full and many present were thrilled to see among them the retired priest from Kerman, who had been imprisoned at one time with Bishop Iraj. It was the first ordination in the Diocese for many years and the first that many present had witnessed. Seroj, the priest for the Teheran congregation, presented the ordinands and guided them through the service. The church's stained glass window, with the evening sun behind it, looked stunning.

When the moment came for washing the feet of the deacons, there was a tangible, poignant hush as the Gospel account of the first footwash-ing was read and the Bishop stooped to wash their feet. A thoughtful engineer from Shiraz told me after the service that he had been unable to stop himself crying through most of it, and especially, for some rea-son, during the administration of the communion. As we processed out of the church (and there is nothing as cheerfully and memorably chaotic as a Middle Eastern Anglican procession) the night sky was suddenly and dramatically filled with the sound and colour of exploding fireworks. Many congratulated Bishop Iraj on the timing of the display. He told us with a delighted smile that Iran must have beaten Thailand in the foot-ball!

(CHAPTER ELEVEN)
POMEGRANATES AND PRAYER IN SHIRAZ

We were seated on the floor eating breakfast, as we had on the previous three mornings in Shiraz. The kitten was on its back under an ancient armchair, playing with a tuft of stuffing that had at last broken through the constraints of the tired webbing. Bahman, our host, whose ordination in Isfahan I have just described, was patiently but determinedly running us through our newly acquired Persian vocabulary. He pointed to items on the coffee table which we were eating – bread, yogurt, boiled egg, honey, fruit – and we gave him back the names in Persian. We did not falter but realised that this was only the opening round. We had hardly taken our first sip of tea and breakfast was always a leisurely business.

We had visited Shiraz once before when we had stayed with long-standing members of the congregation in their lovely villa some miles outside the city. With them we had walked the dusty tracks that weave their way between ancient mud-baked walls, which enclose orchards of pomegranates, plums and grapes and, to our delight learned from our friends how to drink from a pomegranate; squeeze it hard all round without breaking the skin, then pierce it with a sharp thorn or stick and through the hole made, suck out its delicious juice.

During our stay with them, the husband took us to visit the extensive and majestic ruins of the great city of Persepolis, known locally as Takht-é-Jamshid; to the much more modest but still lovely ruins of the tiny abandoned Anglican church of Qalat and to the tomb of Hafez, Iran's celebrated fourteenth century poet in Shiraz. There we looked for, and found around his tomb, tiles with beautiful references to Jesus, which the late Bishop Dehqani-Tafti translated, he said, "somewhat freely" as follows:

> If thou, like Christ, be pure and single hearted,
> The very sun is brightened by thy life imparted.

Another read,
And if the Holy Spirit descend | In grace and power infinite
His comfort in these days to lend | To them that humbly wait on it
Theirs too the wondrous works can be. | that Jesus wrought in Galilee.[1]

On this occasion, we wanted to stay in the famous city of Shiraz itself but we did not want to impose upon the newly-ordained pastor. We knew that his apartment beside the church was very public and that after our previous visit to the church, he had been gently rebuked by the authorities for not notifying them of our presence. It wasn't merely that we did not want to cause him more trouble by actually staying with him, we really wondered how we could sustain four days together with what we perceived to be our limited grasp of each other's language. We arrived fully prepared to seek lodging in any of the nearby hotels, but our proposals were quickly swept aside and our misapprehensions about language rapidly dispelled.

Bahman had gone to considerable lengths to tidy and furnish the normally empty and largely redundant apartment above his own for our visit. The larder had been provisioned simply, two beds made up and the gas-fired heater turned on. We were grateful for the fire and at his insistence it remained on day and night throughout our visit. As Iran is reputed to have the world's second largest reserves of natural gas, we did not feel too badly about it. We were touched by all the trouble he had gone to on our behalf.

Alone with him in his flat, we discovered that he had a very reasonable knowledge of English, though that did not deflect him from making us learn Persian over breakfast, and often late at night over a glass of his home-made wine. It was a wonderfully levelling experience – sitting on the floor being taught by him. We felt privileged to stay with him and were grateful to be drawn so generously and easily into his life and concerns, and those of his congregation. By that last morning, we felt we had become good friends and at ease, Bahman told us an extraordinary story over breakfast. It was prompted by a comment of my own about his three black guard dogs that lived in the sizeable compound, whom I had admired and eventually summoned the courage to stroke.

Four or five years previously, a caller had knocked one evening at his door asking for prayer. The person had seemed very troubled. It was

[1] HB Dehqani-Tafti, *Norman Sharp's Persian Designs*, Sohrab Books, 2001, pages 10,11

apparently not an unusual request, even from a stranger, and the person who had knocked was quite unknown to Bahman. Together they went into the church. While praying with the visitor, Bahman was twice interrupted by a voice distinctly calling his name. The person who was with him seemed quite unaware of the voice. On his third attempt at praying, the voice said quite clearly, 'Bahman, your dogs'. Fearing they had got loose, he left his visitor and ran to find them all securely tied by their leads. One of them though, called Blackie, was very disturbed. Bahman untied him and the dog ran immediately through the courtyard to a little orange grove, where he barked up at the figure of a man crouched in one of the trees. Bahman grabbed Blackie's collar and as he did so heard a car engine start and rev hard in the shadows. He had not noticed it. The man in the tree jumped down and ran for the car, whose back door was opened for him. Then, with the lights blazing, it drove out of the courtyard. When Bahman returned to the church there was no-one there. "I think they had come to kill me," he said simply.

Soon after our arrival in Shiraz we had gone with him and some fifty or sixty church members to the church graveyard on the outskirts of the town to commemorate the first anniversary of the death of a church widow's oldest son, who had died at the age of thirty seven.

Nancy and I somehow got separated on the way there, she ending up in a car with relatives of the family, I on the little bus that had been hired for the occasion. The atmosphere was cheerful, even festive. I found myself seated with two young teenage boys beside the driver, on top of the engine cover. It was warm and noisy.

The graveyard had been well tidied in the week before and as we gathered around the grave, I recognised a stocky man from the congregation putting in hand some repairs to a gravestone. He was cementing back a cross that looked as if it had been broken off. He finished his task quickly, wiped the surplus cement off the cross, washed his hands in a bucket of water, dried them on the seat of his trousers and came over to join us. Someone welcomed us, a brief eulogy was offered and hymns were sung. Our good friend, who had on our earlier visit to the city taught us how to drink pomegranate juice, then led us in several prayers. A further hymn was sung and we dispersed.

Amongst those gathered I thought I spotted a thoughtful, serious young man with whom I had had several long conversations at the retreat in Isfahan three months earlier. He had then impressed me deeply with his grasp of Christian truth and commitment to Christ though he had been a Christian for only two or three years. I say, 'I thought I spotted' because he looked so much older and his face was very drawn and taut. As I approached, and he looked very preoccupied, he turned towards me and I was rewarded as his face broke into a great smile of recognition. We embraced warmly and arranged to meet the following evening. He seemed stunned to see us there and almost embarrassingly grateful for the opportunity to get together to talk.

Many of those who had been at the graveside had, I noticed, made their way back to the home and courtyard of the deceased's mother for tea but a few – some ten or fifteen – lingered on to sing beside another grave, which was at the edge of the cemetery. I was told that it was the grave of Arastoo Sayyah, a previous pastor of the church, who had been murdered in his study by two men in the tumultuous and heady early days of the Revolution. He was the first in a line of new Iranian Christian martyrs. They included Bahram, only son of Anglican Bishop Hassan and Margaret Dehqani Tafti and several distinguished pastors, leaders and members of the Presbyterian and Pentecostal churches of Iran.

Parvis Arastoo Sayyah–Sina was from Isfahan. His first appearance at St Luke's church there, sometime in the late 1940s, was to fetch his sister home. He was determined she should have nothing to do with the church. But later he was to give himself to Christ and to seek ordination. He was ordained priest in 1958 and served in Yazd, Kerman, Isfahan and Shiraz. He married Iris Palmer, who had come out to Iran to work with the Church Missionary Society. On February 19, 1979, two people whom he knew (so-called 'enquirers') called to see Arastoo at about 11.30am in his office, which was in an isolated part of the compound. At 3pm he was found murdered in the office. 'He had,' wrote Bishop Hassan soon afterwards, 'a charming personality and a great love for people and his Lord.'

Some months before his death, Arastoo had contributed to the Diocesan Newsletter an enthusiastic report on a youth camp, which he and the Rev Iraj Mottehadeh, who succeeded Bishop Hassan as Bishop in Iran, had led on the theme of being witnesses for Christ.

> 'Many (of the participants) were from Christian families, others were having to live independently of their families because of their Christian profession and one was a recent believer from Isfahan ... hoping to be baptised shortly.

He was the only one whose family does not live in a city and it was very suitable that one of our evening speakers spoke of Jonah preaching repentance in the great city of Nineveh, since the city is the environment in which most of our Christian youth are called to fulfill the command and promise of our theme, You shall be my witnesses.'[2]

It seemed wonderful to us that 25 years after Arastoo's death, friends should gather at his graveside to remember – and to praise God for him. We did not join them but made our way towards those enjoying tea and cakes. Nancy joined the women inside while I found myself drawn into a lively discussion in the courtyard with five or six young men in their twenties who quickly informed me that they were new believers in Jesus. They were full of questions – about the Bible, its interpretation and application to life today, about the church in Britain and life there in general.

At the time of our visit, Bahman was already well established in Shiraz. He had lived and served the church there for several years before his ordination, which I have described. Arastoo Sayyah was one of his predecessors. To the disapproval of some of the older members of his congregation, he kept pigeons. Each evening we accompanied him as he put them to bed, and in the morning we released them – blinking and talkative – into the sunshine of the courtyard. His apartment was a constant buzz of comings and goings. There were several young men who had taken it upon themselves to help maintain the extensive church grounds and the church building – stunningly lovely in a way that is unmistakably Christian, yet also deeply and sensitively Persian. Sometimes people called wanting to know more about the Christian faith; friends and family dropped in and there were occasional tourists eager to view the church, which gets prominent mention in most guidebooks.

One morning, after one of our memorable breakfast tutorials, Bahman offered to show us around the church, which is named after Simon the Zealot, whom a tradition suggests visited Iran. Bahman, who is an evangelist but no scholar, nonetheless impressed us, not only with his knowledge of the history of the building, but also by his empathy with those who had built it and served its congregation. It was designed and its construction overseen by the Reverend Norman Sharp. He regarded it as his finest work. Its construction was not without incident. An arch collapsed one day, killing three labourers. Norman Sharp was consequently

[2] *The Iranian Diocesan News*, May 1979

put under arrest but released not long afterwards when it was discovered that the contractors had ignored his instructions.

Norman Sharp went out to Iran from England as a missionary with the Church Missionary Society in 1924. He was a Persian scholar of immense learning and distinction, and not only a designer and builder of beautiful church buildings but also a conscientious pastor and priest. 'Sharp loved the members of his church and was touchingly protective of them. I remember going with him,' recalls Bishop Hassan Dehqani-Tafti, 'to visit a parishioner who was in a TB hospital in Shiraz. Without hesitation he drank a glass of sherbet prepared for him by the patient. The risk of catching the disease either did not occur to him or did not concern him. His heart was clearly full of care and love for the young man who was dying. He travelled long distances to make pastoral visits, on a couple of occasions even covering the distance between Shiraz and Yazd on his bicycle. Meanwhile, the journey from Shiraz to Qalat – a forty mile round trip – was frequently taken on mule back, whether in the heat of summer or the thick snow of winter.'[3]

At the time of our visit Norman Sharp's name was still remembered and revered amongst older members of the Shiraz congregation, one or two of whom were sadly not slow to contrast the awesome scholarship of Norman Sharp with what they perceived as the inadequacy of the learning of his Iranian successors.

Inside the church, standing beneath its dome, Bahman pointed out to us a portrait hanging on the wall. It was of Henry Martyn – gentle, youthful and serious. Henry Martyn went to Calcutta in 1805 as Chaplain to Britain's East India Company. While there he translated the New Testament into Persian and Arabic. In 1811 he arrived in Shiraz. There he undertook revisions of the translations. He was just thirty years old. Sir John Malcolm, who knew Martyn well and was later to become the Governor of Bombay, wrote to Sir Gore Ouseley, who was the British Ambassador in Iran, a very warm commendation of the young Henry Martyn.

> 'Mr Martyn expects to improve himself as an oriental scholar. He is already an excellent one. His knowledge of Arabic is superior to that of any Englishman in India. He is altogether a very learned and cheerful man, but a great enthusiast in his holy calling ... I am satisfied that if you

[3] HB Dehqani-Tafti, p.6

ever see him, you will be pleased with him. He will give you grace before and after dinner, and admonish such of your party as take the Lord's name in vain, but his good sense and great learning will delight you, while his constant cheerfulness will add to the hilarity of your party.'[4]

If some of the commendation sounds somewhat quaint and patronising by today's standards, the endorsement of Henry Martyn's intellectual ability is resounding, and respect for his calling – wholehearted.

Canon E J Edmonds, a contemporary, also paid this tribute to him, 'I know no parallel to these achievements of Henry Martyn, the born translator. He masters grammar, observes idioms, accumulates vocabulary, reads and listens, corrects and even reconstructs. Above all he prays.'[5]

Cautioned by his superiors against getting drawn into religious controversy and debate with the mullahs in Shiraz, Henry Martyn found that he could not avoid it! He wrote tracts and he debated, and years after his early death in Turkey in 1812, was remembered in Shiraz with great affection. The local people recognised his sincerity and referred to him as, 'a man of God'.

Our first visit to Shiraz had happened to coincide with an ad hoc party laid on by members of the congregation to celebrate Bahman's ordination. It was a simple, spontaneous and very happy occasion. There were about forty present when it began in the early evening but others slipped in throughout the evening. Nancy and I found ourselves almost overwhelmed with people wanting our attention – by a newly married couple who wanted a blessing on their marriage, by enquirers eager to learn more about the Christian faith and by anxious, troubled people wanting counsel and prayer. I confess I was rather flattered by all the attention, while half aware that we were the focus, almost certainly, of people's attention and hopes simply by virtue of being foreigners. A few present had met us at the Isfahan retreat but none of those who sought us out had seen us until we walked into the church hall that evening. Nancy wisely and firmly warned me that to allow ourselves to be drawn into an evening of prayer and counselling would be no service to Bahman, in honour of whose new ministry the party was being held. We directed those who wanted our help to him, and on most occasions he generously drew us

[4] Vivienne Stacey, *Henry Martyn*, Henry Martyn Insitute of Islamic Studies, Hyderabad, 1980, p. 61
[5] Ibid, p.70

into the conversations that followed.

As the evening came to a close, he came across to ask me if I would formally dismiss the people with a prayer. I was more than happy to do so and suggested we make our way over to the church. Ten or twelve people came with me. After some moments of silence in the semi-darkness of the building, I offered a prayer of thanksgiving. I prayed for Bahman's ministry and commended ourselves and the church to God's shaping and leading. I was kneeling in the aisle in the centre of the church, but just as I was about to get up a young girl's voice broke into a long, fervent extempore prayer in Persian. Other prayers, all in Persian, followed – men and women, boys and girls. Petition, earnest and heart-wrung, mingled with unmistakable outbursts of praise and expressions of love and gratitude. I turned around and opened my eyes. There were nearly thirty people present. As I turned back toward the front of the church, my eyes were caught by the gentle face of Henry Martyn framed in the picture on the wall.

It was a solemn moment. I had studied in Cambridge in the same college, worshipped in the church in the city centre where he had worshipped as an undergraduate and attended prayer meetings in the hall nearby which bore his name. I had read about his work and been stirred by accounts of his sacrifice and love. A few months before his death he had made the following entry in his journal on 18th February, 1812, 'This is my birthday on which I complete my 31st year. The Persian New Testament has been begun, and I may say, finished as only the last eight chapters of Revelation remain. Such a painful year I never passed, owing to the privations I have been called to on the one hand, and the spectacle of human depravity on the other. But I hope that I have not come to this seat of Satan in vain. The word of God has found its way into Persia and it is not in Satan's power to oppose its progress, if he the Lord hath sent it.'[6]

As we knelt in the church that night in prayer, I found myself looking at his portrait and whispering, "Your work was not in vain, listen to these prayers; the word of God has found its way into Persia."

[6] Ibid, p.67

(CHAPTER TWELVE)

ON TO KERMAN

During our few months in Iran, we grew attached to our Lonely Planet Guide to the country. We found its recommendations of places to stay and what to visit very helpful. It had a good selection of useful phrases in it and a lot of down to earth practical advice.

> While traffic in major cities rarely goes fast enough for your taxi or bus to have a serious accident, never underestimate the possibility of dying a horrible death under the wheels of any sort of vehicle while crossing the road. No vehicle whatsoever will stop at any pedestrian crossing at any time. Resist the temptation to amble across an eight-lane roundabout at peak time in downtown Teheran with your back to the traffic as many Teheranis do. Always look for the occasional walkway above or under the road, mainly used by crippled old Iranians or terrified foreigners of all ages. The best idea is safety in numbers ... shuffle across the road in a tightly-huddled group of locals. Drivers are less likely to run over a group of people because of the paperwork at the police station ...

The Guide also had some stunning photos in it and one in particular caught our eye and imagination. It looked like somewhere out of the story of the Arabian Nights or like a set for one of Steven Spielberg's films. It was a photo of a great mud-walled city, dominated by a vast citadel, surrounded by date palms and set in an immense emptiness of desert. It was, we learnt, the medieval city of Bam situated some 120 miles southeast of Kerman, itself in the bottom right corner of the country, getting on towards Pakistan. We resolved to go there. It looked romantic and exotic.

I mentioned that at the Isfahan conference we had met a fine young Iranian couple, Andreas and Elizabeth, newly married and working on behalf of the Anglican Church in Kerman. They had been very keen that we visit them. We were eager to do so and decided to travel on from Shiraz to Kerman and, if possible, to go on from there and explore Bam.

Friends in Shiraz delivered us to the bus station from where we caught a mid-morning bus to Kerman. It was old and had no air conditioning but with only three rather than four seats in each row, pleasantly spacious. Children, of whom there were several, could roam the aisle easily, pausing to climb at times onto the laps of friendly strangers, which they did with trusting, easy cheerfulness and the observant approval of parents. Each of the bus's great windows had huge curtains to keep out the sun's glare and by early afternoon, when it was very hot, we were grateful for them, though I wished I could have seen more through their chinks. At one point we climbed past rugged, bare fields where pistachio trees grew, and later we looked down onto an immense salt lake. At times in the shimmering heat haze the scenery looked surreal and a little like a lunar landscape.

An hour or so into the journey, the ubiquitous video machine was turned on and we found ourselves watching a stockily built young Iranian comedian mimicking a Bollywood, Indian musician to the amusement of our fellow passengers. He was very good. He rolled his head and eyes most dolefully and crooned tragically into the microphone. This he followed up with a graphic demonstration of five popular ways to pick the nose. It was very funny, very vulgar – and we laughed along with everyone else. We learned later that the comedian was Iran's 'Mr Bean' and that occasionally he had had to be curbed by the authorities for overstepping the line of acceptability. It made us curious to know how.

As the afternoon wore on most people dozed. I was glad Nancy was fast asleep when the driver, who was for the most part fairly responsible, entered a sharp corner on a particularly precipitous piece of road far too fast and on the wrong side of the road. He heaved very hard on the huge steering wheel and with much agonised screeching of tyres, the bus bent around the corner. The driver's right shoulder was almost touching his assistant's seat with the effort. Mercifully there was nothing else round the corner. The assistant driver looked fixedly ahead and said nothing. Most of the passengers slept on – oblivious – in the late afternoon heat. At dusk we were passed by a small convoy of military jeeps, each with a heavy machine gun mounted in the back. The soldiers and their vehicles looked purposeful. They were almost the only evidence we saw of the military in all our travels in Iran.

At nightfall, we rolled into Kerman's congested bus yard and not long afterwards took a taxi to the Akhavan Hotel, recommended to us from the pages of our dependable guide book. The room was clean, the manager hospitable and the food imaginative, excellent Iranian fare. All we lacked was a glass of good Bavarian lager and I have a suspicion that the manager might have found some if we had asked him.

We had decided on this occasion, despite any possible protests from our young friends in Kerman, that we would stay in a hotel. We knew that their movements, even more than those of Bahman in Shiraz, were closely observed and that they had sometimes been interrogated by the security services after offering hospitality to foreign Christians. We did not want to cause them trouble.

After supper the hotel manager asked us if we intended going to Bam, and when we said that we hoped to, he arranged for a car and driver to take us there the following day. We agreed to what seemed like the going rate, just twenty dollars, and set out early the next morning feeling quite regal in the back of a modern Peugeot taxi. Our driver drove fast but not recklessly. Most of the traffic was heavy trucks bound, we imagined, either for the port of Bandar Abbas or the Pakistan border. In the middle of nowhere we passed a brand new mosque arising out of the desert. Perhaps it would be joined later by a restaurant and petrol station.

Shortly before Bam, we noticed a sign to Jiroft, home town of Sara, an Iranian Anglican, whom we had met some years earlier studying English first in Birmingham and later theology in Bristol. With her slight figure, dark complexion, large eyes and sharp intellect, Sara is an arresting personality. Her story is also a fascinating one.

Her father was a successful builder and her mother, a dressmaker. She is one of twelve children, the sixth in line after five sons. Two of her brothers have died. Possessed of a very independent personality, which has been at times both a source of grief and admiration to her friends and family, Sara decided at the age of twelve that she wanted to live in a little village outside Jiroft, where the family also had a house. She wanted to sample village life. "I had never suffered," she told us, "and I had always had a heart for the poor." Sara's father indulged her and sent Sara and her mother and the younger children off to the village, much to her mother's dismay. The experiment was short-lived. The children in the village teased and spurned the town girl. She played truant and without the knowledge of her parents, spent school hours at a farm. When the reason for her absence was discovered, she and her mother and the other children returned to Jiroft. Her father never chided her but held the school to blame for his daughter's bad experience.

Back in the mainstream of school in Jiroft, Sara was to show her independence again a couple of years later when, throwing off the teaching of Islam, she adopted and started actively promoting atheism among her classmates. Previously, she said, she had been a strict Muslim, "praying and everything, not letting men see my hair or looking at them." She described her parents affectionately as Iranian traditional Muslims. The catalyst for this dramatic departure from the family's faith was a particular lesson at school. The teacher, the widow of a war martyr, was talking about hell, heaven and paradise. "When she was talking I saw hell was so big that you cannot escape it, while heaven and paradise were so small. I burst into tears when she spoke of hell and shouted in class, "I hate that God." The other children were shocked and it was the start of being an atheist. For a while Sara gave up wearing the chador, the enveloping cover for Iranian Muslim women, but under pressure from the family relented and took it up again. She began to read voraciously, sometimes for as long as ten hours a day. "I spent all my pocket money on books."

She became a dedicated Communist, having long been sympathetic to the cause through the influence of one of her brothers, who was himself an ardent Communist. She was not interested in belonging to any anti-government protest groups but she did want to understand and read about Communism. She even formed a small, caring support group for poor students that actually met in her parents' home. She was very keen that people develop and offer their talents for the benefit of each other. It is a passion she has not lost. Asked what her teachers in school in Jiroft made of her new vocation, Sara replied, "It made my teachers happy because I showed independence."

Later she went to university in Kerman, ostensibly to study literature, while in reality her main ambition was to actively spread atheism among her fellow students. She was soon to discover that the university was less accommodating to her views than her school. Students she spoke to were taken away for interrogation; her room and personal belongings were deliberately trashed. She survived her first term, and during the second she, and a friend called Nadia, discovered that they both needed a Bible for some aspect of their studies. In the end, they tracked one down in a small bookshop run by Daniel, a Christian convert out of Judaism, who was later to show the two girls the church in Kerman. Sara took the Bible on a sale and return basis. After using it for the project she promptly returned it and was refunded its purchase price. She had not wanted it defiling her shelves.

All this we learned from Sara long after our return to Britain, though bits of it we heard from Andreas on the evening after our memorable visit to Bam.

The ancient city did not disappoint us. We passed through the modern town down avenues of eucalyptus and rows of date palms for which Bam is rightly famous. And then, quite suddenly, we were in front of the great mud walls of the old city. We told our taxi driver, a little optimistically, that two hours there would suffice. He was young, very amenable and relaxed and said that we would find him in the shade nearby, even if we took longer. We paid our entrance fee, which though ten times the price nationals pay, was still a lot less than one ticket for Warwick Castle back home.

Our guide book informed us that the original city and citadel were probably constructed in the Sassanian period (224-637 AD), and that in the years immediately before an Afghan invasion of 1722 its population had been in excess of 10,000. Since then, apart from intermittent use as an army barracks, the place has been abandoned. We climbed onto the main wall which circles the entire city and is some two kilometres long. At points along the wall there are small roofed observation towers. The vaulted ceiling in one of them looked to have been newly restored. Through the narrow slit windows we looked out over desert to jagged mountains in the distance and half thought we spied Tolkien's dark riders galloping towards us. At one point the path which had hugged the outer crenellated wall, suddenly ended. We found ourselves on a very smooth, narrow ledge with a great dusty drop below us, and very cautiously indeed edged our way back to safety. We decided to find the next staircase down and to make our way through the streets and up to the citadel which dominates the city.

Restoration work to an old school, mosque and other buildings seemed to be in hand in a leisurely way. We passed restored stables that had once housed 300 horses. As we entered a shady archway below the citadel a very loud and rather aristocratic English male voice boomed out, "Pamela dear, would you like an ice cream?!" We did not hear the reply for almost immediately a very similar voice pronounced the place to be, "a bit like Edinburgh Castle". A moment later a threesome, unmistakably English and fearsomely resolute, strode past. If they saw us, they did not acknowledge us. We felt rather embarrassed, put out too, I think, to realise that we were not the sole British citizens in Bam that day.

On our return to our friendly hotel that evening in Kerman, we found Elizabeth, Andreas' young wife, in headscarf and smart white raincoat waiting in the foyer to take us to their home for supper. The taxi took us down a labyrinth of alleys before stopping in front of a steel gate that led through a little courtyard into their apartment. Andreas was out but Elizabeth's younger brother greeted us warmly while Elizabeth, who had seemed so reserved and quiet in the car, showed herself to be not only a very good cook but also a lively, quick witted and engaging hostess. She and Andreas had been married only a few months. He returned later looking very tired. He had been visiting young families in the neighbour- hood in his self-appointed role as pastor and evangelist in Kerman. In the course of our long, relaxed meal and evening together, we heard how Andreas and Elizabeth had met, of his work in Kerman and among the roaming tribespeople, of his own long and costly journey towards the Christian faith, and of his love and commitment to Iran's little Angli- can church. Elizabeth, meanwhile, plied us with food and added her own timely contributions to the conversation, teasing Andreas when he grew too serious and challenging him nicely when he spoke too long. We asked if it might be possible to look inside St Andrew's Church in Kerman. Andreas was cautious. The church had been closed for several years and was not in good repair. He was also anxious that if he was seen taking us around, local people might think that he was complaining to us about the authorities and their lack of concern for the preservation of an historic church. We did not push the matter further but we were disappointed. Not only was the building well written of in local guide books; it had also been the place of a significant Christian spiritual re- newal some years earlier.

The entry for St Andrew's Anglican Church in the Iranian guide is both intriguing and revealing. 'The Anglican Church of St Andrew, a build- ing easily missed from the street, is hidden in a garden behind a door- way in Shariati Avenue marked with the Persian cross characteristic of all Anglican churches in Iran. The small flock seems largely to have been forgotten by headquarters in Canterbury except for goodwill cards at Christmas and at Easter ... The original building (was) founded by Brit- ish missionaries ... For a few years now they have had to do without a minister, so a small community of lay members sharing the priest's house take it in turn to lead the Sunday service (in Persian).[1]

The comment about Christmas and Easter cards may have been penned in jest but the entry nonetheless betrays a deeply rooted local conviction

[1] M T Faramarzi, *A Travel Guide to Iran*, Yassaman Publications' , Teheran 1997, p.140

that the Anglican Church in Iran is but the tool of Canterbury – which is in turn inseparable from the 'English political' or government. The observation about lay led worship – now sadly long ceased – probably refers back to the time when Andreas and his friends, assisted and guided by Sara, who had by then become a convinced Christian, did lead the weekly worship.

Sara did not, as she would readily tell you, become a Christian in a conventional way. She returned, as recounted, the Bible purchased for her research. She was not very impressed with the Christians she met. Andreas and his two friends, whom Daniel introduced to her at the church, she first thought "silly". Jesus she considered, "a weak man". Andreas and his friends tried to persuade her to pray. She protested that she could not and would not pray to one in whom she did not believe. However, a family crisis was to provoke her to do what she had so firmly told them she would not do.

Sara had an orphan nephew who needed major open-heart surgery. Her family arranged to have him booked into a hospital for the operation. Sara was convinced that he would die if he was operated on in that hospital. A day before the operation was due, Sara was distraught. "For the first time," she recalls, "I needed someone bigger with a miracle hand. I was desperate and I went to church and I cried and said, If you are God, change my parents' minds NOW." He did. "God answered after a few minutes and my sister phoned to say they had decided to cancel the operation for the next day because they thought he would die." That was to mark the beginning of a long, tough struggle, which was eventually to lead to Sara's capitulation to Christ. "I had done many dangerous things and was aware of this fight." In dreams, Jesus came to her, on one occasion expressing his distress at what she was doing. "He kept coming to me – from everywhere – though I shouted, 'I don't need you!' But his love, care and protection amazed me."

Andreas was delighted to discover over supper that we knew Sara and it was then that he began to tell us a little of her story. Later on, we asked Elizabeth how she found living in Kerman. She said simply, "People are not friendly and it is lonely." Back in Britain I was to come across the words of an English missionary, who many years earlier had also felt called to serve the people of Kerman, 'The Kermani is an independent thinker and doer – and Kerman – a difficult place'.[2]

[2] Gordon Hewitt, The Problem of Success: History of the CMS 1910-1942, SCM Press London 1977, Vol 1. p. 377

By 1900, CMS had centres of work in Shiraz, Yazd, Isfahan and Kerman. By the 20s Kerman had a Christian hospital, schools for boys and girls and later, as mentioned earlier, the Anglican Church of St Andrew built in the city. It was another of Norman Sharp's labours of love. Amongst those who served in Kerman in those years was the quite remarkable English missionary, Mary Bird, who died in the city in 1914, and Dr George Dobson, who died there of typhus in 1937 after more than 30 years' service in the country. Both made enduring contributions and were remembered years later with enormous respect and deep affection by local people.

Mary Bird was a character. 'In 1891 she opened a dispensary deep in the Isfahan bazaar where Christians rarely penetrated. She had almost no medical training and yet once the ice was broken people flocked to her. Mullahs preached against her in mosques and encouraged their followers to insult her as she rode unveiled through the bazaars and crowded alleyways. They tried to shut and bolt her door, but with the help of patients she re-opened them.'[3] The Armenian governor of the Isfahan suburb of Julfa was at one time so concerned for her safety that he assigned a policeman for her protection. She was abused and hassled, and there was even an attempt made to poison her but she continued in her work, cheerful and undeterred. She was a phenomenal worker. A new missionary leaving England to join Mary was warned not to follow her example. In her last year in Isfahan before leaving for Kerman, she was reputed to have worked nineteen hour days. The following entry gives an idea of her workload.

> Yesterday thirty women arrived at 6.15am and I began at once but 218 patients with 14 dental extractions kept us both hard at work until 2pm. I broke two teeth but after two attempts I succeeded in getting out the stumps. Sewed up a woman's ear which had been torn by her earring being violently pulled by her fellow wife while fighting – a common accident. Many patients expect me to pray for them and with them, and attribute many cures to this practice, though some repeat their Arabic prayers in a low monotone as an antidote.[4]

Along with her reputation as a tireless worker, Mary also had an enormous zest for life, a keen sense of humour and a remarkable affinity for

[3] Denis Wight, *The English Among the Persians*, I.B. Tauris and Co Limited, 2001, p.120
[4] Clara C. Rice, *Mary Bird in Persia*, London 1916, p.192

those whom society preferred to shun. She wrote in her diary,

> I love and am totally absorbed in the work, and very happy
> in it, only longing to serve better. The other day, when I was
> riding to town, I was wondering if any of the other Euro-
> peans have so much enjoyment in their lives as I have. My
> work, which I thoroughly enjoy, is never wearisome. I have
> loving friends both in England and here – plenty of vari-
> ety … I have good health and only too great an aptitude
> for hammering fun out of everything and oh such countless
> mercies.[5]

One evening, when she was working in Kerman, Mary was called to
attend a woman in the desert outside the town, chained, wild and almost naked. A colleague of hers went with her and later described what
happened.

> Mary Bird went to her unafraid. She unchained her, stroked
> her, kissed her, clothed her, sat long beside her and prayed
> over her – believing simply that God would heal her. She
> gave medicines to her and did not leave until the patient
> was calm and quiet. She went again and again to minister
> to her. Eventually the woman fully recovered and Persians
> marvelled at Khanum Mariam's skill and constantly attrib-
> uted it to Christianity. There were many such cases treated
> by her.[6]

The other name recalled in association with foreign Christian ministry in
Kerman at this time was that of George Dobson mentioned earlier, who
went out to Persia as a young doctor in 1903. We thought about him
when, on our last day in Iran, we visited Teheran's fabulous carpet museum. In the cool of that great bunker-like museum we sat and absorbed
the intricacy of patterns and depth of colour, especially the rich reds and
deep blues. They moved us – as stained glass moves us – deeply – and
yet all the more so as we thought of the small hands that had worked the
looms that made the carpets we looked at.

In the 1920s George Dobson had worked with the government of Iran
to draft simple regulations to limit the age of those who wove, the hours

[5] Ibid, p.192
[6] Ibid, p.192

they worked and the conditions they endured. Bishop Linton wrote in his newsletter in August 1920 – 'these regulations are simple enough, but are just the first step in a land which has hitherto seen no legislation for its workers.' The CMS medical mission in Kerman had plenty of firsthand experience of the plight of weavers in the city. Their records show that in one year there were,

> forty seven cases of deformed carpet weavers, all expect-
> ant mothers under treatment in Kerman. In twenty eight of
> these cases the children died, it being impossible to deliver
> them. In all these cases mothers, who had been several
> days in agony and in states of extreme exhaustion, would
> have died but for surgical help from the hospital. In ad-
> dition there were nineteen operations performed on girls
> for the straightening of limbs. There were also consider-
> able numbers of girls suffering from rickets, paralysis of the
> limbs, and deformities due to carpet weaving not urgently
> needing operations, who were treated as outpatients at the
> hospital.[7]

In due course both the CMS schools and hospital in Kerman were forced to close. In 1934 George Dobson wrote home about the ever-increasing and frequently changing government regulations with which the hospital had to comply. He wrote wryly, 'it will be desirable Jobs and not men of like passion as we are, in the future to Persia.' Three years later he was to die of typhus in Kerman. His legacy was enduring and his name remembered long afterwards with love by both expatriates and Persians. Years after his death an Iranian wrote,

> As I was trying to find information about his origin and fam-
> ily and homeland, it came to me that these sort of people
> belong to no government or nation in particular, but belong
> to everybody. All places are their homeland. Perhaps he
> would have only a flap of bread with a little yogurt or milk
> in the whole of one day. What about his rough coat and
> baggy trousers? You can tell he was a hard worker with no
> thought of his own position. What else? Clearly he was
> a man who lived on another plane. He is standing wait-
> ing ready for the next person and eager to serve him. He
> doesn't know about whether they are Muslim or Christian,

[7] *Iran Diocese News*, September 1921

Iranian, English or foreign. He is looking far away to a region most of us never see.[8]

We spent most of the next day with Andreas and Elizabeth, and with them walked to the university. As we came out of their courtyard into the street Nancy noticed a new white Peykan – Iran's national car based on a once popular British car of the 1970s – parked opposite with two men in the front with white shirts and close cropped hair, "Secret police?" she enquired of Andreas. Four years of living in Hafez Al-Assad's Syria had taught us to recognize plain-clothes policemen and their unmarked cars. Andreas confirmed her suspicions with an easy laugh. He had already been visited since we had called the previous evening. They had been neither difficult nor rude – just fulfilling their responsibility to keep an eye on visiting foreigners. We were glad we had stayed at our hotel, pleased that Andreas had been able to tell them that we had been off to visit Bam and that I was a priest from the same church to which he belonged.

That evening we left Kerman on the night bus and took a tender farewell of our young friends. Sadly the great city of Bam was largely destroyed a few years after our visit by a huge earthquake which killed over 40,000 people. Amongst those who died were all the students of the school in which Sara's brother was then teaching. He had gone home to Jiroft the evening before the earthquake. Andreas and Elizabeth have, as I mentioned, left Kerman. Their legacy is not as obvious as that of Mary Bird or George Dobson but they too gave themselves selflessly in the cause of Christ for the people of Kerman and I am sure are remembered with gratitude and affection in hearts and homes there.

[8] Gordon Hewitt, p.377

O JERUSALEM!
A BRIEF DIGRESSION

In the next three chapters I offer some personal reflections on the background of the Middle East's most protracted and painful problem – Palestine/Israel – and make brief comment on the situation there today. But I begin with a vivid memory of a Christmas visit made by the then Anglican Archbishop of South Africa, Desmond Tutu, to Jerusalem soon after my appointment there as Dean of the Anglican cathedral of St George.

(CHAPTER THIRTEEN)
READY FOR ANYTHING

The Cathedral was packed. The moon was bright. It was reflected on the shiny, dark blue bonnets of the police jeeps parked at strategic points around the perimeter walls of the Cathedral compound, their blue roof lights revolving and their occupants alert and relaxed with the easy, confident nonchalance peculiar to Israeli police and military personnel. It was Christmas Eve at St George's Anglican Cathedral in Jerusalem and the midnight Communion was underway. We were hosting the then newly appointed Archbishop of South Africa, Desmond Tutu, and three of his close friends and colleagues. It was 1989.

It had already been a tumultuous day. Earlier in the evening we had been escorted by police and military vehicles and flanked by the vast slab sided but unmistakable white Volvos of the Shin Bet – Israel's secret police – to the traditional site of the Shepherds' Fields near Bethlehem for the first of three Christmas Eve services. On the way we passed through the once predominantly Christian town of Beit Sahour. It was dark. The steel, graffiti-scrawled shutters on its shops were bolted and locked and its streets deserted. The town had been in the news a lot at that time for withholding taxes, and had been punished with summary visits from Israeli troops instructed to take property and possessions in lieu of the unpaid taxes.

This was at the time of the Palestinians' first 'Intifada', or uprising. As we drove at some speed through the town's darkened streets, we wondered where the population was. We were very soon to discover.

A crowd of over 3000 jostling, smiling, eager, curious, welcoming faces surrounded us as we arrived and stepped, most of us cassock-clad, from a variety of vehicles. The crowd, mostly from Beit Sahour and of all ages, cheered, while some of them – young women – ululated. I recognised friends also from Jerusalem, including a young Jewish rabbi. The Israeli soldiers – and there must have been several hundred of them – struggled good-naturedly to hold back the crowds and to clear a path through them for the visitors. When, after some singing of carols in both English and Arabic, the little Archbishop stepped forward to speak to us, the soldiers listened as attentively as any. It was a remarkable address, shot through with passion and irony, and mischievous touches of humour. It was also self-deprecating and honed, even as he spoke, to the circumstances and experience of his hearers, both Palestinian and Jewish. He spoke about South Africa, as it was then. He did not need to spell out, nor labour, the similarities between the South African situation, and that of his listeners. It was obvious. At one point, with an impish twinkle, he said with deliberation, "Of course, I am speaking about South Africa." His hearers laughed and continued for themselves to make the unspoken tragic comparisons. He spoke also of popular non-violent protest in South Africa and of the rising hopes for change there despite the opposition. Finally, he spoke of the inalienable divine gift of human dignity displayed in the birth of Christ when God took on our human flesh. It was gripping and inspiring, and when it was all over the crowd slipped away - peacefully.

Later the Archbishop's fellow bishop, Michael Nuttall, spoke simply and eloquently on the roof of the Church of the Nativity in Bethlehem to a smaller, less charged congregation of 'bruised pilgrims' about faith in the bright Morning Star, the Christ Child, as the source of their hope and joy.

And it was as our own Palestinian bishop, Samir Kafity, descended from the pulpit after giving his Christmas Eve sermon later still in the evening, in St George's Cathedral, that Stephen, a regular member of the congregation, stepped up to me as I was about to lead the congregation in saying the Creed and said discreetly, but clearly, "I have just been told that there is a bomb under where you are standing." We had anticipated the possibility of something just like this happening and had done our best to prepare for it. Two days earlier we had discovered, to our dismay, that one of the three sets of doors leading out of the Cathedral was firmly locked and that no key for it could be found. The doors in question were rarely used. An aged locksmith was found however and within a few hours had made a substantial new key for us. By the time Christmas Eve arrived all the doors were unlocked, their hinges well oiled, the way to each clear and stewards positioned nearby to open them, if needed, in a hurry.

I announced to the congregation, without explanation, that we would at that point in the service be moving out of the Cathedral and into the courtyard as quickly and smoothly as possible through the doors to which, in turn, I directed different parts of the congregation to go. I felt for one fleeting moment, despite my Christmas ecclesiastical finery, just like an aircraft flight attendant. In less than three minutes the Cathedral was empty and nothing had gone bang. As we came out, four blue uniformed police with sniffer dogs slipped into the Cathedral. As I emerged from the Cathedral, I saw that a table had already been placed efficiently in the middle of the courtyard around which the congregation was beginning to gather. And, as soon as the police, unobserved by many, had given the 'all clear', Stephen and his most conscientious friends - fellow stewards with him - brought out the wine and the chalice, the bread and service book, and the liturgy continued under the clear moonlit sky. After it concluded I overheard a young Australian couple ask an older member of our congregation if the Christmas Eve liturgy was always celebrated in two places. I smiled, but could not hear the reply. The remaining days of the South Africans' visit were not uneventful.

We visited prominent Palestinians and Israelis, though sadly Jerusalem's Chief Rabbi declined a meeting, considering Archbishop Desmond too sympathetic to the cause of the Palestinians. The Minister of Religion did, however, agree to see us though it was to prove, of all our many meetings, the most painful and disturbing.

The Minister welcomed us cautiously, and with encouragement from our delegation, told us the story of his coming to Palestine with his family to escape persecution in Europe in the 1930s. There was no doubt in his mind, nor had there been in the minds of his relatives, that they were coming to a land which was by divine right their own land. But it was, he told us with sadness and astonishment, a conviction not shared and indeed strenuously rejected, by the Arabs, who he said - rather pathetically, I thought - "did not welcome us". Had he really expected - we wondered together later - their Arab neighbours, whose lands they coveted and were scheming to appropriate, to have welcomed their arrival with singing, garlands and dancing?

Later Naim Ateek, friend, colleague and Canon of the Cathedral, told his family's story of eviction at gunpoint in 1948 from their Palestinian ancestral home in the Jordan Valley by members of the Jewish Stern Gang.

It was a terrible meeting and the air was charged with mutual mistrust and great anxiety. In the middle of it, John Allen, the Archbishop's press secretary, asked to be excused for a moment. He looked distressed. After a few minutes I went to find him. He was standing in the corridor - sobbing. He was a big man, but he was overcome with grief at what he had witnessed of suspicion and misunderstanding. After some minutes we returned to join the others. Very soon afterwards the meeting ended. As we went down the stairs from the Minister's office, a young religious Jew lent over the stairwell and spat on us. We returned to St George's Cathedral for lunch and a break, noticing once again as we turned through the gates, the slogan that had been daubed on the outside walls of the Cathedral compound overnight, 'Tutu is a black Nazi pig'.

For the most part, the visit of Archbishop Desmond Tutu provoked violent hostility in the Israeli press, verging at times on hysteria. But there were exceptions: one columnist, describing the visit for those who took the trouble to travel with the Archbishop and to actually listen to what he said, as a visit of 'deep spirituality, humanity, and hope'.

After a rather subdued lunch the delegation, whose fourth member, Winston Ndungane, the Archbishop's Executive Officer and seven years later his successor as Archbishop of Cape Town, went to their rooms for rest before the final afternoon of meetings across the city. At the time I had set for us to re-gather, I could find none of the delegation in the place where I had arranged for us to meet. I went to each of their rooms in turn but all were empty. As I returned to the courtyard I could see the two blue police escort jeeps outside the gate waiting for us. Anxious and a little rattled I asked Nagi, the gateman, if he had seen the little Archbishop and his friends. "Yes," he replied cheerfully, "they are in the church." Nagi missed little, was a shrewd observer of human nature, could do wicked imitations of one or two pompous clerics whom we knew and once described himself, under interrogation from a rather fervent Christian pilgrim, as an 'Anglican Muslim'.

I went into the Cathedral - a very modest building - and quickly saw the four in the side chapel kneeling in a row in front of the altar - two purple cassocks, one black one and a blue lounge suit. I sat at the back, looked at my watch and fretted at the possible disruption to my carefully choreographed afternoon programme. But it soon became clear that the four were not yet done. The minutes slipped by, and I let them. I sensed, even in my distracted fretfulness, that this was where we were meant to be. After perhaps a quarter of an hour they rose, Desmond Tutu leading them down the short aisle. He beamed warmly at me and said with a chuckle, "Now we are ready for anything," and they were.

(CHAPTER FOURTEEN)
PALESTINE -
LAND OF PROMISE...

In 1921, Winston Churchill visited Jerusalem. He had just been made Secretary of State for the Colonies. He spoke with both Arabs and with Jews. He spoke expansively to the former of the ability of Palestine to support 'a larger number of people than at present'. The larger number he alluded to were of course, in his mind, Jewish immigrants. He went on and assured his hearers that, 'no Arabs would be dispossessed'.

After addressing his Arab hearers, he went to speak to a Jewish delegation about the future of Zionism. He was full of confidence and hope for its future. He spoke of Zionism as 'a great event in the world's destiny' and wished it every success in overcoming 'the severe difficulties in its path'. He continued, 'if I did not believe that you were animated by the very highest spirit of justice and idealism and that your work would in fact confer blessings on the whole country, I would not have the highest hope I have that eventually your work will be accomplished.'[1]

Two days later, on 29 September 1921, Churchill planted a tree at the site of the future Hebrew University on Mount Scopus. There he spoke movingly and hopefully to his Jewish listeners of the future that might be theirs. 'The hope of your race for so many centuries will be gradually realised here, not only for your own good, but for the good of the entire world.' Perhaps Britain's famous prime minister had intimation of the struggles, terrible pain and ceaseless conflict that lay ahead for he went on to caution, 'the non-Jewish inhabitants must not suffer. Every step you take should therefore be for the moral and material benefit of all Palestinians – Jew and Arab alike. If you do this, Palestine will be happy and prosperous – and peace and concord will always reign – it will turn into a land of milk and honey in which all races and religions will find a rest from their sufferings.'[2]

On 23 September 2011, almost ninety years to the day since Winston

[1] Martin Gilbert, *Churchill: A Life*, Minerva, 1991, p. 435
[2] Ibid, pp. 435,436

Churchill's words on Mount Scopus, Mahmoud Abbas, the President of the Palestinian Authority stood and spoke at the General Assembly of the United Nations and made there a passionate plea for Palestine to be granted full membership of the United Nations. It was a bold, even a risky move, but one which Abbas and his followers hoped might prove a significant step towards the realisation of their long cherished dream of an independent, sovereign Palestine on a pitiful rump of the land that was once theirs and of which Churchill promised their forebears they would never be dispossessed.

And it was in that same forum of the United Nations General Assembly in New York, that sixty three years earlier, on 29 November 1947, the vote was taken in favour of the Partition of Palestine. Ironically, while it was the United Nations General Assembly that hosted and made possible that historic vote – so strenuously worked for by the Zionists and their supporters and so fiercely resisted by their opponents – that Israel's current, outspoken Prime Minister, Benyamin ('Bibi') Netanyahu has denounced it during his time in office as 'a theatre of the absurd'. It was that vote which precipitated what Israel has come to call its 'War of Independence' and led on 14 May 1948 to the declaration of the founding of the State of Israel, a day before Britain's mandate for Palestine expired. The behind-the-scenes lobbying by both sides of the leaders of nations, prior to the vote, had been prodigious.

Some years later, American President Truman spoke of the pressure movements at that time around the United Nations, which were unlike anything that he had seen before, while the White House too was subjected to constant barrage. I do not think I ever had so much pressure or propaganda aimed at the White House as I had in this instance. The persistence of a few of the extreme Zionist leaders – activated by political motives and engaging in political threats – distracted and annoyed me.'[3]

Truman was not the only leader riled by the antics of fervent Zionists. Jawaharlal Nehru spoke with anger and contempt at the way the UN had been lined up. He said the Zionists had tried to bribe India with millions and, at the same time, his sister Vijayalahmi Pandid had received daily warnings that her life was in danger, 'unless she voted right'.[4] President Truman may have been disturbed and annoyed by the Zionists but his Administration nonetheless swung behind the vote for partition sought

[3] George Ienczowski, *American Presidents and the Middle East*, p. 157

[4] Heptulla Najma, *Indo-West Relations: The Nehru Era*, p. 157

by them and bullied others to do the same. During the last four days before the vote Haiti, Liberia, and the Philippines – all heavily dependent on the United States financially – agreed, not surprisingly, to support the partition plan. Liberia's ambassador to the United States complained vigorously that the US delegation had threatened to cut aid to several countries if they voted differently to their benefactor.

In the months and weeks prior to his speech at the United Nations, President Abbas, his supporters and sympathisers, were strongly pressured by the United States Administration not to make a bid for Palestine at the United Nations. The pressure was not as brutal or as blatant as that exerted by President Truman's Administration in favour of the partition vote but it was strong, and punishment for going against the President's wishes, in the form of cuts in American aid to the Palestinian Authority, was threatened. In the decades that have followed the creation of the State of Israel the pressure on American presidents to bend to the wishes of Israel's leaders and its supporters – and particularly to America's Christian Religious Right – has grown enormously. Few American presidents can have raised the hopes of more people for an enduring peace in the Middle East and for a resolution of the question of Palestine than Barack Obama. But those hopes, so unrealistically high, have been comprehensively dashed. In the eyes of most people in the Middle East he has, in regard to the Palestine/Israel issue, been thoroughly snubbed by Israel's Prime Minister, let down by his Secretary of State and, in a bid to outdo the extravagant pro-Israel rhetoric of potential Republican presidential rivals sounded, in the opinion of Israel's own media, more Israeli than an Israeli.

There was one occasion when President Obama, exasperated by Israel's relentless building of settlements, eventually elicited from Binyamin Netanyahu the promise of a sixty day freeze on settlement construction – something the latter bragged no previous Israeli Prime Minister had ever done. It was a very small gesture for which Netanyahu extracted from Secretary of State, Hillary Clinton, a very generous reward, which included the promise of new top of the range fighter aircraft and a pledge to veto any attempt to win recognition for a Palestinian state at the United Nations Security Council. During the designated sixty-day freeze, construction continued unabated on existing settlement units and plans were prepared for the construction of new ones.

On 5 October 2011 former American President Jimmy Carter was interviewed by the BBC's Jon Snow in London's Royal Albert Hall. The hall was full. The interview was far-ranging and later there were questions from the audience. Carter listened to each attentively and answered with great warmth, generosity and refreshingly down-to-earth common sense. He appeared a most youthful eighty-six year old. He lamented the radical and, he considered, almost unprecedented polarisation of political opinion in America, and conceded that America's very powerful conservative news channel, Fox News, had contributed much to the polarisation. Asked mischievously by Jon Snow if he had appeared on Fox News, Carter replied with a smile that he was 'still waiting for the invitation'. The interview encompassed the Middle East and President Obama's perceived attitudes and policy with regard to it. Asked whether he thought Obama had shelved the hopes and views expressed in his speech at the famous AL Azhar mosque in Cairo at the start of his presidency, Jimmy Carter thought not. On that occasion, on 4 June 2009, President Obama said, 'the United States does not support the legitimacy of continued Israeli settlements. This construction violates previous agreements and undermines efforts to achieve peace. It is time for the settlements to stop.' Jon Snow then volunteered that the White House's present incumbent had little room to manoeuvre and was subject to great pressures. Jimmy Carter paused before replying quietly, "yes, the pressures are incredible, and to people outside America, incomprehensible."

The speech of Mahmoud Abbas referred to already was a long, impassioned and somewhat repetitive recitation of the plight of the Palestinian people – from the 'nakba' or catastrophe of 1948 when he said, 'we left, carrying only our keys, belongings and memories and a vibrant and cohesive community was destroyed' – up to the construction of Israel's annexation wall, which continues. The speech had neither the flair nor its deliverer, the elegance of Haider Abdul Shafi, head of the Palestinian delegation, when he had addressed the Madrid peace talks which were convened on 30th October 1991, in the aftermath of the first Gulf War and jointly sponsored by the USA and Russia. He said, 'We, the people of Palestine, stand before you in the fullness of our pain, our pride, and our anticipation, for we have long harboured a yearning for peace and a dream for justice and freedom. For too long the Palestinian people have gone unheeded, silenced and denied – our identity negated by political expediency, our rightful struggle against injustice maligned, and our present existence subsumed by the past tragedy of another people.' He continued, 'We come to you from a tortured land and a proud, though captive people, having been asked to negotiate with our occupiers, but leaving behind the children of the Intifada and a people under occupation, and under curfew, who enjoined us not to surrender or forget. As we speak, thousands of our brothers and sisters are languishing in Israeli prisons and detention camps, most detained without evidence, charge or trial – guilty only of seeking freedom or daring to defy occupation. We speak in their name, and we say, "Set them free".'

Mahmoud Abbas's speech probably lost a lot in translation. Abdul Shafi, whose home in Gaza I visited on more than one occasion, was supremely articulate in both Arabic and English, and the words I have quoted were those of his English text he had written for the peace conference. I have the full text beside me. I cut it out of The Jerusalem Post on Friday, 1 November 1991, when we were still living in Jerusalem. It is curling up at the edges and a little brown in colour. Mahmoud Abbas's speech – more rough, dogged and desperate – reflects, perhaps faithfully, the additional frustration, bewilderment, disappointment, anger and pain of the long and seemingly futile years of struggle between the Oslo Peace Accords and the present day.

'Israel,' he said, 'continues to besiege the holy city of Jerusalem, preventing worship at our mosques and churches.' He condemned the criminal actions of Israeli settlers and the protection afforded them by the Israeli army. He spoke of the restrictions on the movement of Palestinian people and goods and of the taking of their water. He mentioned the Oslo Accords, signed eighteen years earlier, which were linked with letters of mutual recognition of Israel and Palestine. The Accords were the outgrowth of the 1991 Madrid Peace Talks. 'But,' he said, 'every initiative (for peace) and every movement shattered on the rock of the Israeli settlement project.' Despite all this he said his people were ready to adopt the path of 'relative justice', settling for just 22% of all the territory taken by Israel in 1967. He spoke also of the building of Israel's monstrous separation wall, whose construction continues, as mentioned, to this day. He ended, 'with only dreams, hopes and slogans in the face of bullets … our efforts are not to delegitimise Israel – only the occupation and the logic of ruthless force.'

Benyamin Netanyahu's reply in the United Nations to the speech of Mahmoud Abbas was bellicose. He began with the extravagant assertion that, 'Israel has extended its hand in peace from the moment it was founded.' There was certainly no evidence of that extended hand in peace amongst those who fought so strenuously for the creation of Israel in the tumultuous months following the Partition Vote and there has not been a lot of evidence of it since.

Over the last few decades several distinguished Israeli historians have turned their energies to re-examining the accounts of the events that led – in the months referred to – to the founding of the State of Israel. The results of their labours, reluctantly accepted now by many brought up to believe that the departure of the Palestinians from their lands was a convenient coincidence, aided by their own fearfulness and their leaders' hysterical urging, show it was rather the result of a ruthless and meticulously planned programme of eviction and expulsion. Ilan Pappé – author of The Ethnic Cleansing of Palestine, 'strips away the last, tattered remnants of all the myths which Israelis have sedulously cultivated about their War of Independence – from the earliest and most plausible of them – that the Palestinians had fled the country on the orders of their leaders, to the latest and least implausible… that their flight was, 'the unplanned consequence of war.'[5] In fact, Pappé says it was the other way round; the original objective was the removal of the Palestinians and the war was the consequence, the means to carry it out.

One Joseph Weitz, in charge of the colonisation and settlement of the about-to-be-declared State of Israel, was straightforward and candid about the way to proceed: 'the only way is to cut and eradicate (the Arabs) from their roots; not a single village or a single tribe must be left.'[6] Under Weitz' direction and with enormous attention to detail the staff of the Jewish Agency prepared to dispossess an inconvenient and unnecessary people of the homes they lived in and the fields which they and their families had cultivated for centuries. In March 1948, Ben Gurion, who was soon to become Israel's first Prime Minister, launched Plan Dalet for the systematic and total expulsion of the Palestinians from their homeland. Every Hagannah commander received a list of villages and neighbourhoods in his zone and precise operational instructions about how and when to attack, occupy and destroy them and evict their inhabitants. By early 1949 the Palestinian exodus was complete. Anything between 700,000 and a million of the land's 1,300,000 population had left. For those who had planned and carried out the expulsion it was a most satisfactory outcome.

Tragically, almost the same number of Jews, perhaps as many as 800,000 were, in the years immediately leading up to the founding of the State of Israel and following 1948, forced from their homes across

[5] David Hirst, Beware of Small States, Lebanon, Battleground of the Middle East, 2010, p. 45, reprinted by permission of Faber and Faber Ltd.
[6] Ibid, p.46

the rest of the Middle East, where they too had lived – in some cases for thousands of years. In many of the Arab countries where they had lived they had been accepted, respected and appreciated and, for the most part, treated far better by their Muslim neighbours than their fellow Jews had been over centuries in Christian Europe. Palestinian author and publisher, the late Naim Attallah', received a congratulatory letter from Moshe Menuhin, father of the famous Yehudi Menuhin, after the publication of his book, The Palestinians. Moshe Menuhin applauded the writing of the book describing it as an act of courage and a service to humanity. He explained that as a Jew who had grown up in Russia with a sense of fear and alienation, he had felt a natural affinity with the Palestinians. Furthermore, 'history had taught him that during the previous 1,500 years, Arabs were practically the only people who had welcomed Jews into their midst, when they were being persecuted in almost every other part of the world.'[7]

If there is little evidence of the 'extended hand in peace' in the years leading up to Israel's Declaration of Independence – and in fairness to Netanyahu, he was not referring in his speech to that period – it is hard to find a lot of evidence for it in the years since.

I once had the responsibility of taking the Most Reverend George Carey, who was at the time the Archbishop of Canterbury, and a small delegation, to visit the Prime Minister of Israel, the late Yitzhak Shamir. He was born in Poland in 1925 and emigrated to Palestine in 1935. There he joined the Irgun Zvi Leumi, an extreme Zionist military group opposing British rule in Palestine with, one might dare to venture, the same passion and resolve with which Hamas today opposes the rule of Israel.

We found the Israeli Prime Minister alert, engaging, witty and welcoming. He reminded me of an energetic little stoat or weasel. At some point in our meeting the Archbishop deftly probed the President's past, asking with a disarming smile whether he had not at one time in his life been a terrorist. At this point our conversation had moved on to discussion of the then raging Palestinian Intifada – or Uprising. Yitzhak Shamir seemed quite unfazed by the question; I'm sure it was not the first time anyone had put it to him. He replied, also with a smile, and to the effect that there had been a lot at stake then.

There was indeed, and to those who had escaped the ovens and death camps of Germany or Poland, or the pogroms of Russia, neither the fading might of Britain, nor the massed, if badly led and poorly equipped, armies of the surrounding Arab nations would wrest 'Israel' from their grasp. And after Independence there would be little patience with any person or peoples who resisted the new state or whose opinions, in their minds, threatened its future. Such were to be resisted and where necessary destroyed. Israel's Prime Minister, with whom we met, was one of three men who authorised, after Israel's Independence, the murder of the United Nation's representative in the Middle East, Count Folk Bernadotte, viewed by Shamir and his colleagues as anti-Zionist and considered an obvious agent of the British.

Author David Hirst, in his book, Beware of Small States, referred to earlier, suggests that from its outset Israel has opted for the exercise of force rather than negotiation with its frequently hostile neighbours. 'Force,' he writes, 'became the instinctive, automatic remedy for every problem – more effective than diplomacy, negotiation or the mediation of outsiders and security became the great shibboleth in whose name it was applied.'[8] Moshe Sharett, Israel's first Foreign Minister, lamented this outlook. He spoke of the choice before Israel of being, 'a state of law' or 'a state of piracy'. He deplored the moral corruption that reliance on force engendered and the subordination of purity of arms to a policy of revenge, 'elevated to a sacred principle of state'.[9]

One day, after a busy morning in the office in Aden, we returned to our apartment for lunch. We turned on CNN to watch the latest news. The Israeli Defence Force was engaged in one of its periodic incursions into Gaza. Footage showed rows of Israeli self-propelled guns shuddering as they sent shell after massive shell into Gaza. Ariel Sharon, impetuous and swaggering and at the time Israel's Prime Minister, was interviewed at the scene. He promised further massive retaliation for any Palestinian Katyusha rocket that fell on Israel. We winced and changed television channels. The contrast between what we had just been watching and what we now saw could not have been greater.

In what looked like a courtroom, three black South African youths sat in a half circle facing a thin white man. He was between 40 and 50 years old and was addressing the young men. He invited them to look in his eyes and to listen closely to his words. He said, "I forgive you from the

[8] David Hirst, p.57, re-printed by permission of Faber and Faber Ltd.
[9] Ibid, p.53

bottom of my heart for what you did to my wife." They had murdered her. We had dropped in to a clip of the proceedings of South Africa's Truth and Reconciliation Committee. A few minutes later, roles were reversed as a stout white South African policeman asked a different group of black youths if they could forgive him for roasting a friend of theirs over an open fire to extract information.

In his inflammatory speech at the United Nations, Israel's Prime Minister, Binyamin Netanyahu, spoke of a growing malignancy 'between East and West that threatens the peace of all. It seeks not to liberate but to enslave, not to build but to destroy.' He continued provocatively, 'that malignancy is militant Islam. It cloaks itself in the mantle of a great faith yet murders Jews, Christians and Muslims alike with unforgiving impartiality.'

His words were intemperate, and at that extraordinary moment in the history of the Middle East, more than usually inappropriate. Militant Islam, made up of various strands, does indeed pose a very great threat to very many people but at the time of Netanyahu's speech, with almost the whole of the Middle East caught up in the initial euphoria, turmoil and excitement of the Arab Spring, militant Islam appeared to have been wrong-footed and for a moment briefly eclipsed. Much has happened since then, and Muslim organisations, having been on the sidelines at the beginning, have now become closely involved in all the revolutions, and have managed to exploit the uprisings and come close, in some places, to taking them over altogether. But the watch words of the young revolutionaries and their supporters at the start – from Tunisia to Yemen – were freedom, liberty, human rights, human dignity and democracy. 'Their cry,' wrote a friend from his home in Jerusalem, 'is against corruption, dictatorship, abuse of power, nepotism, misuse of state funds, poverty, oppression of people, restriction of civil liberties and many others.' And there are many in Israel today, both Israeli Arabs and Jews, who would identify with those concerns and wish to see them addressed in their own backyard. The majority of the revolutionaries are, of course, Muslim but among them are also Arab Christians. The things they seek are not the exclusive possession of any faith – rather the aspiration of all peoples everywhere, of any faith and of none. Neither militant Islam nor, thankfully, militant meddling Western powers appear to have had much bearing on the birth of these momentous developments. Netanyahu would not be the first prime minister who, seeking to divert clamour for change at home, has tried to deflect attention to what he portrays as a more urgent priority elsewhere.

He also raised the spectre of Iran's president having control of an arsenal of nuclear weapons (as of course Netanyahu himself has). 'Can you imagine that man who ranted here yesterday? Can you imagine him armed with nuclear weapons? If Iran is not stopped we shall face the spectre of nuclear terrorism, and the Arab Spring could well become the Iranian Winter.' It was again, highly inflammatory stuff, intended to elicit maximum sympathy and support from Israel's champions in America and his own constituency at home. Still, the prospect raised of President Ahmadinajad's finger poised over a nuclear button or closing around the nuclear trigger was an alarming one, though even he must know that to launch a nuclear attack on Israel would be to guarantee the incineration of much of his own nation within minutes. Critical observers of the State of Israel point out that an Iran with nuclear military capability would undoubtedly put a severe constraint on Israel's freedom of military movement in the region. At the moment Israel can threaten and bomb its most troublesome neighbours with relative impunity – and sometimes does.

Israel today is beset with numerous problems and awesome challenges both within and without. It has always been. At present controversy rages within the country over who exactly qualifies to be called a Jew. The rapidly growing numbers of Orthodox Jews – with their peculiar privileges and distinct perspectives on how society should be ordered – arouse anger and resentment among many secular Israelis. Reports of corruption at high levels in society and government are commonplace. Then there is 'The Occupation' which the majority of Israelis prefer not to think about. And, on the wider front, looking beyond Israel itself, there is deep and understandable anxiety and fear, particularly in relation to the state's immediate neighbours and to Iran, with its dark threats, just over the far horizon. These latter fears are fuelled by the extravagant threats of her most outspoken enemies, quoted by her most constant supporters, and used by Prime Minister Netanyahu and others to justify policies which former President Jimmy Carter said could lead only to catastrophe. And then there lie, behind the contemporary fears, the long and bitter centuries of persecution, pogroms, the gas chambers and the death camps. The story of the last and most awful of these ghastly chapters is constantly repeated, still avidly devoured and by some, shamelessly exploited.

Jeffrey Goldberg, journalist and Jew from New York, wrote a fine book, Prisoners, from which I shall quote more extensively later, in which he describes, honestly and sensitively, his own experience over several years of living in present-day Israel. In the opening chapters he speaks of the fears to which I have just referred and from which he suggests even New

York Jews are not immune. 'I am not the only Jew who divides the Gentile world into two camps; the Gentiles who would hide me in their attics when the Germans come – and the Gentiles who would betray me to the death squads. The Jews of America, when they go to the polls, are voting against memories, memories of Cossacks, Nazis and blood libels.'[10]

A friend recently told me a Jewish joke to add to the stock I have acquired over the years and cherish: The father of a five year-old called Moshe was coaxing his young son to jump out of a tree into whose lower branches he had managed to scramble. 'Jump, I'll catch you,' his father said. 'Just jump!' With some trepidation the youngster cast off and jumped. His father stood aside, and an indignant and pained Moshe hit the ground. 'Papa,' he bawled, 'you promised you'd catch me.' Father replied, 'Now you've learned an important lesson – trust no-one in this world, not even your own Papa.'

In his novel, To the End of the Land, Israeli author David Grossman describes a young Israeli boy questioning his mother about Israel's friends and enemies in the world. 'What do you tell a six year-old boy, a pip squeak, Ofer (his name) who, one morning while you're taking him to school, holds you close on the bike and asks in a cautious voice, "Mummy, who's against us?" His mother lists all the Arab countries and then remembers Indonesia and Malaysia, Pakistan and Afghanistan and probably Uzbekistan and Kazakhstan too – none of those 'stans' sound so great to you – "and here we are at school, sweetie." Later his mother finds Ofer listening surreptitiously to the news and sobbing with anger at another bombing in a Jerusalem market place. He then demanded to know where the friendly countries were. She took down an atlas and showed him the USA and then turned over the pages and pointed out some European countries. He looked at her in astonishment, 'but they're all the way over there!' he shouted in disbelief at her stupidity. 'Look how many pages there are between here and there!'[11]

In their respective addresses to the United Nations, both Abbas and Netanyahu accused the other side of wrecking past peace talks. Both sides

[10] Jeffrey Goldberg, Prisoners, A Muslim and a Jew across the Middle East divide, p. 8, copyright © 2006, 2008 by Jeffrey Goldberg. Used by permission of Alfred A. Knopf, a division of Random House, Inc. Any third party use of this material outside of this publication, is prohibited. Interested parties must apply directly to Random House, Inc. for permission

[11] David Grossman, To the End of the Land - A Novel, published by Jonathan Cape, London, 2010, pp.373,374, re-printed by permission of The Random House Group Ltd.

have played their part in the wrecking. Totting up the respective scores in that game is a futile process. Palestinian doctor, Izzeldin Abuelaish, wrote a profoundly moving book, I Shall Not Hate, in the aftermath of the deaths of his three daughters and a niece in an Israeli army assault on Gaza where he and his family were then living. At one point in it he writes of the pointlessness of indulging in blame and counter blame in the long, tragic story of the Israel/Palestine conflict.

> 'It sounds simplistic, but it's the only way to get out of the mud our feet are stuck in. The occupation and the oppression of the people in Gaza is like a cancer, a disease that needs to be treated. It's all about the will to solve the problem rather than the determination to keep the anger front and centre. Arguing over who did what and who suffered more is not getting us anywhere. We have to move on; we have to build trust and mutual respect between the peoples. You can't respect someone you don't know so let's get to know one another by listening and opening our eyes to the other side. We need to encourage kavod (respect) and shivyon (equality).'[12]

Neither Palestinian nor Israeli have been very well served by their leadership and while the perils along the path to peace are great, the danger of not making peace is surely greater – with potentially cataclysmic consequences for the entire world.

At another point in To the End of the Land, Ofer's mother expresses her frustration with the political leadership across the Middle East. At the time of her outburst she is at home preparing a salad. She begins by castigating past Palestinian leaders, Hajj al Amin al-Husseini and Arafat amongst others. She has a swipe at Scud missiles and Katyusha rockets, mentions Deir Yassin, the Palestinian village, many whose inhabitants – men, women and children – were brutally killed by Jewish fighters in the immediate lead-up to the foundation of the State of Israel, and concludes with a crescendo of contempt for Israel's political leaders – dead and alive – including Golda Meir, Menachem Begin and Bibi Netanyahu.

> 'She grabs a sharp knife, swings it and lands it down furiously to dice Abd al-Qader al-Husseini with Haj al Amin al-Husseini and Shukeiri and Nimeiri and Ayatol-

[12] Izzeldin Abuelaish, I Shall Not Hate, Walker and Company, New York, 2007, p.123

lah Khomeini and Nashashibi and Arafat and Hamas and Mahmoud Abbas and all their kasbahs, and Qaddafis and SCUDS; she slaughters them all together: Katyushas and intifadas and martyrs' brigades... Feverishly brandishing the knife she finally chops up Khan Yunis and Sheikh Munis, Deir Yassin and Sheikh Yassin. She pounds them all indiscriminately like a hornet's nest that must be destroyed and she adds Baruch Goldstein, and Yigal Amir and with a sudden revelation she also throws in Golda and Begin and Shamir and Sharon and Bibi and Barak and Rabin and Shimon Peres too – after all, don't they all have blood on their hands? Did they really do everything they could so she could get five minutes of peace and quiet around here?'[13]

The land which Winston Churchill hoped might become a land of milk and honey has become a land of tears and bloodshed in which few have found rest from their sufferings.

---

[13] Grossman, pp.530,531, re-printed by permission of The Random House Group Ltd.

(CHAPTER FIFTEEN)

WHAT PRICE ZION?

It was a scramble to get there and when we did, there was not a lot to see. The buildings of the little hilltop village of Bayt Baws on the rapidly expanding edge of Sanaa were mostly abandoned, their roofs collapsed and the courtyard walls broken down. The guide book informed us that the village dated back to the time of the prominent Sabaean Kingdom, and that there were inscriptions from that period still to be found on some of the ruined buildings in the village.

We had not come to look at the inscriptions but at the remains of a Jewish synagogue in what had once been the Jewish quarter of the village. Two cheerful, grubby, barefooted boys had spotted our arrival and guessing rightly the purpose of our visit led us to the 'Jewish house of prayer'. They pointed out what others must have told them were the remaining Jewish features of the little building, including a large raised Star of David carved onto one of the walls. We thanked the two boys for their help, gave them a packet of biscuits and some small money. They smiled winningly and scuttled away.

In 1900 there were 80,000 Jews living in present-day Yemen – 5,000 of them in Aden. Now there are probably just a few hundred, at the most, living with difficulty in the area of Saada, north-west of the capital of Sanaa. It is a region where for several years now a vicious low-level civil war has been going on between government forces and those usually described as 'Houthi rebels'. There is speculation that they are funded by Iran, with whom they have religious and other ties. The conflict has claimed at least 5,000 lives and displaced several hundred thousand more from their homes.

A quick glance in the index at the back of our much-fingered tourist guide to Yemen for 'Jew' gives more than twenty references. They describe the Jewish legacy in Yemen of beautiful buildings and fine craftsmanship across the country from Mahweet in the Haraz mountains, where there is a prominent old house known as Bayt al Imam, which used once to be the home of a distinguished Jewish family to Ibb, further south, where in the old part of the city substantial and lovely wooden doors – the work of Jewish artisans – still swing easily on their hinges.

The lives and welfare of the Jews of Yemen depended, as have the lives of fellow Jews down the centuries and around the world, on the whim and the wishes of those who held the reins of power in the lands where they lived. In 1656, the first Turkish occupation of Yemen ended. It had lasted over one hundred years. The Turkish presence had been resented and resisted. Opposition to the occupation had been brutally suppressed. It was a time of great hardship during which many people, including Jews, moved to find security, food and work in Sanaa. While it was a necessary move for the Jews, it proved a problematic one. After the departure of the Turks, power had been reclaimed by the city's powerful local imams who, resentful of the increased Jewish presence in the city, resolved to 'take them in hand'. The building of synagogues was forbidden and numbers of Jews were forced to become Muslim. But many more resisted pressure to convert, and in anger and frustration the ruling Imam banished all Jews to Mawza on the Red Sea. It was a short exile. Within a very short time the Imam discovered that with the Jews gone, there was no-one left in Sanaa capable of making even the simplest kitchen utensil, let alone jewellery, for which the Jewish silversmiths were rightly famous. He quietly asked them to return. By the time they did so, all their homes had been taken.

The lot of the Jews in Yemen over the centuries has not been an easy one. They were valued for their creative skills, but they were bullied and imposed upon, forced to live in certain parts of towns and cities, locked up at night and forbidden to enter some towns in the same way in which today non-Muslims are prevented from entering Islam's holy cities of Mecca and Medina. They were, furthermore, expected to go barefoot outside their Jewish quarter, to wear distinctive clothing, and if they rode a donkey, to dismount on passing a Muslim. Jews were not permitted to ride horses. And, in conformity with a law passed in 1806, Jews had to carry away dead animals and clean the public toilets on Saturdays. This decree remained in force until the Jews of Yemen left for Israel in 1949 and 1950.

The situation of the Jews in other parts of the Middle East was often very much better than that of the Jews of Yemen, as the following description of the life of Jews in Baghdad makes clear.

> 'Jews had been here for over 1000 years when the Islamic armies conquered Mesopotamia, and for many of the centuries following that fateful conquest they had flourished. From Ottoman times until the middle of the last century,

Jews dominated trade and finance in Baghdad. They enjoyed religious and communal autonomy, hobnobbed with tribal dignitaries and government officials and, in almost every sphere of life they, were conspicuous, prosperous and influential.'[1]

For these Jews, comfortable and confident of their position in society, and proud of their lineage in the land – from the patriarch Abraham to the prophet Ezekiel – the annual Passover recitation, 'next year in Jerusalem', was taken only as a matter of form. No-one actually hoped they'd be spirited away from Baghdad to witness some grand restoration – except a handful of Jews who bought cemetery plots in Palestine thinking that even if they didn't get buried there, their certification of purchase would guarantee them a place in the after-life.'[2]

For the relatives and well-connected Jewish friends of the author of Last Days in Babylon, the Zionist project seemed, when it impinged upon them, a distant irrelevance and its advocates, unwelcome irritants. And it was a relative of the author's family – a lawyer, Yusef Elkabir – who wrote to the Iraq Times dismissing the Zionist movement in Europe through and through. He attacked its foundation philosophy that demanded Palestine as a homeland for the Jews simply because it had been their homeland some 2000 years before. As Elkabir saw it, 'Reconstructions of historical geography, if accepted as practical theory, were patently absurd for if their legal basis was accepted then we would presently have the world ruled by militant archaeology.'

It was not only Jews in Iraq who in the 1920s and 30s expressed scepticism about the movement to found a Jewish state on the land of Palestine. Fred Uhlman, a distinguished German Jewish artist who fled to London in the 1930s, tells in his book Reunion – an extraordinarily beautiful and poignant story – how the father of the book's main character Franz savaged, as Elkabir had done in his article, a Zionist who had come to their home in Stuttgart to collect money for the cause. 'My father,' he wrote, 'abhorred Zionism. The whole idea seemed to him stark mad. To claim Palestine after 2000 years made no more sense to him than the Italians claiming Germany because it was once occupied by the Romans. It could only lead to endless bloodshed, and the Jews would have to fight

---

[1] Marina Benjamin, *Last Days in Babylon*, Bloomsbury, 2007, Prologue XVII. Printed by permission of Bloomsbury, (David Higham) 2007.

[2] Ibid, p. 44

the whole Arab world. And anyway what had he, a Stuttgarter, to do with Jerusalem?' Asked by his unwelcome visitor what he made of Hitler – Franz's father replies with a robust, if tragically misplaced confidence, 'This is a temporary illness, something like measles, which will pass as soon as the economic situation improves. Do you really believe that the compatriots of Goethe and Schiller, Kant and Beethoven will fall for this rubbish? How dare you insult the memory of 12,000 Jews who died for our country?'[3] But, the compatriots of Goethe and Beethoven did fall for 'the rubbish'. The book, though a novel, is highly autobiographical.

Neither the urbane and integrated Jews of Baghdad, nor the accomplished and assimilated Jews of early 20th century Germany, had been exposed to the pitiable, hopeless, widespread grinding poverty or the savage, unpredictable bouts of cruel persecution that so many of their fellow Jews in Russia, Poland and other parts of Eastern Europe had suffered. It was out of an acute awareness of these sufferings that the architects of Zionism planned, persevered and plotted. As indicated elsewhere, they would stop at nothing and do anything to gain Palestine. In his magisterial and eloquent book, A People Apart: The Jews of Europe 1789 - 1939, author David Vital writes of the attitude of the authorities in Russia towards the Jews at the end of the 19th century: 'alone of all the major European powers, the Russian autocracy founded its approach to everything that touched upon Judaism as a faith, and as a culture, and upon Jews as a people – on a fundamentally Jewish hatred. This was all the more powerful for its being extraordinarily complex and shot through at the same time with a deep intuitive and, so to speak, generalised xenophobia in which fear, contempt and suspicion of the alien were all combined.'[4]

Jews in Russia in the late 1880s were forced, with few exceptions, to live within the officially demarcated Pale of Jewish settlement, where an entirely fresh set of laws, rules and regulations aimed, 'to constrain and confine the Jews within the stated territorial and professional spaces', were inaugurated. Some were petty, but nonetheless painful - like those forbidding Jews to make or sell Christian religious artefacts such as crosses or icons, or even candles. Others had far more serious consequences like the May Laws introduced in May 1882 purportedly as tem-

---

[3] Fred Uhlman, *Reunion*, p. 40 published by Harvill Press. Reprinted by permission of The Random House Group Limited.

[4] David Vital, *A People Apart, The Jews in Europe 1789-1939*, Oxford, 1999, p.81. Printed by permission of Oxford University Press

porary regulations, but never to be revised or revoked. These suddenly made it illegal for Jews who lived within the Pale, which was almost entirely rural, to actually live, work or own land in the countryside. The language of the legislation was complicated and convoluted, but this in essence is what it came down to. Its effect was to crowd the Jews into the towns without any real regard for their possible employment or housing, 'and to separate them to a very great extent from those with whom they had traditionally traded and for whom they had long provided various commercial services'.[5] There are, I think, some similarities between the treatment of the Jews in Russia at that time, and that of the Palestinians in Israel/Palestine today.

The introduction of the May Laws coincided with the Russian pogroms – what the Oxford English dictionary describes as, 'organised persecution or extermination of an ethnic group, especially Jews'.

By the end of 1881, at least 200, and possibly as many as 250 Jewish communities in southern and south western Russia, had been subject to violent attacks which left many dead and thousands traumatised. A journalist working for the Russian newspaper, Galas, described his impressions of the city of Balta after rioters had been given free rein in the Jewish quarter of the city between 10 April and 12 April 1882. In the rioting, nearly a thousand Jewish homes, and several hundred Jewish shops, taverns and workplaces were destroyed. 'What I saw,' reported the journalist, 'defies description. It took me seven hours by the clock, walking and riding in my carriage, to traverse the most important parts of the town - in which, in one word, everything that had belonged to the Jews had been demolished, destroyed, sacked. Nothing remains standing, other than the carcasses (of buildings), the walls and roofs.'[6]

A Jewish survivor of an earlier assault on his home city of Odessa wrote soon afterwards in his diary: 'it is as if we were besieged. The courtyard is bolted shut. We sleep in our clothes ... for fear that robbers will fall upon us and so that we can then quickly take the little children ... and flee wherever the wind will carry us. But will they let us escape? Will they pity the infants who do not yet know that they are Jews, and that they are unfortunate...till when O God of Israel?'[7] Sometimes the perpetrators of pogroms were punished for their rampages. Often they were not. On one

[5] Ibid, p.294. Printed by permission of Oxford University Press
[6] Ibid, p.284. Printed by permission of Oxford University Press
[7] Ibid. Printed by permission of Oxford University Press

notorious occasion, after the terror and destruction visited on Odessa, the city's governor punished both Jews who had been attacked, and those who had attacked them. When the Jews protested their treatment, the governor explained his behaviour - brazenly stating that he had ordered Jews to be shipped to sea along with their tormentors, 'to show I do not favour the Jews'. He continued, 'it would be madness on my part, to show any sympathy for the Jews, since they drain the blood of the Christians.' He concluded by addressing his hearers, both Jew and Christian - 'I do not blame you Christians in the least for having attacked you .... you richly deserve it.'[8]

The Russian pogroms were terrible but they brought about among many Russian Jews a radical reappraisal of their inherited understanding of their calling and destiny as Jews. In particular, they began to question openly their long established and unquestioning acceptance of oppression and suffering as their divinely ordained lot. Of this development, David Vital writes,

> 'Remarkably, the pogroms were followed with very great rapidity by an entirely unprecedented movement both of ideas and of people, a movement in which independent, personal, secular volition replaced self-abnegation as the supreme determinant of conduct. There had been no such precedent for such a transformation in the recorded history of the Jews in their Exile.'[9]

Despite these profound stirrings, the traditionally held fatalistic perspective of the Jewish vocation in exile prevailed amongst most Jewish religious leaders. Any change in the circumstances of the Jewish people would, the advocates of this position believed, be brought about by God himself. In the meantime good and strict behaviour was 'everything'.

There are devout Jews today who continue to believe passionately that this remains the true and proper vocation of all Jews, and who regard the State of Israel as a grievous denial of their calling and an act of reckless defiance towards God. Beside me I have the transcript of a talk given by one Rabbi Ahron Cohen, international spokesperson for an organisation called Neturei Karta - a mouthpiece for 'Jews united against Zionism' -

[8] Ibid, p.292. Printed by permission of Oxford University Press
[9] Ibid, p.290. Printed by permission of Oxford University Press

delivered a few years ago in Beirut in May 2005.

> 'Now I mentioned earlier that we **were** given a land but under certain conditions. The conditions were basically that we had to maintain the highest of moral, ethical and religious standards. The Jewish people did have the land for approximately the first 1,500 years of their existence. However, regretfully, the conditions were not fulfilled to the required degree and the Jews were exiled from their land. For the last 2,000 years or so the Jewish people have been in a **state of exile decreed by the Al-mighty** because they did not maintain the standards expected of them. As was foretold in our Torah, this state of exile is the situation that exists right up to the present day. **It is a basic part of our belief to accept the Heavenly decree of exile and not to try and fight against it or to end it by our own hands.** To do so would constitute a rebellion against the wishes of the Al-mighty.'

The rabbi delivered a lecture at the University of Aberystwyth in March 2012. Frail in body, his spirit was indomitable and his views on the State of Israel and the Jews' true calling – unchanged.

Alarmed by the pogroms and in many instances victims of them, thousands of Russian Jews – inspired by the new spirit of Jewish self-determination and anxious to make a better life for themselves and their families – headed for America. 750,000 Russians migrated to the United States between 1889 and 1900. Some did make their way to Palestine, but at that early stage in the Zionist vision, the steel mills of Pennsylvania held out more promise than the bare hills and malaria-infested swamps of Palestine. In 1914, out of the 3 million Jews in the USA, only 1,200 belonged to a very loose 'federation' seriously supporting Zionism. In New York the movement had only 50 members.

In our time in Jerusalem, we frequently hosted groups of pilgrims – British and American mostly – some of whom had newly discovered the Palestinian cause and had taken it up with zeal. They wrapped themselves round with black and white Palestinian headscarves, outdid one another in swapping stories of Israeli military brutality and oppression, and sought eager audience with prominent Palestinian leaders – Muslim or Christian. It usually fell to me to set up these meetings and I was glad to do so. But I sometimes wished that those for whom I made these arrangements could try to take on board the enormity of the forces that were at work – of oppression, dispossession, humiliation and persecution – stretching back century after century, and long before the Holocaust, the British mandate for Palestine and the Balfour Declaration, which eventually gave birth to the present State of Israel, and in which Christians often played a significant and shameful role.

'There is,' wrote the late Max Warren – theologian, author and missionary – 'a terrible Christian responsibility for centuries of persecution of Jews, for the very conception of the ghetto – for the pogroms in so many professedly Christian countries. Suffice it to say that, had Christians made their witness to the Jews with a fraction of the grace and patience and courage and wisdom with which they made it to the Gentiles, history would have been very different.'[10]

But, a Christian's awareness of the long and often terrible treatment Jews have met with in the past at the hands of fellow Christians, ought not, I believe, to stifle any criticism of the State of Israel today by Christians, though I hope such an awareness will make them pause awhile before offering it. In this context, I recall an interesting conversation I had with a young Jewish rabbi, whom I also invited from time to time to meet with our visiting pilgrim groups. He told me about a young German Christian pastor who had just come to see him in Jerusalem, who was distraught at what his country had made the Jews suffer. "I have no right to criticise Israel again," he protested almost tearfully, a sentiment I have heard often voiced by staunch American Christian supporters of Israel also. "NEVER again?" countered our friend. He then directed his anxious and rather surprised German pastor to a chapter in Dietrich Bonhoeffer's, Ethics, entitled, 'What do we mean by telling the truth?' Truth, explained the rabbi, drawing on his reading of this chapter, isn't relative but relational. The one who wants to tell the truth must first know from where his listener is coming. "Yes," he added, "you as a German have a burden when criticising Israel. But you must not hold Israel up to different standards than those to which you hold other regimes in the world. But to be silent, is not the truth."

Gideon Levy, an Israeli journalist writing for the Israeli daily newspaper Haaretz, said a very similar thing at the 2012 Greenbelt Christian arts festival where he was one of many guest speakers. "It is your duty to criticise – for the sake of Israel," and he added, "What sort of a friend is

[10] Max Warren, *I Believe in the Great Commission*, Hodder Christian Paperback, 1979, p.75

the friend, who shrinks ever from offering criticism to a friend?"

The Old Testament book of Proverbs has challenging words about the wisdom of receiving criticism: 'Well meant, are the wounds of a friend', says a contemporary rendering of Proverbs chapter 27 verse 6. Criticism, my Jewish rabbi friend said, may be offered, and should be heeded when made, as this quotation indicates, by one who has shown himself a friend.

I referred earlier to the honest and helpful insights into the current Israeli/Palestinian predicament I found in Jeffrey Goldberg's book, Prisoners. In the book he recounts experiences of his time in the Israeli army and in particular his tour of duty at a huge detention centre where he served guarding Palestinian prisoners.It was called Ketziot. 'It was,' he said, 'a place bleached of colour and bereft of kindness – an island of small mindedness and cruelty in a brown sea of sand.'[11] Some prisoners held at Ketziot were forbidden visitors for between two and three years. While he was a guard there, he worked hard to make friends with some of the prisoners, and to a degree his overtures were reciprocated. He did his best to understand their concerns and aspirations. And it was at Ketziot that he was confronted for the first time in his life with the bleak, uncompromising philosophy of radical Muslim fighters implacably opposed to the state of Israel, and imbued with a bitter hatred of all Jews. Their experience of Ketziot did nothing to lessen their opposition to Israel or their professed loathing of Jews.

It was also there in the prison that Goldberg got an unexpected and uncomfortable perspective on the Palestinian story. It came in the course of a very ad hoc Passover celebration arranged in haste for the Jewish Israeli guards in Ketziot. 'The Seder consisted of hurried readings, empty of feeling. Ignoring the chanting, I read a bit of the book of Exodus to myself. The first of the Ten Commandments – I am the Lord your God, who has led you out of the land of Egypt, the house of bondage. The house of bondage? Here we were celebrating Jewish freedom in a prison filled with Arab captives. We had built a prison and planted it right along the pathway of Jewish freedom and filled its cages with Palestinians who were demanding only what the Jews themselves demanded in the time

[11] Jeffrey Goldberg, Prisoners, A Muslim and a Jew across the Middle East divide, p. 25, copyright © 2006, 2008 by Jeffrey Goldberg. Used by permission of Alfred A. Knopf, a division of Random House, Inc. Any third party use of this material, outside of this publication, is prohibited. Interested parties must apply directly to Random House, Inc. for permission.

of Exodus – and today – freedom.'[12] It was a train of thought he found deeply unsettling and which he struggled in his mind to contest, reasoning that Israel was NOT Egypt, nor the Palestinians SLAVES.

Ketziot, if it still exists, is a very long way from the ruined Jewish village of Bayt Baws in Yemen with which this chapter opened – more than two thousand kilometres away. And the too long, protracted and terribly painful Palestine/Israel conflict is a long way from the minds of most Yemeni people, for most of the time. They support, almost as an article of faith, the legitimacy of the Palestinian cause and with it hold a general disapproval of Jews, but these are not matters that touch upon their daily lives. There are much more pressing matters to hand. Some years ago, the Yemeni government called on its people to give money for the relief of the people of Gaza, once again under siege and bombardment. The request was for money for medicines. A reporter from the English language newspaper, The Yemen Observer, asked a mother of six in Sanaa what she would be contributing towards the alleviation of suffering of her fellow Muslims in Gaza. "Nothing," she replied, "I do not have enough money to buy the little I must have tonight to feed my children." There are hundreds of thousands – probably more – young mothers in Yemen tonight who are faced with the same acute dilemma. A good friend, a Palestinian Christian, who worked for nearly ten years with a large well-known international Christian relief agency in Israel/Palestine, and particularly on the West Bank, visited us for a week in Aden. We went to refugee camps, polyclinics, the offices of other international relief agencies and the main government hospital. When he left he said sombrely, "The situation here in Yemen is much worse medically than where I have worked these past years."

The sudden and dramatic flight of hundreds of thousands of Jews – valued and often respected in the Arab countries in which they and their ancestors had long lived – to Israel in the years both preceding and immediately following its founding, was part of the human cost of the realisation of the Zionist dream. Of course in the popular writing of Israel's advocates, their departure was not portrayed as a tragedy – which on many levels it was – rather as the miraculous snatching of desperate Jews from the snapping jaws of the Jew-hating Arab peoples.

I have also heard it suggested by Jews and Israelis and by supporters of the State of Israel that the dispossession and driving out of the Palestin-

[12] Ibid, p.169

ians in 1947 and 1948 was exactly matched by the Arabs driving out the Jews from the Arab lands where they too had lived. 'If,' the argument goes, 'that's how the Arabs treated us Jews, what right have you Arabs to protest that we Jews did the same to you?'

But it was the creation of the State of Israel, and the stormy decades of conflict between Arab and Jew that preceded its founding, that turned Arab neighbour against Jewish neighbour in city after city across the Middle East, where for years they had lived, often as friends, and in many places worked together as colleagues. The flight of the Jews from the Arab countries, used now in retrospect to justify the expulsion of the Palestinians, also played very conveniently into the hands of Israel's founders, desperate as they were to boost the Jewish population of the new-born state. It was a flight they also did their best to promote.

The exodus of Baghdad's Jews had been preceded by anti-Jewish riots, the widespread pillaging of Jewish property and the deaths of at least two hundred Jews. Their troubles began in the late 1920s and increased with intensity through the succeeding years - fuelled by the arrival in Iraq of refugees from Palestine, Syria and Lebanon, displaced by the conflict and convulsions in Palestine. Some of those who came were not slow to suggest that the same treatment, which they perceived had been meted out to them in Palestine by Jews, should be visited in turn upon the Jews of Iraq. Those responsible for encouraging emigration to Israel did their part to work on the fears of the Jews tempted to linger in Arab countries after the State's founding. Some have suggested that bombings of Jewish interests in Baghdad in the wake of Israel's founding were actually the work of Israeli agents or their proxies. Whoever was responsible for what came to be known as the 'Baghdad Bombings', they certainly hastened the exodus. And at the same time, the Zionist movement issued a manifesto calling on Jews to sign up for immigration. It began with the following, 'O Zion, flee daughter of Babylon', and concluded, 'Jews, Israel is calling you. Come out of Babylon!' Between 1949 and 1952 Operations Ezra and Nehemiah airlifted, via Iran and Cyprus, between 120,000 and 130,000 Iraqi Jews to Israel. During the same period, 10,000 Jews left Lebanon for Israel, and between June 1949 and September 1950 British and American transport planes made 380 flights from Aden to Israel carrying 49,000 Yemeni Jews. This airlift, officially called 'Operation on Eagles' Wings' - its name based on a line from the book of the prophet Isaiah - was also more popularly called 'Operation Magic Carpet'. The operation was not made known to the world until it was completed.

Most of Yemen's Jews had never seen a plane before they boarded their flight in Aden. An observer of the airlift wrote movingly of what he saw: 'the local authorities require no formalities and the Yemenis sit on their cases until the moment comes for embarking. They have complete patience and complete fearlessness. Mothers with babies at the breast, old men and children wait eagerly for the word to climb into the plane...' The writer was deeply impressed by the quiet rapture of all as they sat on long wooden benches, innocent of safety belts, flying over the Red Sea. At sunset, the men rose together to say the evening prayer led by the elders, and when the prayer was over, then in their places they sang their songs, and a few danced their solemn religious dances... they were excited when we could tell them we were looking over the land of Israel, passing Aqaba and the Negev and looking down on the lights of Beer-sheba and Gaza.'[13]

Ironically, during the 1930s, Jewish Yemenis wanting to emigrate to Israel – and 15,837 did emigrate between 1919 and 1948 – stood a much higher chance of getting there than either Polish or German Jews. In all, many more Polish and German Jews went to Israel during that time but they represented a smaller percentage of the total Jews of those countries than the Jews of Yemen. There were three reasons why the Jews of Yemen were so favoured. First of all, they had a reputation as hardworking agriculturalists, and they were badly needed to farm the land purchased or taken by the new Jewish immigrants from the Arab Palestinians. In the minds of the European Zionist settlers in Palestine, Yemenis were better suited to the work than others. One wrote patronisingly, 'our Yemeni brother is fit by nature to do work which is a hardship to his fellow, who comes from the more liberal countries of the Diaspora'.[14] Secondly, the Jews of Yemen were ignorant of the role of unions, and of regulations relating to the rights of workers and those matters with which their European counterparts had long been familiar. It was hoped their ignorance would make them a pliable and uncomplaining workforce. The third reason Yemenis were favoured was that they had very large families.

The snuffing out of the last tiny community of Jews in Beirut was a terrible thing. When we arrived there in early 1983 during the aftermath of Israel's costly invasion of Lebanon in the summer of 1982, not many more than a dozen Jews remained in Beirut. By the time we left two years later

[13] Norman Bentwich, *The Jewish Exodus from Yemen and Aden,*

[14] Aviva Halamish, *A New Look at the Immigration of Jews from Yemen to Mandatory Palestine.*

there were none. When the taking of foreign hostages in Lebanon became a popular, high-profile pastime for radical groups in the country, Beirut's remaining Jews were taken by them too. Thousands of Lebanese were taken hostage also during Lebanon's long and awful civil war – most never to be seen again. Their disappearance was eclipsed and largely forgotten in the publicity and attention inevitably given later on to the few Western foreigners who were kidnapped.

A group called the Organisation of the Oppressed of the Earth took the Jews – eleven of them. The group had a policy that whenever any Shiite civilian died at Israeli hands in the south of Lebanon, a Jewish hostage would die too. They died, one by one, amongst them Elie Hallack, known as 'Doctor of the poor' for the way he cared selflessly for the homeless Shiite squatters, who lived then in the utterly desolate and bomb-scarred old Jewish quarter of Beirut. Today, the old commercial heart of the city, ravaged in the civil war, has been lavishly and beautifully restored. The mosques and churches in the area once bruised by shells and peppered with shrapnel, have been restored too, along with an old and beautiful synagogue. No-one recites prayers in Beirut's synagogue now. No-one prays either in the ruined synagogue of Bayt Baws; the Jews who did have all long gone.

(CHAPTER SIXTEEN)
WINDSOR TERRACE

Nadia is lovely. She has a beautiful round, open, smiling face and lives with her husband and their family just ten minutes' walk away from the church. When I first met them they were sharing a two-bedroom apartment with her brother-in-law. The apartment was in an ugly complex of rundown buildings, which I was sure must have been built in the Soviet era. It was a conviction I lived with for a long time until one day I took a short cut with Dr John to the beach, where he wanted to swim. As we passed the buildings just mentioned I noticed on the wall of one the sign, 'Windsor Terrace', and concluded they must, after all have been built by the British, probably in the early 1960s. The story of how Nadia came to work with us is intriguing.

One night, she had a dream of entering the church compound past which she and her family must have walked daily on their way, either to school, or the shops and markets of Tawahi. In the dream she went through the little metal gate beside the main gate of the church and the clinic compound. She found to her amazement, that it was full of light. She recounted the story to one of our Ethiopian staff, who later relayed it to us. At the time of the dream Nadia was desperate to find work and a salary to supplement her husband's meagre income as a policeman. Stirred by her dream, Nadia set out two days later to visit the church and to seek work from the director. She was taken on immediately as a cleaner for the eye clinic. She has worked there now for several years and is held in warm affection and respect by all the staff. When the workload is heavy, as is often the case when visiting surgeons come to operate, her husband and often one or other of the older daughters are to be found cleaning and clearing beside her. They are a happy and close-knit family. At the time of writing, her husband has just narrowly escaped being killed by a suicide bomber, who entered the police station where he works, not far from the clinics, just moments after he had gone out to buy lunch for some of his colleagues. He returned to find two of them dead and parts of the bomber strewn in the debris.

A few years ago in calmer times, one of our staff, Dereje, mentioned earlier - an Ethiopian, head of our maintenance team and a most sincere Christian - came to tell me that Nadia and all her family had been put out of the accommodation they had been sharing and were now living on the street. Their eviction had followed a heated argument with the brother-in-law. Dereje added that Nadia's oldest daughter was due to be married in less than six weeks' time. In the afternoon, and with Nadia's approval, I went with Dereje to investigate the situation.

The 'street' was in fact a fifteen metre wide strip of dusty waste ground between the old apartment block and the road which led to one of the president's occasionally occupied seaside palaces. On the open ground, a shack had appeared, made of upturned wooden pallets, discarded sheets of old plywood, some other rough pieces of wood, some short rusty sheets of corrugated iron and a large, slightly torn and faded blue plastic tarpaulin. I noticed that a cable had been connected to an overhead power line and that a black polythene water pipe snaked its way from the apartment building through the dust to the back door of the hut. Yemeni people are very resourceful. Two of Nadia's smallest children had been watching out for us at the side of the road and ran - shy and giggling - to tell their mother of our arrival. She greeted us warmly, and despite our every protest, despatched the two youngsters to a nearby kiosk to purchase chilled cans of Coke and a packet of custard cream biscuits. They returned quickly with the purchases and six small, curious, barefooted friends. Nadia, smiling and gracious as always, directed us to a strip of carpet on the dirt floor and invited us to sit. She took a small black plastic bag with the purchases from one of the children, pulled the rings off the Coke cans, gave us one each and emptied the biscuits onto a plate, which she brought out from a wooden box in the corner of the little hut. We looked around us. In another corner of the room - about the size of a lounge in a small suburban English home - was a pile of foam mattresses with a colourful piece of Somali cloth covering them. In the corner where the wooden box was, from which our plate came, was a blue plastic box with kitchen utensils, then some pots and beside them a washing-up bowl, a Jerry can, and further along a single gas burner and gas bottle. I could see a lot of light through the gaps in the roof and was glad it rained only four or five times a year in Aden. Nadia did not complain about her lot, but she did express anxiety on behalf of the bride-to-be, who would be married from the flimsy, hastily constructed shed in which we sat. "In'shallah," she said, with her eyes turned heavenwards, "kulshi tamaam", which means in English, 'God willing, all will be well'. We promised her that we would do all that we could.

A month later, in good time for the wedding, and on a somewhat enlarged footprint of the original hut, stood a substantial little house - with cinder block walls, three windows, a metal front door and a gently sloping roof of shiny new corrugated iron. Inside, there was a tiny bathroom with a western toilet – ingeniously connected to the mains – a small kitchen and a sizeable sleeping/living area. Five years on and occupying a little more of the wasteland, the building still stands. I do not know if Nadia's husband receives any utility bills from the municipality. I do know that the building of the annex to Windsor Terrace was a very wonderful thing in which all our staff were involved and to which they all gave generously, readily and most sensitively. It was all done with the minimum of fuss – and the wedding when it came, was beautiful.

Not long after our arrival at Christ Church, I discovered behind the eye clinic an enormous heap of rubbish. It included broken chairs, the carcasses of old air-conditioning units, great lengths of metal piping, discarded aluminium door and window frames and, to my great curiosity, a lot of old, broken metal crutches. I thought flippantly that perhaps one of my predecessors had exercised a regular healing ministry and that the crutches were evidence of its effectiveness! I went in search of Gashu, confident that he would give me the authoritative word on the matter. He giggled deliciously when I put forward my suggestion for the presence of so many old crutches behind the clinic. He explained that the priest at Christ Church usually kept a supply of new crutches in the back of the vestry to replace those broken or worn out by their users, most of whom were refugees, and some of whom had lost a leg or foot, having trodden somewhere on a hidden mine. It was not long after I had had the presence of the crutches explained that Naughty Mohammed, as we came to call him, passed by asking for a new pair of crutches. He was a Somali refugee, spoke fluent English and Italian, appeared to know all the Western foreigners, who were, at that time very few and to depend largely upon their generosity for his livelihood. His crutches were pitiful. One arm grip had broken, the two handgrips were bandaged where the rubber grips had once been and the tips of the crutches, at one time covered by little rubber caps, were now very sharp, bare aluminium. I gave him a new pair of crutches from the little cache in the vestry I had been told about and took the old ones from him. He seemed delighted and hopped with vigour around the courtyard, testing them out. We did, incidentally, clear the rubbish from behind the clinic but on a recent return visit to Aden found a new heap had taken its place. It is just such a convenient corner to put unwanted things.

Within two weeks of being presented with the new crutches, Mohammed was back, but this time perched on a ghastly pair of heavy green metal crutches. I asked what had happened to the crutches I had given him.

He replied breezily that he had sold them. When I asked him why he had sold them, he told me that he had taken a new wife and had needed some money. I remonstrated with him, but still gave him another pair, insisting he sign for them, date his signature and not return for another year for new crutches unless – I jested – he had within the year covered 5000 kilometres.

He came back within a year, but not for crutches. Once he turned up when we had a rare group of tourists visiting, who wanted to look around the church. They were all Italian and spoke not a word of English or Arabic. I did not think that any of our staff had Italian and I was in a dilemma about what to do. But at that moment, Mohammed, who had been observing the arrival of the Italians with some interest from a shady corner of the courtyard, hopped over and asked if he could help. He did help and accompanied me and the tourists around the church, translating my simple commentary into passable and clearly understandable Italian. When the group came to leave, their grateful leader turned to Mohammed and asked if he was a Catholic, "No," came the cheerful reply, "a Muslim."

When we returned recently to Aden for a short tour of duty – after an absence of three years – Naughty Mohammed appeared within twenty four hours. "He smelt you," said Dr Nada. I hoped not. On sighting me Mohammed smiled and explained that it was very good to see Nancy and myself, especially as all his foreign friends had sadly left, and with them his main source of income. That was the nice thing about Mohammed. You always knew where he was coming from and what he wanted, and if one said no to a request from him he accepted it and would then ask immediately when he could try again. With some others who came to our gates wanting help it was harder to know exactly where they came from, or what they really wanted.

It was like that with Ephrem and Hamid, who appeared in the middle of one hot, busy morning. Ephrem was short, and very slight, balding, and with a prominently broken front tooth. He wore flip-flops, long baggy khaki shorts, and a long white shirt worn outside his shorts. He looked about forty years old. Hamid was five, bright, smiley and handsome. Ephrem told me that they had just crossed over by boat from Bosasso but that his wife, the mother of Hamid, had drowned in the surf when the boat they were in had tried to land its exhausted passengers. It was a tragically familiar story. From a wallet he produced a photograph of a young woman whom he said was his wife. The photograph, which was in a clear plastic envelope, looked as if it might have been in the sea. It was wrinkled and creased. The UNHCR had already found them accommodation in a hut in the sprawling refugee camp of Basateen on the edge of town. Sometimes they attended church on Fridays. Hamid loved the company of the other children at the church. Occasionally, they attended a Bible study group that met on Sunday nights in our home. Ephrem contributed thoughtfully, but wanted us to know that he was definitely not a Christian.

One day, Ephrem phoned on his mobile to tell us that some young men had tried to set fire to his hut during the night because they wanted them out of the area. Ephrem said that they had done it because he and the boy were Oromo and disliked by many Somalis and by fellow Ethiopians, who came from a different tribal background. I went to see them as soon as I could, bumping down the camp's potholed roads in our bus, anxious to see how they were. There were signs of a small fire having been lit against a wall of the hut, and while I was there a neighbour looked in to tell me that he'd seen several boys making the fire before he had shouted at them and chased them away. Hamid seemed completely unfazed by whatever had happened during the night, and remained happily absorbed in reading a book given to him by one of the young German children in our Sunday School. From time to time he chuckled delightedly to himself as he read, and looked at the pictures in the book. Ephrem, meanwhile, muttered darkly about persecution of the Oromo and of needing 'relocation'. I went to see the Protection Officer in the United Nations office, responsible for security in the camp. She was sceptical of Ephrem's story, telling me, "Refugees will go to almost any lengths, do anything and say anything that they think will get them out of where they are and on to what they consider a better place." I was shocked by her words. But over the years I have reluctantly come to acknowledge the truth of them. Our own clinic staff, who came to know Ephrem and Hamid quite well, and whose judgement I respected on many matters, remained deeply suspicious of Ephrem's claim to be the father of Hamid. One day Ephrem came to me and announced that they were off to Oman to find a better future there. I tried to dissuade them but failed. Later I learned that they had been imprisoned for several months in Oman before, incredibly, turning up at the compound of Holy Trinity in Dubai, where they told my astonished colleague, the Reverend John Weir, that they had come from Christ Church in Aden. The last time I heard of them they were back in Yemen, in the capital Sanaa. Ephrem may or may not have been the young boy's father. Whatever the truth, he looked after young Hamid conscientiously. The child seemed well adjusted and intelligent and had a keen sense of humour. He always looked clean and healthy. However, I thought he was quite shamelessly used by Ephrem to elicit sympathy, practical help and financial assistance wherever he went and that the child's best interests were certainly not served by being dragged to and fro across the Arabian Peninsula. We grew fond of Hamid. But not all who came knocking at the door for help were refugees or Yemenis who had fallen on hard times.

One afternoon we received a phone call from a good friend who worked in the main office of the UNHCR in Aden, asking anxiously if we could give temporary refuge to an American mother and her three children, whom she had seized back from her estranged Yemeni husband in Sanaa a few days earlier. It was a story as bizarre as it was tragic.

The American mother, whom I shall call Sarah, had met a Yemeni man when she had been living briefly in Japan. He had followed her back to America and there they had got married. Between them they had three children. At some point the husband had had a run-in with the authorities for mistreating the children. Then some time after 9/11 he was taken and held for a while as a terrorist suspect. On his release he went back to his wife and family but one day when Sarah was out, he took the children, left the States and flew with them back to Yemen. All this we learned from Sarah during the days that she and the family spent with us at Christ Church.

Distraught at the loss of the children, Sarah began to hatch a plan to kidnap them and take them with her back to America. It was a desperately reckless plan and involved the assistance of an accomplice, whom I shall call Dan, who was also an American and an ex-Marine. They had flown over from the States together and had managed to take the children, without any drama or objection from the children, while their father was away. The kidnappers had then hired a taxi and driven with the children to Bab al Mandab, where Yemen's western Red Sea shoreline edges closest to Africa's. There they had unpacked and blown up an inflatable dinghy intending, incredibly, to paddle a perilous twenty miles and more through one of the world's busiest shipping lanes to Djibouti, where they hoped that the American Embassy would prove more sympathetic to their plight than the one in Sanaa, which they had already approached. The children's American passports had apparently been destroyed by their father, when they had returned to Sanaa from America. When Sarah had gone to her Embassy in Sanaa for help on her arrival in the country she had been turned away, one American embassy official apparently describing her to his counterpart in the British Embassy later as, 'a mischief maker'.

Unsurprisingly, the sight of two very obviously foreign adults accompanied by three young children, inflating a dinghy on the lonely, windswept beach at Bab al Mandab, did not go unnoticed. Those who intercepted them and thankfully thwarted their plans, whether police or soldiers, were remarkably kind and helpful and suggested that the little party try to take a regular boat from Mocha to their intended destination. They took the advice, but even the port officials in windy, laid-back and almost forgotten Mocha could not embark passengers without passports, and they were turned back. And it was then that the taxi driver wisely proposed that they head to Aden and the office of the United Nations there. Though it would have been another four hours' drive on to Aden in his old taxi, he would have been very glad of the unexpected fare. It was in Aden that they met our friend, who phoned us and asked for our help. We readily agreed to take the little family in, for a few days, until we could decide together what to do next. Our local staff were quite used to foreign families staying in the guestrooms or apartments, and it was into one of these that we put them. The children, who were delightful and aged between seven and twelve years old, soon made themselves at home, quickly discovering the table tennis table and later the garden. Sarah asked if she might go out shopping, assuring us that she had enough Arabic to do so and that she would cover up comprehensively so that no-one would know that she was foreign. We agreed, but anyone watching her walk down the street would have known she was not Yemeni for she walked so terribly fast in the late afternoon heat and so very purposefully. When we went later that night to look in on them, all were fast asleep on mattresses on the floor curled up around each other like kittens in a litter. We never did set eyes on Sarah's accomplice and expect that he headed for the first travel agent he could find in Aden.

The next morning, I telephoned an acquaintance working in the British Embassy in Sanaa and asked if he could possibly make discreet enquiries in the appropriate section of the American Embassy there about Sarah and her situation. He seemed happy to enquire on my behalf and phoned back within half an hour, but with a less than encouraging response. "Consular business," he was told, "is not for discussion." Only a few minutes later, our friend at UNHCR received a phone call on her mobile from Sarah's husband in Sanaa, asking very politely about his children. She was shocked and a little frightened. We had learned that Sarah's husband was not only well-connected but also a forceful character. I do not know whether the phone call she received was in any way related to the call I had made to our embassy and to the one made by my contact there to the American Embassy. I think it probable. Twenty minutes later, I too received a call from Sarah's husband. He was charming and solicitous, and when I told him how the children were and what they had been up to he seemed grateful and told me he would be in touch.

While the children and their mother had been relaxing and had spent the morning on the beach, another good friend of ours had been exploring safer ways for our friends to take passage to Djibouti. In the evening he called round to discuss the results of his research. There were several options but none of them was straightforward, and all of them were risky. Sarah listened closely, but later said simply, "I think we must take the children back to Sanaa. Whatever route we take the trail will lead back here, and that I know will cause you many problems." We could not disagree. It just happened that we were due to make one of our occasional trips to Sanaa the very next day and it was quickly decided that we should all travel there together. I hated waking the little family early the next morning.

The journey to Sanaa was thankfully uneventful and relatively easy. The children chatted, dozed, and sometimes told us dreadful jokes. Sarah was quiet. We dropped the three children off with their bags within sight of their home and saw them enter the front gate. We took Sarah to a little hotel we knew of some distance away. She expected to fly home within two days. She wrote to us later from America. It was a good letter – warm, thoughtful and realistic. She told us that she could speak to the children at leisure once a fortnight, and that sometimes her husband listened in.

It was an extraordinary episode. While we were relieved that the original attempted sea crossing had had to be abandoned and were saddened by the whole complicated story, our abiding emotion is of grief and bewilderment at the attitude of the American Embassy and of those there involved in Sarah's case. I expect that in pursuit of 'the global war on terror', the predicament of a lone American mother and her children counted for little; the well-being and potential usefulness of her ex-husband to the cause, a great deal more.

Dealing with the beautiful Somali mother of seven, who appeared towards the end of our first Ramadan in Aden, was a simpler case. The staff told me I should help her and gave me three reasons why. First, Ramadan was coming to an end and the Eid fast approaching, for which she would be in need of extra money for celebratory food and new clothes for the children. Secondly, they had discovered that the woman, like so many other Somali women, had not seen her husband nor heard from him for over two years. Thirdly, they knew that she and the children, who had accompanied her, had a long journey back to Kharaz camp west of Aden. I did as instructed, and every year at the same time she returned with the children to collect her dues. It was her annual visit, and though the money we gave was modest, she and the children always seemed enormously grateful. We would have missed them if they had not come.

On another occasion I was approached by an anxious mother also from the distant refugee camp, who came to see me with her twelve year-old son. Through one of our Somali staff we discovered that the boy had a rather embarrassing medical problem for a young man and that it needed sorting out promptly. We asked the couple to wait while we phoned two hospitals to find out what the small operation that he needed might cost. It was not a lot, but it was outside the remit of the UNHCR department responsible for refugee welfare. We agreed to pay for the operation from the funds we set aside for work with refugees. Within a week, all that needed to be done for the young boy was done. Several months later, I spotted him and his mother seated in the shade in the clinic courtyard. I was apprehensive that they had come back to us for another favour, and I asked them, I think rather brusquely, what they wanted. "Nothing," replied the mother, "we just came to say thank you." I felt chastened and a little ashamed of my attitude to them. They had come a long way just to say thank you.

There was one time when the number of refugees coming to us threatened to swamp our normal work completely. I cannot remember what it was that provoked the flood – maybe a rumour that attendance at the clinics could facilitate exit from the country to Europe or America. Amongst desperate people, rumours – good or bad – spread fast. We quickly put in place some guidelines on the refugee cases which we could and could not see, reminded those coming to us of the medical provision – good, but limited – available to them in the camps, and pointed out to those who could take it in that we were a charity committed first and foremost to serving the poor in our immediate area of Aden. The flood receded and the numbers coming to us for help became manageable.

Some may question as they read what I have written, the wisdom of helping out the people I have described, in the way that we did. But those who came to us, particularly for humanitarian help of one sort or another, often came to us as a last resort. Relatively few of those whom we helped we saw again. Naughty Mohammed and the Somali mother of seven were exceptions. The amount spent each month, whether on bags of rice or sugar, emergency rent for a room, the occasional operation or medicines, even the cost of a passage in an open boat to bring a family member over from Somalia, rarely exceeded a couple of hundred dollars. I was also aware, at some times more acutely than at others, that the opportunity to help, in however small a way, might not always be there, and that it was important to do what we could, while we could. There were certainly times when it would have been easier to have refused to help, or to have postponed giving help, but when we had the means to help and a case looked deserving and genuine - something I nearly always checked out with the local staff - it seemed wrong to either refuse or delay assistance. And it was I confess, in Aden that I first consciously stumbled across a little verse in the Old Testament book of Proverbs, which read; 'Do not withhold good from those to whom it is due, when it is in your power to do it. Do not say to your neighbour, "Go and come again tomorrow and I will give it", when you have it with you.' (Proverbs chapter 3 verse 28). It was a verse that had an awkward way of coming to mind when I was tempted to tell someone who wanted help, to push off and come back another day. And then there were to hand the many demonstrations of open-handed generosity we witnessed in Aden towards the poor by those who themselves had very little, which were a challenge. I will end this chapter with an example.

Dereje and Elias came to the office one morning looking both solicitous and hopeful. I cast an eye up to the calendar over my desk prepared to tell them that they could not, at that early stage in the month, have an advance on the coming month's salary. Anticipating my thoughts, they quickly told me that while they wanted money, it was not this time for themselves. They explained that a week earlier they had found a very sick Eritrean man of their own age, whom they recognised but had not seen for several years. They had found him lying on a strip of cardboard in the entrance of an old crumbling apartment block and had taken him in a taxi to the main government hospital in the city. In the hospital he had received scant attention. Dereje and Elias had brought in food, washed him and paid for a few preliminary tests and investigations, but had now run out of money and were looking to me to help out. When the clinics closed, we set off together to see their friend whose name was Abdul-lah.

He was in a long, low, single-storey building some distance from the main block. He was small, emaciated and in considerable pain. We were instructed by a doctor on the ward to take him off for an x-ray and to pay the accountant for it on our way. It was not an easy undertaking. We were expected to wheel him there on the hospital bed. The bed had one missing wheel and sat down at that corner. We lifted the corner off the ground and wheeled the bed as best we could, lifting it completely over those parts of the concrete path that were badly broken. Abdullah whimpered with pain as we moved him. After the x-ray was taken and the fee paid, someone else took blood samples. These we were told to take to a laboratory down a side alley outside the main gate. We found the place and tapped on a hatch set in the door. It flicked open, a gloved hand reached out for the blood samples and a veiled face told us to return for the results after two hours. We went off to a noisy little restaurant and ordered ourselves chicken and rice and three cans of cold drink. We did not hurry over our meal. After eating, Elias went home. He lived nearby. Later, Dereje and I collected and paid for the laboratory report and then went in search of the young lady doctor overseeing the Eritrean's case. We found her studying his x-rays. She spoke to us in excellent English and in a superior tone. She informed us that the patient needed an operation and told me that I should make my way immediately to the cashier, pay for the operation - and she told me how much to pay - and return to her with the receipt as proof of payment. I went off as directed and had to wait a while for the cashier to come to his office. As I sat in that sad, dark corridor with its peeling paint and dirty, bare concrete floor of what had once been proudly known as Queen Elizabeth Hospital, one of the most modern and prestigious when it was built, I thought of the statistics that I had recently read, showing that while almost a quarter of the country's budget was spent on security and keeping the President in power, barely four percent was spent on its health. The President himself was reputed to travel to Germany or Saudi Arabia when he needed to see a doctor. When the cashier returned to his post he told me that the cost of the operation was considerably more than I had been told by the doctor. I was very angry and did nothing to conceal it. The whole situation was just so sad and shabby and mean and squalid. And on every street down which we had driven to the hospital there were hanging, at the time, huge and expensive banners portraying the President and heralding the forthcoming general election. Each banner, I had been told, cost over one hundred dollars - about the cost I had originally been told I should pay for the Eritrean's operation. I remonstrated with the cashier and told this to him. I also told him that the patient was a refugee, without relatives, and that he had to date been fed, washed and cared for in the hospital by fellow refugees and that though I was now involved, I had never met the patient until that afternoon. The cashier looked briefly embarrassed. I counted out the notes that the doctor had told me would cover the cost of the operation and, giving the man my most severe stare, walked off. As I left, he said in English, "I'nshallah all is ok now?" I did not reply.

I had been told that Abdullah would be moved to a ward in the main hospital before the operation. A kind orderly from whom I asked directions took me there himself. The ward was small and light and tidy. I was glad. I found Abdullah with Dereje seated beside him, sleeping peacefully. He looked much more comfortable. "He is not afraid," whispered Dereje, "he is Christian." In turn, we prayed for him briefly as he slept. Then I slipped away and took an ancient taxi home. The driver was no more impressed with the presidential banners that lined our route and fluttered in the evening breeze than I was. I did not follow all that he said, but I knew that it was about the President and noted that the Arabic word for thief cropped up frequently.

Abdullah was taken to theatre soon after I left. He died a few hours after the operation in the early morning. Dereje was with him. Later in the day, he made him a simple coffin.

(CHAPTER SEVENTEEN)

TO THE END

The lecture theatre was comfortable and well filled. There was a cheerful buzz of conversation and a tangible sense of excited anticipation. The majority of the audience looked Middle Eastern – the men mostly middle-aged in smart suits, the women well dressed, some with tasteful headscarves draped with casual elegance over their hair. Also scattered among the gathering were students from London's nearby School of Oriental and African Studies, and others whom I thought were probably aspiring young British diplomats in suede chukka boots, corduroy trousers and old tweed jackets.

We had come to listen to Yemen's newly created Nobel Peace Prize winner, Tawakol Karmon – mother of three and indefatigable and cheerful champion for peaceful change in Yemen. The organisers of this memorable meeting asked that the contents of it be not widely made known but suffice it to say, it was a spirited, encouraging and happy occasion. Standing and speaking on the podium, Tawakol reminded us of the young lady doctors in the clinic – attractive, articulate and convinced. They, with millions of others of their fellow Yemenis, would share her vision of a happy and uncorrupted Yemen and her resolve, not to go back. We wish them well, but the odds are heavily stacked against the realisation of their dream. While the dire predictions of the country's descent into civil war have mercifully not been realised, and the long and irresponsible rule of President Ali Abdullah Saleh for which the young revolutionaries protested is thankfully over, huge challenges remain – political, economic and humanitarian.

Our involvement with Yemen – albeit with a very small and scruffy corner of it - came about quite unexpectedly.

The Iran chapter in our lives was sadly a very short one. We had just begun to study Farsi in language school in north Teheran. Our class was very mixed – the wife of the Japanese Nissan representative in Teheran, two tediously talkative Syrian diplomats, a Turkish businessman, a gentleman from Iceland and a British lady MP were just some of our fellow students. Our teacher was fun, energetic and creative. Her headscarf was frequently slipping down to reveal her slightly greying hair.

One day in the middle of a class I was summoned to the director's office. There he handed me back our passports apologising, I think sincerely, for the fact that despite his intervention and best efforts on our behalf, the Foreign Ministry had declined our request for permission to study. Friends – local and foreign – commiserated, and five days later we flew home, spending our last Iranian money on a lovely tablecloth, which we bought in Teheran's Mehrad airport lounge. We learned before leaving that the study visas for two other students in our class, both with very different backgrounds to our own, had also been declined. On one of our remaining days in the city we happened to meet up with a very kind and gracious Roman Catholic bishop, himself an Iraqi citizen, who had lived and worked in Teheran for several years. "Don't give it any more thought," he wisely counselled, referring to our situation. "You may think of twenty-four reasons why your visa was refused and I could think of even more and it will be none of them. Travel well, and may God bless you."

We returned to our home in north Wales – to wild, wintry weather, stunning views across the Mawddach Estuary and glimpses of Cader Idris, our nearby mountain, through the mist. Not long afterwards, the former Bishop in Cyprus, Clive, invited us to take up a chaplaincy post in the Gulf. We accepted and made preparations to leave. But only days before we were due to depart, Nancy discovered a lump where it is not good to have a lump and within a week was under the conscientious care of Bangor hospital's excellent oncology department. Little did we imagine, as she began a long course of chemotherapy, that we would ever return to the Middle East – least of all to Yemen.

Soon after Nancy began her regular visits to Bangor hospital, I was invited to help the then Archdeacon of Ystumaner, the Reverend Arfon Williams, who was also the Rector of St Mary's in Dolgellau, to help him in the parish of St Mary's. For those unfamiliar with Anglican ecclesiastical terminology, most bishops have archdeacons – usually fellow clergy of some seniority, who are his chief administrative officers – sharing the pastoral care of clergy, supervising the care and upkeep of buildings, often sitting on too many committees and sometimes, like Arfon, having additional responsibility for a congregation or two. In one English diocese where I served, one archdeacon was known as 'Herr Flick' for the striking resemblance he bore to the German officer of the same name in the once popular TV series, 'Allo, Allo'. Another archdeacon was known as 'The Rotweiler'. Neither of them was as intimidating as their nicknames suggest and the fact that they were given them speaks of the affection in which they were both rightly held. In some Anglican parishes the minister or pastor is referred to as the 'Vicar', in others as the 'Rector'.

The two years attached to St Mary's, Dolgellau, were happy ones. The congregations were welcoming, supportive and forbearing, and in Arfon and his wife Carol, we could not have had more wonderful friends and colleagues. The time there also exposed us more knowingly to the fragile and temperamental state of the Church in Wales. It was towards the end of our two years and the successful completion of Nancy's treatment that another invitation was extended to us, again by Bishop Clive, to return to the Middle East to fill in in Aden in the absence of a permanent Chaplain and Clinic Director. We went, and after only one week found ourselves respectively summoning courage to broach to the other the conviction that we thought we should offer for the post long-term. It was rather wonderful. The offer which we made to the Bishop at the end of our six week stint and which a number of friends, Yemeni and expatriate, had by then encouraged us to make, was accepted with alacrity and enthusiasm by the Bishop. There were no other contenders.

What followed, I have tried in the preceding pages to describe – I hope with the gratitude and enthusiasm we share for the work at Christ Church and with the affection which our time in Yemen has stirred in us for the country and its people. I will curb any lapse into sentimentality for on any reckoning Yemen remains a very harsh and difficult place.

I had not expected when I started writing, to include the chapters on Iran, nor to have drifted into the dark and dangerous currents of the Middle East's most intractable problem of Israel and Palestine. I touched on Iran because our brief encounter with the country and its people was such a wholly unexpected and happy one, which at a time like the present, when Iran is constantly castigated and threatened in the world's media and by most of the world's leaders, it seemed worthwhile to share. It is a great country with a cherished, ancient culture and history. We met there, as I have recounted, with extraordinary kindness and generous hospitality from all sorts of people. We were moved by the courageous and tenacious witness of the Iranian Christians whom we met, who in many cases opened both their hearts and their homes to us, and of whose long and often precarious presence in Iran many in the West are quite unaware. On our return to Britain we read up avidly on the history of the little Anglican church of Iran and found ourselves challenged and inspired by the faith, dedication and love of its pioneering founders on whose diaries, papers and reports I have drawn.

My brief digression into the Palestine/Israel issue was largely provoked by conversations with friends and family in America while on holiday. It is also a subject which at one level or another impinges on almost any conversation about the Middle East. There were moments when I feared our discussions on holiday about the issue would damage our friendships irreparably. They have not, and thankfully those friendships have remained intact! Some with whom we met were convinced that Israel could do no wrong; others remain equally convinced that it can do no right. It was with both in mind that I wrote the chapters that I did. I offer them merely as reflections and observations on this most fraught and painful conflict. Many, many others have written more comprehensively and more competently on it .It remains a most daunting and divisive subject . The chances of reaching a just and enduring resolution of it at this time look slim, and thoughtful observers of the situation sadly consider a third Palestinian uprising or Intifada a real possibility .

A week ago we received from a young English friend, currently studying Arabic in Egypt, a cheerful update on his progress and some astute observations on post-Mubarak Egypt. He also told us of a private conversation which he had just had with his well-educated, middle-class Egyptian, Arabic, language teacher which had turned to Israel and the Jews. Our friend, widely read and politically aware, was utterly stunned by the vehement hatred she expressed for the State of Israel and all Jews. It did not sound sadly that she had had any first hand contact with either.

In Yemen, there are reportedly hundreds of unsupervised mosque schools where hatred of the West and of Jews are part of the curriculum. Perhaps such hatred is more easily fomented in the hearts of those distanced from the immediate conflict, who can keep in their minds a popular caricature of the enemy without risk of actually meeting the enemy and possibly having that caricature shattered.

The Palestinian doctor, Izzeldin Abuelaish, from whose book with the wonderfully defiant and hopeful title 'I Shall Not Hate', I have earlier quoted, condemns the futile policies and actions of all those – Palestinian and Israeli – which condone, extend or inflame the conflict. It is a truly remarkable book written out of the rubble of Gaza, the smell of death and cordite and the destruction of his own close family.

Four girls – his daughters Bessan, Aya and Mayar and their cousin, Noor died when two Israeli tank shells were fired into their bedroom. Another daughter, Shalha, in her last year of high school, was also seriously wounded along with another cousin, Ghaida, and Nasser, a brother of Izzeldin. What followed immediately after the shelling was broadcast live on Israeli television. At the time Dr Abuelaish was on the staff of the Sheba Hospital in Israel to which he commuted daily from Gaza. The Israeli military would allow no journalists into Gaza at this time, but Israel's Channel Ten, like all news channels eager to know what was going on in Gaza, had contacted Abuelaish for daily bulletins and updates on the situation. Moments after the attack he got through to Channel Ten's anchor man – one Shlomi Eldar – who was doing a live broadcast. He decided to take the call immediately on the air. It must have been the most anguished and electrifying of interruptions. Within moments the footage went round the world – with dramatic effect.

An Israeli woman from Sderot, the town in Israel on which the rockets sent from Gaza were largely falling, spoke bravely and honestly of the broadcast: 'The Palestinian pain, which the majority of Israeli society doesn't want to see, had a voice and a face. The invisible became visible. For one moment it wasn't just the enemy – an enormous dark demon who is so easy and convenient to hate. There was one man, one story, one tragedy – and so much pain.'[1]

During the times of Israel's military incursions into Gaza – which left in their wake such destruction and death, and strewed in the rubble and detritus of war the inevitable bitter seeds of revenge - Izzeldin Abuelaish held in mind his youthful memories of a summer vacation he had spent working on an Israeli moshav and the great kindness of the Jewish family with whom he lived at the time. 'It was,' he writes, 'so completely unexpected.' As he looked out from his home, years later in Gaza, on helmeted Israeli soldiers moving through the city's mean streets and watched their armoured bulldozers demolishing the pathetic homes of fellow Palestinians, he realised that he had to commit himself to finding a peaceful bridge between what he saw before him and the thoughtful, generous hospitality of those whom he had met during that faraway summer vacation.

In medicine – in the relief of suffering and the promotion and enabling of new life, particularly through his work as a gynaecologist - he had found a bridge between himself and the Israeli doctors with whom he worked. And he had discovered in the course of the work he shared with them that differences of nationality and religion were of very little

[1] Izzeldin Abuelaish, *I Shall Not Hate*, Walker & Company, New York, 2010, p.19t

consequence.

Towards the end of the book, where Izzeldin again laments the loss of his daughters, he speaks of his determination not to hate, despite his great loss and searing grief,

> 'My three precious daughters and my niece are dead. Revenge, a disorder that is endemic in the Middle East, won't get them back for me. It is important to feel anger in the wake of events like this, anger that signals that you do not accept what has happened, that spurs you to make a difference. But you have to choose not to spiral into hate.'[2]

In Prisoners, quoted from already, Jeffrey Goldberg describes a meeting with an American Jewish couple who made their home in the Israeli settlement at Tekoa on the West Bank. Their names were Seth and Sherri Mandrell. Seth is an Orthodox rabbi and they moved with their young family to Israel from Maryland, USA in 1997. One day, some time after they had established themselves at Tekoa, their 14 year-old son, Koby and a friend of his of the same age played truant and skipped school. Their bodies were found in a cave in a steep ravine not far from the settlement the next day. They had been beaten to death with rocks. I will let Goldberg tell of their meeting:

> 'I asked Seth how he kept his faith. He said, "the world is full of pain. But without God it is only pain. I can't imagine a world without God." He's a skeptic about the possibility of peace with his Muslim neighbors. "This does not mean," he said, "that peace is impossible – it is just not available at the moment. Of course I have my hopes. To believe in God is to have hope," he said. "Should the day come when the Muslims seem ready to have peace," he would be willing to hand Tekoa over to his neighbours. This would be no small thing for Seth Mandrell to say.'[3]

These rare voices of hope come, significantly, from hearts scarred deeply by the conflict.

[2] Ibid, p. 196

[3] Jeffrey Goldberg, *Prisoners, A Muslim and a Jew across the Middle East Divide*, pp.305, 306, copyright © 2006, 2008 by Jeffrey Goldberg. Used by permission of Alfred A. Knopf, a division of Random House, Inc. Any third party use of this material, outside of this publication, is prohibited. Interested parties must apply directly to Random House, Inc. for permission

Jerusalem, I once heard described as, 'The city of claim and counter-claim'. It is a tragically apt title. I do not want to add further grounds for it, but in relation to Jerusalem and what many devoutly call, 'The Holy Land', I venture to say that Jesus, to whom Christians look for their inspiration, guidance and ultimate authority, said little about real estate – at least in relation to the possession of the land of Israel but a great deal about the dangers of greed and covetousness, a fair amount about the peril of not settling grievances and much about the preciousness of human life.

Towards the end of his book Goldberg offers a surprising reflection on his favourite Psalm – 137, with its beautiful, aching, opening lament, 'By the rivers of Babylon, there we sat down and wept when we remembered Zion.' 'If,' he says, 'the first two verses remind us not to forget Jerusalem, the third verse is an inadvertent reminder of the cost of loving it too much. It is the verse that speaks of revenge against Babylon and of the wish to dash its children against the rock.'[4] On this he comments pertinently, 'The Jews in captivity dreamed of revenge against the Babylonians. This is natural. The horror of this verse is the wish to see the death of Babylon's children as well. But the horror instructs: The holiness of the land can poison the man who sanctifies only stone and forgets the supreme value of life.'[5]

Some months ago a friend gave us a book, The Islamist, written by an English Muslim called Ed Husain. In the book he explains why he joined radical Islam in Britain. He describes what he found inside the network that promoted it and tells us why in due course he left its ranks. It provides a very detailed and disturbing picture of active, very extreme, ruthless cells of disaffected young British Muslims set on causing mayhem and destruction in the name of Islam, in the country which has given them a home and the freedom to follow their own religion. But it is more than that; it is the story of one man's spiritual pilgrimage – powerfully told. In the end it was not only the mindless brutality of the radicals to whom he belonged that drove him from them but also his awareness of the spiritual wasteland inhabited by these people with whom he had been so thoroughly involved. At one point in the book he recalls wistfully the beauty of his childhood upbringing in the Muslim faith and contrasts that with the raucous, radicalism into which he had been drawn. 'In my childhood I heard melodious chants glorifying God and the Prophet, but now we

---

[4] Ibid, p.304

[5] Ibid

had done away with the Prophet and melody. All that was important to us was God, an angry God.'⁶

I once parked in the shade of a small mosque in Aden's Crater district and, waiting for Nancy to finish at the hairdresser, listened in the car to a CD of some beautiful instrumental playing of well-known Christian hymns and songs. The car windows were closed, the air-conditioning was on and the music was low. I closed my eyes to enjoy the music but a sharp rap on my window brought me abruptly from my reverie. I lowered the window and an old and angry man addressed me. I assumed that he was upset because I had taken his parking slot. I had not. I had been listening to music in the proximity of the mosque. It was, he said, shaking his finger, "Haram" – forbidden. I protested in Arabic that what I had been listening to was the music of Heaven. It was a rather provocative and undiplomatic thing to say, but he was not polite. He scowled and I turned it off. The Ayatollah Khomeini is reputed to have said sternly, "There is no joy in Islam".

I think that is true of the Islam he espoused. But his was not the kind of Islam which we often encountered in our corner of Aden.

There was the incident of the threatened burning of the bus. Once we gave sanctuary to a head-strong Sudanese refugee, who had taken it upon himself to distribute Christian tracts outside the mosque in the camp where he was living and who received death threats as a result. It was one of our own Muslim staff, who lived on the edge of the same camp, who urged me to take seriously the threats to the Sudanese and to take him in. On another occasion, when we were visiting a long-abandoned and extensive European graveyard near to one of the President's palaces, the local friend, who was showing us around, apologised to us for the state of some of the graves. "The long-beards," he explained, and added, "Hard Muslims have broken down all the crosses that stand up. They do not like crosses that stand up." I looked around me and took in what he had said. I did notice one cross, though, that was still standing. It was big and appeared to have been made from the substantial timbers of an old ship.

Back at the clinics, we had a cross on the wall of the community centre, another in the main office above the medical clinic and, when we

⁶ Ed Husain, THE ISLAMIST, Why I joined radical Islam in Britain; what I saw inside and why I left, Penguin Books, 2007, p.143. Re-produced by permission of Penguin Books Ltd.

created the laboratory in the corner of the courtyard and needed extra natural light, we put the transparent glass bricks into the wall, in the shape of a cross. It was Dereje's idea, and a good one. The cross was readily visible to all who entered the courtyard, and as far as I know, no one ever objected to it.

Most of the staff in the clinics were Muslim. There were no 'hard Muslims' among them, but all of them were, I believe, devout Muslims, big-hearted and generous too – quick to acknowledge God's goodness and express their dependence on him. Once, I sought out Dr Nada, eager to thank her, quite literally, for saving the life of a pitifully thin and sickly Somali mother. When I told her how grateful we all were to her, she replied modestly, "God healed her. I was useful." It was rare that a morning passed when I did not hear from the lips of one of our staff – cleaner, doctor or technician – a sincere and heart-felt, 'Al Hamdulilaah' – 'Thanks be to God' – on hearing, for example, of the safe delivery of a relative's baby, the correct diagnosis of a patient's ailment or, on meeting unexpectedly with an old friend.

Sometimes Nancy and I felt challenged, as did our fellow Christians on the staff, by the attitudes and actions of our Muslim colleagues. When we came finally to leave Aden, Mansour escorted us to the airport, diligently oversaw the processing of our baggage and walked us through the departure lounge. He joked a little as we walked and he expressed the hope that we would be back again, Inshallah – God willing. Then he paused and stood still, his head slightly bowed, his hands clasped before him and said, "Mr Peter, Mrs Nancy, if there is anything I have done to upset you, I ask you now to forgive me." We felt choked beyond words.

Our association with the Middle East goes back now some 40 years. We met in 1973 in the courtyard of a small house on an unpaved, pot-holed, dusty street in Jordan's port city of Aqaba. I was then teaching as a volunteer in a school in Jordan. Nancy was doing the same in Beirut. We had both newly graduated from our respective universities. My parents had met in Palestine in 1947; my father was serving with the British Army's Sixth Airborne Division and my mother was a nurse in a great military camp at Sarafand. But it is not nostalgia that has continued to draw us back to the region.

In the third term of my first year at university I attended a course of lectures in the theology faculty where I was studying, entitled, 'The Triangle of Monotheism'. They were delivered by the enormously erudite, eloquent, passionate and godly Bishop Kenneth Cragg, prolific author, lifetime student of Islam and friend. The lectures dealt with the relationship between Christianity, Judaism and Islam. I found them both intellectually demanding and inspiring. At the same time, I read one of Kenneth Cragg's earliest, and I expect the most influential, of all his books, The Call of the Minaret. The following extract I know almost by heart.

> 'How sadly attenuated is the Christian prophet as Islam knows him ... the mystery of his self-consciousness as the Messiah is unsuspected, the tender searching intimacy of his relationship to his disciples undiscovered ... where are the words from the Cross in a Jesus for whom Judas suffered? There is in the Quran neither Galilee nor Gethsemane, neither Nazareth nor Olivet. Is, 'Come unto me all you who are weary ... and I will give you rest ...' an invitation that need not be heard, and is Jesus' taking bread and giving thanks a negligible tale? Should not all humankind be initiated into the meaning of the question, 'Will you also go away?' In sum, must not the emasculated Jesus of the Quran be rescued from misconception and disclosed in all his relevance?'[7]

The obligation to rescue Jesus from 'misconception' and to disclose him 'in all his relevance' remains as important and demanding a task today in Britain, as in the Middle East. The deep affection we continue to feel for our Muslim friends and colleagues, and the respect we hold for their faith, has done nothing to diminish that sense of obligation. It has, if anything, deepened it. It is that obligation, heard when a student of the late Kenneth Cragg, that continues to draw us back to the region where Nancy and I first met, but also to give shape and direction to our lives and ministry wherever we are.

We left Aden and our post there nearly four years ago and did not expect to return. We were tired and were glad to hand over to our able younger successor, Nigel. It had been the happiest and most rewarding of assignments, but when Nigel and his wife Catherine left we felt that we should at least offer to return as 'stand-ins'. We have been back several times since then. Each visit has brought with it a predictable mix of grief, heartbreak, laughter and joy. Early on in the first visit back, I had

[7] Kenneth Cragg, The Call of the Minaret, Orbis Books Maryknoll New York, 1956, p.235

to conduct, as always in the Middle East – at short notice – the funeral of a refugee. It affected me deeply and the next day I wrote about it to friends.

'The gravediggers were wreathed in dust as they furiously scraped, shovelled and filled the grave. I was standing only feet away but they were almost invisible in the swirling cloud. For a brief moment I caught sight of a red peaked cap, a yellow T-shirt and a raised shovel. The service at the graveside had been a simple thing. None of the twelve men and women gathered there minutes earlier around the rough plywood box knew or had even seen the deceased except when they collected her from the hospital freezer, put her in the box and loaded her onto the back of an old pick-up truck. I had not known or seen her either. We only learned her name, Shawa, from the death certificate held in the hands of the young, faithful keeper of the cemetery. The certificate had been issued by the UNHCR, who had phoned the previous evening to say that they had the body of a Christian Ethiopian woman for burial. I then contacted Nasser, the cemetery keeper, to ask him to prepare the grave. Somehow the leaders of the Ethiopian congregation, who worship at Christ Church on a Thursday evening, all of whom are refugees, undertook to make a coffin and help with the burial. And so it was, in late afternoon, as the day cooled and the sun began to set, that we buried Shawa. I was very proud of the twelve friends who had come across the city to pray and to help. I later learned that Shawa had only arrived on the shores of Yemen a few days earlier, having made the dangerous crossing over from Somalia in a little open boat. She had made it to the main refugee camp on the outskirts of Aden, where she was found slumped and semi-conscious, lying against the wall of a little clinic. From there she had been brought to the old government hospital in the centre of town, where she died soon after admission. At the graveside, I spoke of Jesus' teaching of God knowing even when a sparrow dies and told them God knew and noticed when Shawa died. Alone in death, I thanked those gathered – fervently – for being her family for the minutes we were there together at her graveside. They had, I said, done a good thing. I know them all.'

Two days before we left at the end of that first return visit, Elias the Ethiopian, who has featured often in these pages, came to ask me if I could conduct his marriage. He was shocked when I told him we would be leaving in two days. I think he had assumed that we had returned for good. I knew that he and his bride, Tigist, had been prepared for marriage by their pastor, Jabir, whom I knew well. I assured Elias that if I could come up with a simple, authorised form of service that we could have translated in the course of the wedding into Amharic and Arabic and meet any other legal requirements, I would hold the wedding at the end of the clinics' working morning before we departed.

All that had to be done was done – in time. The clinics closed an hour early. The staff and a few friends attended. The bridegroom looked magnificent and his bride gorgeous, if a little dazed. It was not a lavish affair. Cake and Coke were served afterwards in the hall. The joy was very great.

Now home once again in Wales, we are considering with anticipation and apprehension the possibility of another return visit. We look towards it with anticipation – to be again with colleagues and good friends; with apprehension – because the situation there in Aden, in Yemen, remains so unpredictable.

We shall go as we have gone to every assignment in our life together, whether to leafy Warwickshire, north London suburbia or embattled Beirut, trusting in the mercy and goodness of God and in his promise that, 'even there his hand will lead us and his right hand hold us fast.' (Psalm 139.10) I end with some lines – slightly adapted – from an old and popular Christian hymn.

> O Jesus thou hast promised to all who follow thee
> That where thou art in glory, there shall thy servant be
> And Jesus we have promised to serve thee to the end
> O give us grace to follow, our Master and our Friend.

(BIBLIOGRAPHY)

Abuelaish, Izzeldin, *I shall not hate, A Gaza doctor's journey on the road to peace and human dignity*, Walker and Company, New York, 2010

Aithie, Patricia, *The Burning Ashes of Time: From Steamer Point to Tiger Bay,* Poetry Press Limited, 2005

Bat, Ye'or, *The Decline of Eastern Christianity under Islam From Jihad to Dhimmitude*, Farleigh Dickinson, Madison, NJ: University Press, 1999

Benjamin, Marina, *Last Days in Babylon, The Story of the Jews of Baghdad*, Bloomsbury, 2007

Bosch, David J., *Transforming Mission*, Orbis Books, 1991

Boyd-MacMillan, Ronald, *A Faith that Endures, The Essential Guide to the Persecuted Church*, Sovereign World, 2006

Brown, John, *A Way in the Wilderness – A Bishop's Prayer Journey through the Arabian Peninsula*, Christians Aware, 2008

Chapman, Colin, *Cross and Crescent*, Inter- Varsity Press, 1995

Clark, Victoria, *YEMEN – Dancing on the Heads of Snakes*, Yale University Press, 2010

Cragg, Kenneth, *Common Prayer, One World, A Muslim-Christian Spiritual Anthology*, Oxford, 1999

Cragg, Kenneth, *The Call of the Minaret*, Orbis Books, Maryknoll, New York, 1956

Dehqani Tafti, H.B., *Norman Sharp's Persian Designs*, Sohrab Books, 2001

Dehqani Tafti, H.B., *Unfolding Design of My World*, Canterbury Press, Norwich, 2000

Faramarzi, M. T., *A Travel Guide to Iran*, Yassamin Publications, Teheran, 1997

Fazzina, Alexandra, *A Million Shillings – Escape from Somalia*, Trolley, 2010

Finkelstein, Norman G. *The Holocaust Industry*, Versó, 2000

Flapan, Simha, *The Birth of Israel, Myths and Realities*, Pantheon Books, New York, 1987

Fromkin, David, *A Peace to End All Peace – Creating the Modern Middle East, 1914-1922*, Penguin Books, 1991

Gairdner, W.H.T., *The Reproach of Islam*, The Foreign Mission Committee of the Church of Scotland, Edinburgh, 1909

Gilbert, Martin, *Churchill: A Life*, Minerva, 1991

Goldberg, Jeffrey, *Prisoners, A Muslim and a Jew across the Middle East divide*, Alfred A. Knopf, New York, 2006

Greenaway, Paul & David St Vincent, *Iran*, Lonely Planet Guide, 1998

Grossman, David, *To the End of the Land – A Novel*, Jonathan Cape, London, 2010

Harney, Desmond, *The Priest and the King, An eyewitness account of the Iranian Revolution*, I.B. Tauris, 1999

Hewitt, Gordon, *The Problem of Success: History of the CMS 1910-1942.* SCM Press London, 1977

Hinchcliffe, Peter, John T. Ducker, Maria Holt, *Without Glory in Arabia – the British Retreat from Aden*, I.B. Tauris, 2006

Hirst, David, *Beware of Small States, Lebanon, Battleground of the Middle East*, Faber and Faber, 2010

Historical Encyclopaedia, *"Meadows of Gold and Mines of Gems"*, ca. 956 Mas'udi Ali-Abu'l Hassan, London: Printed for the Oriental Translation Fund of Great Britain and Ireland, 1841

Husain, Ed, *THE ISLAMIST, Why I joined radical Islam in Britain; what I saw inside and why I left*, Penguin Books, 2007

Ingrams, Leila, *Yemen Engraved*, Stacey International, 2006

Keay, John, *Sowing the Wind, The Seeds of Conflict in the Middle East*, John Murray, London, 2003

McElwee Miller, William, *My Persian Pilgrimage*, Pasadena: William Carey Library, 1989

McLaren Ritchie, David, *The Church of Scotland South Arabia Mission 1885-1978*, Tentmaker Publications, 2006

McLaughlin, David, *Yemen*, The Brandt Travel Guide, 2007

Moffatt, Samuel Hugh, *A History of Christianity in Asia, volume 1*, Orbis Books, 1995

Mother Theresa, *Love, Joy and Peace*, Fount, 1998

Musk, Bill, *Kissing Cousins?*, Monarch Books, 2005

Nuttall, Michael, *Number Two to Tutu – A Memoir*, Cluster Publications, 2003

Padwick, Constance, *Temple Gairdner of Cairo*, SPCK London, 1929

Peskett, Howard and Vinoth Ramachandra, *The Message of Mission*, Inter-Varsity Press, 2003

Rice, Clara C., *Mary Bird in Persia*, London 1916

Smith, Tim, *Coal, Frankincense and Myrrh, Yemen and British Yemenis*, Dewi Lewis Publishing, 2008

Stacey, Vivienne, *Henry Martyn*, Henry Martyn Institute of Islamic Studies, Hyderabad, 1980

Uhlman, Fred, *Reunion*, Vintage Books, 2006

Vital, David, *A People Apart, The Jews in Europe 1789-1939*, Oxford, 1999

Warren, Max, *I Believe in the Great Commission*, Hodder Christian Paperback, 1979

Watson, David, *One in the Spirit*, Hodder Christian Paperbacks, 1973

Wright, Denis, *The English Among the Persians*, I.B. Tauris and Co Limited, 2001